THE CAMBRIDGE APPLIED LINGUISTICS SERIES

Series editors: Michael H. Long and Jack C. Richards

This series presents the findings of recent work in applied linguistics which are of direct relevance to language teaching and learning and of particular interest to applied linguists, researchers, language teachers and teacher trainers.

In this series:

Computer Applications in Second Language
Acquisition

ONE WEEK LOAN

Computer Applications in Second Language Acquisition

Foundations for teaching, testing and research

Carol A. Chapelle

Iowa State University

CAMBRIDGE
UNIVERSITY PRESS

PUBLISHED BY THE PRESS SYNDICATE OF THE UNIVERSITY OF CAMBRIDGE
The Pitt Building, Trumpington Street, Cambridge, United Kingdom

CAMBRIDGE UNIVERSITY PRESS
The Edinburgh Building, Cambridge CB2 2RU, UK
40 West 20th Street, New York, NY 10011–4211, USA
10 Stamford Road, Oakleigh, Melbourne 3166, Australia
Ruiz de Alarcón 13, 28014 Madrid, Spain
Dock House, The Waterfront, Cape Town 8001, South Africa

http://www.cambridge.org

First published 2001

Printed in the United Kingdom at the University Press, Cambridge

Typeset in Sabon 10.5/12pt   System 3b2   [CE]

A catalogue record for this book is available from the British Library

Library of Congress Cataloguing in Publication applied for

ISBN 0 521 62637 4 hardback
ISBN 0 521 62646 3 paperback

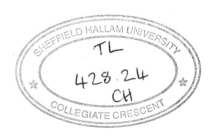

For my parents

Contents

Series editors' preface

Perhaps no single area of applied linguistics has seen such explosive growth over the past 15 years as computer-assisted instruction. Books and journal articles on the subject abound – indeed, new journals have appeared dedicated exclusively to it. Rapid developments in computer hardware and software are obviously a driving force, but so, too, is the increasing number of computer-literate people entering the field, whether as graduate students or language teachers.

Amidst all the excitement and innovation, however, a degree of healthy skepticism has survived in some quarters. Just how much of the work has produced genuine advances in language sciences? How much has really been a case of computer-buffs in search of a justification for their love of the technology, or worse, computer manufacturers in search of new markets for their products?

Carol Chapelle is a rare and valuable blend of enthusiast and skeptic. She is unquestionably one of the leading authorities on computer-assisted language instruction, and sees exceptional opportunities in computer-aided research for applied linguists. However, she is equally well known, and justifiably so, as an expert on second language acquisition, language teaching, and language testing, in each of which area she had published extensively before her work with computers in applied linguistics began, and in each of which she has continued to publish since. Her knowledge in those fields enables her to review research and practice involving the new technology fairly, but critically – to distinguish substantive contributions from commercial gimmickry. In particular, she regards research in second language acquisition as both a field in which computer technology can be of immense value, and as a valuable source of knowledge for researchers and practitioners working in the related areas: language teaching and testing.

Professor Chapelle's new book, *Computer Applications in Second Language Acquisition: Foundations for Teaching, Testing, and*

Research, provides a comprehensive analysis of past and current work in the field. It is well organized and clearly written, and should provide an invaluable resource for language teachers, language testers, and SLA researchers alike. It is a substantial contribution to knowledge, and a valuable addition to the Cambridge Applied Linguistics Series.

Michael H. Long
Jack C. Richards

Thanks

I am indebted to all members of our profession who have identified and addressed substantive issues of practical relevance to language teaching and assessment, especially Lyle Bachman, Mike Long, Teresa Pica, and Peter Skehan. I hope the influence of their work is evident and constructively built upon in this volume.

I thank my colleagues and friends who got me interested in the topics covered in this volume over 20 years ago, especially Lyle Bachman, Doug Brown, Bob Hart, and Joan Jamieson. I hope each of them sees this work as a worthwhile product of their teaching. I also thank Mike Long and Alison Sharpe for encouraging me at the start of this project as well as Julia Harding for her careful editing.

I am grateful to the many people who commented on segments of drafts, including Roberta Abraham, Lyle Bachman, Mickey Bonin, Pete Boysen, Jack Burston, Susan Conrad, Graham Crookes, Graham Davies, Catherine Doughty, Dan Douglas, Dan Eignor, Larry Frase, Debra Hoven, Joan Jamieson, Sue Otto, Dana Paramskas, Peter Skehan, Rex Thomas, Mark Warschauer, an anonymous reviewer, members of the GRApES research seminar at Iowa State University, and students in classes at University of Hawai'i, Northern Arizona University, and Iowa State University.

I thank those who waited patiently for so many years while I worked on this project, especially Tess.

Abbreviations

CACD	computer-assisted classroom discussion
CASLA	computer applications in second language acquisition
CALICO	Computer-Assisted Language Instruction Consortium
CALL	computer-assisted language learning
CALT	computer-asssisted language testing
CASLR	computer-assisted second language research
CAT	computer-adaptive testing
CMC	computer-mediated communication
ESL	English as a second language
IRT	item-response theory
ITS	intelligent tutoring systems
LAN	local area network
MTMM	multitrait multimethod
SLA	second language acquisition
TESOL	Teachers of English to Speakers of Other Languages
TOEFL	Test of English as a Foreign Language
UCLES	University of Cambridge Local Examinations Syndicate

1 Historical foundations of CASLA

At the annual TESOL convention in San Francisco in 1980, interested and curious participants attended Joan Jamieson's and my workshop introducing the use of computer software for teaching English as a second language (ESL). Joan and I had intended the workshop as a demonstration of existing ESL teaching software with an explanation of how such software is written and used in the curriculum. As newcomers to the profession, we had probably accepted uncritically the fact that the computer *was* used for teaching in the ESL program where we worked. We were therefore intrigued by questions from the audience about whether the computer *should be* used for language teaching. Various forms of this question – whether or not computers should be used for language teaching – were echoed throughout the following decade, but during the 1990s the question gradually changed from 'Should the computer be used in second language teaching?' to 'How can the computer best be used in language teaching?' As we enter the 21st century, everyday language use is so tied to technology that learning language through technology has become a fact of life with important implications for all applied linguists, particularly for those concerned with facets of second language acquisition (SLA).

Forward-looking members of the profession have suggested that the nature of communicative competence has changed in a world where communication occurs with computers and with other people through the use of computers. Writing about communicative competence in the 21st century, Rassool points out:

in a world increasingly driven by (a) the need for innovation through research and development (R&D), (b) the multilevelled changes brought about in our everyday lives as a result of the nature and speed of technological developments, (c) the volume and range of information available, and its open accessibility, (d) the multimodal features of electronic text as well as (e) its interactive nature, we require significantly *more* than just the ability to read and write in a functional way. (1999: 202; emphasis in original)

If, as Rassool suggests, 'communicative competence refers to the interactive process in which meanings are produced dynamically between information technology and the world in which we live' (Rassool, 1999: 238), language learners are entering a world in which their communicative competence will include electronic literacies, i.e., communication in registers associated with electronic communication (Murray, 2000; Warschauer, 2000).

As a consequence, anyone concerned with second language teaching and learning in the 21st century needs to grasp the nature of the unique technology-mediated tasks learners can engage in for language acquisition and how such tasks can be used for assessment. Language learners typically use computers at least to write papers, receive and send e-mail, and browse the World Wide Web; one challenge for language teachers is to shape some of their computer-using experiences into language learning experiences. To meet the challenge, the study of the features of computer-based tasks that promote learning should be a concern for teachers as well as for SLA researchers who wish to contribute to knowledge about instructed SLA. Many learners will be required to prepare for computer-assisted language tests such as those developed by the Test of English as a Foreign Language (TOEFL) program and the University of Cambridge Local Examinations Syndicate (UCLES) as well as the many Web-based language tests, including those being developed for languages of the European Union through the Diagnostic Language Assessment (DIALANG) project. Therefore, test users need to understand the issues involved in selecting such tests and helping learners prepare for them; equally critical is the knowledge of computer-assisted language testing required of test developers and researchers who construct and evaluate these new testing procedures.

To date the need for an understanding of computer-related issues in SLA has not been met by a coherent set of principles for examining past work and plotting fruitful directions. Instead, cross-disciplinary perspectives have been applied to individual efforts at development and evaluation of computer applications in second language acquisition (CASLA) – perspectives which may enrich the knowledge base concerning computer capabilities and potentials for design and evaluation. Despite the value of cross-disciplinary input, the array of computer-related methods, concepts, and initiatives presented to applied linguists can be overwhelming. Moreover, substantive progress in CASLA requires that its identity be defined, including principles for evaluation drawn from relevant work in applied linguistics. This book lays out such principles to delineate the domain of CASLA as defined through computer-assisted language learning, computer-assisted language testing, and computer-assisted second language acquisition research. This chapter and the next begin by defining CASLA first through historical development in each of these areas and then in relation to other fields that have influenced CASLA. The following chapters focus on evaluation issues pertaining to computer applications in each area, and the final chapter suggests directions for future work on the basis of needs identified across areas.

CASLA before the microcomputer

CASLA began with projects exploring development and use of computer-assisted language learning (CALL)[1] within the field of educational technology and was therefore shaped by perspectives in education as well as by computer hardware and software developed for purposes other than language instruction (Kerr, 1996; Saettler, 1990). In the US, computer-assisted instruction was first used in the 1950s, but examples of CALL are not documented until the 1960s, when a number of projects were undertaken to explore how the computer could be used for foreign language instruction in higher education. With a few exceptions, such projects were initiated by an individual who used computer equipment and software which had been acquired on campuses for other purposes. For example, Collett (1980), in New Zealand, reported that the idea for his French program came from a colleague in physics who had used the university's mainframe for computer-assisted instruction. Boyle, Smith, and Eckert (1976) reported a computer-based diagnostic French test also developed on a mainframe computer at a university. In the 1960s and 1970s, these small-scale individual projects, along with a few larger efforts, comprised the first experiences with CASLA.

CALL in the 1960s was supported by mainframe computers connected to terminals on a single campus or by telephone lines to terminals off campus. Computer-based learning activities, called 'courseware' were developed using programming languages and were stored on a mainframe for students to access as needed. The mainframe computers and their general-purpose programming languages of the 1970s were able to support the basic interaction

---

[1] Computer-assisted language learning (CALL) was the expression agreed upon at the 1983 TESOL convention in Toronto in a meeting of all interested participants. I have retained this term throughout this volume to refer to the area of technology and second language teaching and learning despite the fact that revisions for the term are suggested regularly.

required to implement the instructional design for this era of CALL. By today's standards, courseware was not technologically sophisticated even though it was often carefully planned. The fact that the software was stored on a single mainframe at an institution allowed for record keeping in a central location and communication among users. The mainframe also meant, however, that expenses were incurred for writing and using courseware. Because early CALL users were participating in expensive innovation, pressure existed to ensure that CALL was time well spent for learners.

Despite obstacles such as cost, individual language teachers throughout the world were fascinated by the prospects CALL appeared to offer. In the UK, for example, Rex Last and Graham Davies had each been exploring the construction of authoring software (which would simplify production of CALL) for years before they met in 1979.[2] Their individual experiences (e.g., Last, 1979) later became a valuable resource for an early commercial producer of language learning software in the UK. Davies' experience also made him the logical choice to head the government-funded National Centre for Computer Assisted Language Learning established in 1985.

The best-known early CALL project in North America was initiated as one part of a larger computer-assisted instruction project at Stanford University in the Institute for Mathematical Studies in the Social Sciences directed by Richard Atkinson and Patrick Suppes. The project began in collaboration with IBM, and later received funding from federal government sources. Atkinson's early research on learning foreign language vocabulary (Atkinson, 1972), still cited as having useful implications for principled design of CALL (N. C. Ellis, 1995a), was based on his mathematical learning theory rather than on then-current foreign language pedagogical practices. Atkinson (1972) found that learning, as measured by a test a week after the instruction, could be optimized significantly by having a computer program select items for practice on the basis of learners' past history of performance and item difficulty.

The work at Stanford was important also because its directors, Atkinson and Suppes, went on to form the Computer Curriculum Corporation in 1967, which continued to provide instruction in English as a second language (Saettler, 1990: 308). IBM also initiated an early project at the State University of New York at Stony Brook by funding experimental CALL materials for German (Elling, 1995).

---

[2] I am grateful to Graham Davies for the historical information he provided. For an account of past work in Europe, see Davies (1989; 1993).

Another early project began in Canada through a coordinated effort among three Ontario universities, Western Ontario, Guelph, Waterloo (and later the University of Alberta) resulting in CLEF (Computer-Assisted Learning Exercises for French), a series of 62 lessons covering basic French grammar (Paramskas, 1983), which would later be used by over 200 institutions in Canada and more abroad (Paramskas, 1995).

These are just a few of the many CALL projects that were undertaken by individuals on their university's mainframe computer during this period. Holmes and Kidd (1982) review some important ones, describing them as 'modest', emphasizing 'pedagogical principles and practical applications.' The pedagogical principles tended to go beyond the behaviorist/audio-lingual paradigms of early teaching machines by providing learners with grammatical explanations and specific feedback about their responses. For example, a German CALL project of this era at Massachusetts Institute of Technology was described as follows:

[The] tutorial to teach German reading uses the computer as a source of information to be consulted by the student as needed; the [other aspect of the program] . . . uses a model of the structure of the language being taught to enable the program to determine whether a response is correct and to provide the student with useful error analysis if it is not. (Nelson, Ward, Desch & Kaplow, 1976: 28)

The practicality and efficiency of computer use were seen as essential by instructors who were using expensive mainframe computer time. Decker (1976), for example, described his innovative approach, which involved having the computer illustrate how to perform particular grammatical operations on French learners' sentences. He then explained how this innovation would be sequenced as the first step of a process including illustration, drill, and testing to ensure that the learners had benefited. As Decker's application illustrates, and Holmes & Kidd (1982) concluded, CALL of this era was seen as a supplement to rather than as a replacement for classroom instruction. Multiple initiatives around the world explored ways in which instructional goals could be accomplished more efficiently through the use of the computer.

These projects formed the profession's initial perceptions of CALL, but what was perhaps the greatest impact on the field in this era resulted from the major commitment made in the early 1970s by the US government to support computer-assisted instruction across the curriculum. Saettler (1990) described the irony of the decision that precipitated this significant phase in the evolution of CALL.

Despite the decline of [computer-assisted instruction (CAI)], the federal government, through the National Science Foundation (NSF), decided to determine whether CAI could be made effective and available to as many teachers and schools as possible. This was the viewpoint behind the $10 million made available in 1971 to two private companies, Control Data Corporation (CDC) and Mitre Corporation, with the idea that the two companies would compete with each other and that at least one viable CAI national system would emerge. (1990: 307)

Control Data Corporation worked with the University of Illinois at Urbana-Champaign to develop the hardware and software for the PLATO (Programmed Logic for Automatic Teaching Operations) system; the Mitre Corporation contracted with Brigham Young University in Utah to develop the TICCIT (Time-Shared, Interactive, Computer-Controlled Information Television) project. These projects, providing mainframe computer systems and software designed specifically for instruction, impacted the evolution of CALL in two ways. First, each system included major CALL components. By early 1980, TICCIT had an extensive collection of courseware that was used as an adjunct to classes in ESL, French, German, Spanish and Italian (Hendricks, Bennion & Larson, 1983) and PLATO had courseware for those languages in addition to many others such as Arabic, Chinese, Hindi, Hebrew, and Swedish (Hart, 1981a).

Second, each provided laboratories for investigation of CALL and sowed the seeds for future professional infrastructure. The TICCIT project produced a core of faculty in language teaching prepared to contribute to the evolution of technology in SLA. By the late 1970s they were pioneering videodisk technology, which resulted in one landmark project in the evolution of CALL (Schneider & Bennion, 1983). Brigham Young faculty were also leaders in computer-adaptive testing for foreign languages (e.g., Madsen, 1991). In addition, a faculty member of Brigham Young University, Frank Otto, was founder and executive director of the professional organization Computer-Assisted Language Instruction Consortium (CALICO), which has provided a forum for intellectual collaboration and growth in the field since 1984.

The PLATO project also contributed to the professional expertise in CALL. The courseware developed on that system, which supported audio (input to learners), graphics, and flexible response analysis, was the product of language teachers' best judgement of what supplemental course materials should consist of in the late 1970s. As a result of his many years of developing courseware on PLATO, Robert Hart summarized the accomplishments and identified directions for growth in 1981:

Eight years of intensive development have brought the PLATO IV grammar drill design to a high state of sophistication, so much so that further work in this direction will bring diminishing marginal returns. If we wish to make [CALL] a more powerful tool for language instruction, we really must begin to investigate qualitatively new design possibilities. (1981b: 16)

The new design possibilities he suggested were the following: (1) use of artificial intelligence techniques for analysis of learners' language in order to provide an appropriate instructional strategy, (2) diagnostic assessment of grammatical competence, (3) exploration of games and simulations which require use of 'non-trivial grammar while remaining interesting and computationally tractable' (1981b: 20), and (4) task analysis of language production, comprehension, and learning in CALL.

In retrospect, these experience-based suggestions proved to be ahead of their time. Because so few were engaged in the development and use of CALL in 1981, evolutionary progress resulting from professional discussion was not yet possible. The large majority of those who had experimented with CALL on a mainframe, or who were beginning to learn to program a microcomputer, seemed focused on the challenge of getting general-purpose hardware and software to perform for language instruction. However, primitive computer equipment and lack of professional organization were only two reasons why the early 1980s saw minimal work on these research directions. A third was perhaps that research in applied linguistics was not yet mature enough to offer principled guidance.

It would be difficult to document the many seeds sown during this period that would develop into the first attempts at computer-assisted language testing projects and computer-assisted SLA research. However, it was not an accident that early examples in the US were at Brigham Young University, where Harold Madsen and Jerry Larsen were the first in the early 1980s to report on efforts to develop computer-adaptive language testing, and the University of Illinois, where Nina Garrett began her work on computer-assisted SLA research investigating German syntax through data collected on the PLATO system (Garrett, 1982). Despite these and a few other pioneering efforts in testing and SLA research, the pre-micro-computer era of CASLA was devoted primarily to exploration of CALL.

The first microcomputers

Computers became widely available to language teachers in the early 1980s. Since microcomputers did not require users to be attached to a mainframe computer maintained by a university or business, any academic department, language school, or individual teacher could purchase one and explore its potentials for language teaching. During this period, some became interested in computer-assisted language testing (CALT) and computer-assisted second language research (CASLR), but the primary activity continued to be in CALL.

Because of the microcomputer, just three years after the inquisitive participants gathered at the San Francisco workshop, CALL had gained enough professional visibility that those working on CALL converged to discuss methodological issues, and begin formal professionalization of CALL. The 1983 annual TESOL convention in North America included papers arguing methodological issues in CALL,[3] and a suggestion was made to establish a professional organization (CALICO) devoted to the issues involved in language learning technology. By the following year, TESOL members were working to establish a CALL Interest Section. One year later in the UK, the British Council sponsored a course on CALL at Lancaster University which proved so popular that subsequent gatherings were organized to discuss and learn about CALL. The 1986 gathering turned out to be the founding meeting for the EuroCALL professional organization, which later received funding from the European Commission to act as a pan-European organization for CALL. In Europe, North America, and Australia, CALL's status had developed from a local curriculum or classroom issue to an international professional concern. The need was evident for teacher education through courses such as the one the British Council sponsored in 1984 at Lancaster University. In addition, a market had developed for production of introductory materials explaining computers and their classroom uses, and within a four-year period a large number of such books were published.[4]

By coincidence, this period overlapped the height of Steven Krashen's[5] popularity and hence it was fashionable to invent CALL that could be claimed to promote 'acquisition' rather than 'learning.'

[3] Prior to 1983, there had been only one or two sessions each year at the TESOL convention concerned with computers and language teaching.

[4] The following books are among those based on work of the early 1980s that were produced for teacher education: Ahmad, Corbett, Rogers, & Sussex, 1985; Brumfit, Phillips, & Skehan, 1986; Cameron, Dodd, & Rahtz, 1986; Davies, 1985; Hainline, 1987; Higgins & Johns, 1984; Hope, Taylor, & Pusack, 1984; Jones & Fortescue, 1987; Kenning & Kenning, 1983; Last, 1984; Leech & Candlin, 1986; Underwood, 1984; Wyatt, 1984.

[5] Krashen's view of SLA, laid out in his 1982 book, depicts two separate and unrelated processes: unconscious 'acquisition' and conscious 'learning,' the former being the most effective, in his view.

During this time, much of CALL's history was lost because what might have been the best accomplishments (e.g., perhaps Atkinson's optimal vocabulary acquisition paradigm) as well as suggested research needs (e.g., Hart's suggestion for diagnosis of grammatical competence) of the previous decades were labeled as 'learning-oriented' and therefore irrelevant to acquisition – and to CALL's future (e.g., Cook, 1985; Sanders & Kenner, 1983).[6] The two most influential books of this era attempted to promote CALL by explicitly attempting to dispel the idea that it must be limited to activities focusing on 'learning.' Higgins and Johns denounced the link between CALL and explicit teaching as follows:

The computer, some say, serves only the conscious process of learning, and can do nothing to facilitate acquisition . . . [W]e hope to be able to show that this view is wrong, and that the computer is quite flexible enough to serve a variety of learning theories. (1984: 17)

Underwood made the same point as follows:

It is important to stress here that this negative view [of computers as useful only for explicit learning through drills and tutorials] by no means reflects limitations in computers themselves, but rather limitations in the programs being written . . . Although much of the literature is devoted to arguing that the computer cannot do this or cannot do that, what is meant is that no one is doing it. (1984: 50)

'It' according to Underwood referred to developing 'Communicative CALL,' which he defined with 13 premises intended to be consistent with Krashen's prescriptions for creating an environment for acquisition (e.g., communicative CALL will not judge all of the language students produce). Central to Underwood's approach to creating communicative CALL was the use of techniques from artificial intelligence (i.e., natural language processing) to recognize learners' input to the computer and to generate responses in order to create a 'meaningful' conversation between computer and learner.[7] These two books are considered seminal works in the evolution of CALL because they supply novel ideas for CALL – programs such as games and activities based on collaborative learning – which the authors saw as providing good contexts for acquisition.

The strand of SLA research stemming from Krashen's ideas about acquisition without explicit instruction failed to provide guidance for

[6] At the same time, some researchers continued to work on substantive technical issues of response recognition and analysis (Pusack, 1983; Lian, 1984).

[7] The microcomputers widely available during the early 1980s did not have enough memory for successful implementation of the type of AI approaches (real-time written conversation) Underwood advocated.

empirically based evaluation. Evaluation of CALL tended to be comprised of the developers' or users' opinion about the extent to which an activity seemed communicative on the basis of the type of tasks it asked learners to engage in. One type of task argued to allow for communicative language practice was based on text reconstruction, which consisted of variations on cloze exercises (Higgins & Johns, 1984). Variations included the following features: words deleted on a fixed-ratio basis, words deleted on the basis of some criteria, or all words deleted;[8] texts that the teacher entered into the program, texts that came with the program, or texts other learners constructed; with help options and scoring, or with simple yes/no judgements concerning the correctness of the learners' entries; with the end result being the completed text, or the end result responses to comprehension questions about the text. Advocates of 'acquisition-oriented' activities saw text reconstruction as sufficiently 'communicative' and 'learner-controlled' to argue for their pedagogical value. But two factors equally instrumental in their popularity were the computational simplicity of the program required to construct such learning activities and the fact that instructors were able to input their own texts, thereby producing customized CALL materials.

Another novel invention of this era was the computer-assisted concordancer activity. Borrowed from corpus linguistics, which had already been established as a mode of inquiry in linguistics when microcomputers became widespread in the early 1980s, concordancer software is used to identify words or expressions requested by the user and display them with reference to the lines in which they occurred in a text. Higgins and Johns (1984) suggested extending the practice of concordancing to language classrooms by showing the learner how to use the concordancer to retrieve the same types of linguistic data that teachers and linguists draw from. This activity was argued to empower the learner to investigate questions of vocabulary use and grammatical collocation on their own.

Although the primary impact of SLA theory was contributed by Krashen's ideas in the early 1980s, another influence came from research on individual differences (H. D. Brown, 1980). In particular, studies looked at hypotheses from SLA about the role of individual differences on the effectiveness of different instructional approaches (Abraham, 1985) and desirability of CALL (Chapelle & Jamieson, 1986). Investigating learning style and task variables in CALL,

---

[8] Jones and Fortescue (1987) claimed that among the various text reconstruction programs, the type in which all words are deleted, called a storyboard, was the most flexible and popular.

Abraham (1985) found that field-independent learners performed better on post-tests when they had used a rule presentation (deductive) approach and field-dependent learners performed better after using a lesson presenting examples of the structure (inductive). Investigating the same learner variable, Chapelle and Jamieson (1986) found field-independent ESL students tended to have a more negative attitude toward the CALL they investigated, while the field-dependent students had more positive attitudes. Related research combined CALL with SLA through examination of learner strategies in CALL (Curtin, Avner, & Provenzano, 1981; Jamieson & Chapelle, 1987).

In short, the early 1980s was an active time in the evolution of CALL because of the diversity of ideas proposed and the growing professional discussion. This progress, however, was coupled with the regression inherent in setting aside what had come before. Loritz aptly describes the early microcomputer phase as 'the adolescence of CALL . . . a time of exploration, a time of energy and exuberance, a time when old ways are discarded, a time when new identities are born and born again' (Loritz, 1995: 47). Despite the professional visibility of the 'communicative CALL' movement, the innovative work done in the UK, and some pioneering efforts in video, many CALL developers and users during this period appeared to be reinventing the CALL of the 1970s rather than building on experience, and they did so on microcomputers which were limited in memory size and in fundamental capabilities such as audio or display of foreign language character fonts.

Sophisticated microcomputers

The frustrations resulting from limitations of early microcomputers were short lived because of rapid developments during the 1980s. Throughout the decade, affordable machines came equipped with more and more memory, as well as capabilities for audio, graphics, and video. It became clear to many that computers were going to find a permanent place in language teaching and research. By the late 1980s, CALL had developed through a number of ambitious projects, professional infrastructure including teacher education, and more explicit treatment of evaluation issues. Work in CALT and CASLR began to appear as well.

Computer-assisted language learning

Developments in hardware and software made tenable Hart's (1981b), Underwood's (1984) and Phillips' (1985) suggestion that artificial intelligence in CALL be explored. Some also believed that the more sophisticated hardware and software would radically change the nature of CALL and its development:

[T]he possibilities [opened up by the more sophisticated microcomputers] are qualitatively different from those offered by the simpler equipment. It is not just a matter of having more memory to play around with: the more sophisticated machine calls for more sophisticated programming. The day of [do-it-yourself] CALL, of the hobbyist programmer, the teacher enthusiast presenting his class on Monday morning with the exercise he has spent the weekend programming, may be over. We are moving into an entirely new phase, the most distinctive feature of which is the Intelligent Tutoring System or ITS for language learning, Intelligent CALL. (Farrington, 1989: 68)

In retrospect, Farrington's characterization has been true of only one branch of CALL. The more sophisticated machine, it has turned out, can be equipped with more sophisticated software in the form of authoring tools so the 'hobbyist' and 'enthusiast' were able to communicate with the more sophisticated machines to produce more polished-looking software than had previously been possible. Even more important, however, was the fact that many CALL developers and users did not embrace the philosophy behind the intelligent tutoring system (i.e., that instruction should be designed to explicitly focus on learners' linguistic needs) and therefore pursued other CALL applications such as corpus exploration and computer-mediated communication activities.

Software development

Others tenaciously held the goal set out by Underwood (1984) that the computer could and should be programmed to 'communicate' with the learner through the natural language processing methods developed by the computational linguists working within artificial intelligence. One instructional design using these methods was modeled after a *microworld* which is intended to create an environment for learners to explore principles of math and physics.[9] The software Papert (1980) designed was a computer programming language called Logo which allowed children to see geometry in action by writing commands which would instruct the computer to draw shapes and designs of their choosing. This microworld, 'math-

---

[9] In Papert's own example of a microworld for language learning, he described an activity in which children program grammatical rules into the computer, which the computer then used to create poetry. He described what is learned as an understanding of grammatical concepts.

land,' allowed children to acquire math concepts through experimentation and play in an environment which showed them the immediate effects of their mathematical statements. The idea of acquisition through manipulation of a responsive environment was attractive to CALL developers in the early 1980s who were seeking ways in which the computer could create contexts suitable for implicit 'acquisition' in Krashen's sense. Higgins and Johns (1984), for example, proposed a 'grammarland' which would 'create a miniature universe of discourse and a program which would manipulate things in that universe, answer questions about it, ask questions, or do any of these things at random if the user merely want[ed] a demonstration' (p. 75). Attempts to extend the microworld principle to CALL have taken many different forms, which vary considerably in their levels of sophistication (e.g., Ashworth & Stelovsky, 1989; Coleman, 1985; Culley, Mulford, & Milbury-Steen, 1986; DeSmedt, 1995; Durrani, 1989; Sanders & Sanders, 1995).

The software made possible by the more sophisticated microcomputers also prompted development of text analysis programs (also called grammar checkers), which were designed to provide an automatic analysis of surface features of a learner's writing and feedback about grammatical and stylistic errors. Research into text analysis had actually begun on the mainframe computers of the 1960s, when US researchers explored the capabilities of text analysis software for automatically scoring L1 English students' essays for testing (Brock, 1995; Wresch, 1993) and for providing stylistic L1 guidance to technical writers. These programs used a combination of word and phrase pattern matching and syntactic parsing to provide writers advice on how they could improve the clarity and style of their documents. In the late 1980s, similar technologies were applied to ESL learners. Dissatisfaction with the quality of the feedback provided by L1 products to L2 learners (Brock, 1993; Liou, 1991; Pennington & Brock, 1992) resulted in a number of independent efforts to develop software which would identify the types of syntactic errors that particular L2 learners make (e.g., Cook, 1988; Liou, 1991; Levin, Evans, & Gates, 1991; Loritz, 1986; Sanders, 1991).

The realities of such projects were often frustrating, as researchers attested at annual conferences, and yet the rapidly evolving technologies of this time offered high hopes for development of CALL by combining research in educational technology (particularly hypermedia), artificial intelligence, computational linguistics, and speech recognition technologies. One such vision – a CALL program for learners studying Spanish in the US – was described by Underwood (1989):

The scene is the carrel of a multi-media lab. A student is sitting in front of a color video monitor connected to stereo headphones and a tiny microphone; at her fingertips are a computer keyboard and mouse. Out of sight is a powerful computer CPU and something which looks like a CD player with a stack of 5 1/4-inch disks. Using the mouse, the student points at a little square on the screen, clicks, and the screen fills with the sights and sounds of Madrid. A voice asks her (in Spanish) if she is ready to continue; speaking into the microphone, she answers, 'Si.' She asks to talk to Javier, one of the characters she had met before, because he might have some information she needs. The screen now shows the street in front of Javier's apartment. She rings the doorbell with a mouse-click and Javier appears on the screen. 'Buenos dias,' he says. The student begins to ask him questions. At times Javier seems reluctant to talk and she must rephrase her questions to get him to respond. At other times, he says that he is sorry, but he is unable to answer such questions, for political reasons. (1989: 80)

With sights set on images such as Underwood's, a number of large CALL projects were launched during this period. The highest profile of these in the late 1980s was the industry-funded Athena Project at Massachusetts Institute of Technology in the US. The intention, as reported in 1985, was to draw upon research conducted at the Artificial Intelligence lab and other campus-wide computer resources to create a 'discovery-rich environment for the student to explore and interact with' (Kramsch, Morgenstern, & Murray, 1985: 31) through the combination of video and natural language processing technologies. In a frank retrospective account of this project, which officially ended in 1994, the emphasis on software-focused research is evident (J. H. Murray, 1995). This emphasis is underscored in a description of the natural language processing (NLP) facet of the work:

NLP is hard. When we initiated our project, we naively thought that we could successfully build an NLP system in two to three years that could analyze and respond in real time to [written] input in any one of four European languages, up to the level of a fourth semester student. Instead, it took us five years to build a system that can process second- to fourth-semester level input pretty well and often in something approaching real time . . . Grammar writing eventually expanded to fill all available time, preventing us from implementing more than prototypes of the numerous applications based on NLP that we had originally intended to create. (Felshin, 1995: 271)

The Athena project was the most ambitious, but there were a number of others of that era focused on use of either natural language processing or video. For example, researchers at the University of Delaware received funding to explore the natural language processing technologies for developing a foreign language adventure game

(Culley, Mulford, & Milbury-Steen, 1986). To produce video-based CALL materials for several foreign languages, IBM funded a consortium of universities led by the University of Iowa. Products from this project have been widely used and have served as models for subsequent work. In the UK, the Technology Enhanced Language Learning (TELL) Consortium, consisting of 15 development centers and other affiliated evaluation centers, received substantial funds for developing multimedia language learning materials. A number of small projects were also undertaken in Canada during this period (Craven, Sinyor, & Paramskas, 1990).

Professional issues

As research and development continued in laboratories world-wide, CALL's professional infrastructure continued to expand. The Computers and Teaching Initiative Centre for Modern Languages (CTICML) was established in the UK at the University of Hull in 1988, and its journal, *ReCALL*, appeared shortly thereafter. Euro-CALL continued to hold regular meetings and to seek appropriate funding – an effort which finally succeeded in 1993. Another CALL conference in Europe at the University of Exeter became a regular event and a journal based there, *Computer Assisted Language Learning: An International Journal*, appeared in 1990. In Australia the journal dedicated to CALL, *On-CALL*, appeared in the mid 1980s, and another North American journal, *CÆLL Journal*, dedicated to CALL for English as a second language, appeared in 1989.

The content of the CALL books published during this period had evolved from introductions to CALL for teachers and applied linguists who had never worked with computers to more focused treatment of a particular facet of CALL. Methodologically oriented books with practical classroom techniques continued to appear but with less introduction to the computer and more focus on the pedagogical issues of CALL (e.g., Hardisty & Windeatt, 1989; Tribble & Jones, 1990). As Farrington had predicted, some researchers probed the uses and limits of artificial intelligence in CALL (Last, 1989; Swartz & Yazdani, 1992; *Computers and the Humanities*, 1989; Bailin, 1991; Holland, Kaplan, & Sams, 1995). Others worked toward philosophies and theoretical underpinnings for CALL (Higgins, 1988; Kenning & Kenning, 1990). Perhaps the most telling indication that CALL was evolving as a professional area of concern was a more explicit treatment of evaluation issues in some publications.

Evaluation issues

For the first time since the early CALL projects of the 1970s, explicit treatment of CALL evaluation and research issues began to appear in some CALL volumes (Dunkel, 1991; Smith, 1987; Pennington, 1989; Pennington & Stevens, 1992). Some of the suggestions that had come out as a result of experience with PLATO in the 1970s began to be taken up in a serious way. In 1981, conclusions drawn from the PLATO project were summarized as follows:

It is obvious that the developers of computer-based language materials have
given far too little attention to evaluation . . . If the issues are so complex
that conventional procedures (e.g., those employing group mean
differences) are inappropriate for providing an answer, then we should
present clear arguments why that is so and provide alternative analyses
(e.g., based on individualization or optimization features). (Hart, 1981b:
16)

Several edited volumes prepared at the end of the 1980s contained papers explaining difficulties with 'conventional procedures' and laid out rationales and procedures for examining CALL from the perspectives more consistent with second language classroom research. It was clear to many at that time that 'comparative research that attempts to illustrate the superiority of computers over some other medium for language instruction should forever be abandoned' (Pederson, 1987: 125).

Alternatives to assessing technology by isolating its effects within a learning environment were drawn from work in second language classroom research (e.g., Day, 1986; Gass & Madden, 1985) and ethnographic research (e.g., Watson-Gegeo, 1988; Davis, 1995). Influenced by the qualitative classroom research tradition, CALL researchers advocated study of CALL within its larger classroom and sociocultural context. Referring to the CALL research of the prior three decades, D. Johnson (1991) noted the following:

The bulk of research on computers and learning in educational
environments has focused on the cognitive aspects of learning. Yet, theory in
second language acquisition and research in second language acquisition
classrooms indicate that the social interactional environments of the
classroom are also crucial factors that affect language learning in important
ways. (1991: 62)

These suggestions from the 1980s have slowly but surely been taken up, yet the control-comparison group design seems to die hard in regular discussion at conferences and on Internet discussion lists.

Computer-assisted language testing

During this period, some language testing researchers attempted to apply some of the relatively new theory and computer methods from other types of tests to language testing. Concerns were also raised that computer-assisted testing should be seen as an opportunity to extend beyond common-place types of language test items and uses.

Computer-adaptive testing

The first-developed and most widely known use of the computer for interactive testing is a computer-adaptive test. Computer-adaptive language testing became possible through a combination of test theory for obtaining robust statistical information on test items and computer software for calculating the item statistics and providing adaptive control of item selection, presentation and evaluation (J. D. Brown, 1997; Green *et al.*, 1984; Tung, 1986; Wainer *et al.*, 1990). Harold Madsen, a professor at Brigham Young University, was among the first to apply these procedures to second language testing. He described a computer-adaptive language test as follows:

a very basic psychometric procedure which enables the examiner to measure language proficiency efficiently and with considerable precision. The adaptive or 'tailored' computer test accesses a specially calibrated item bank and is driven by a statistical routine which analyzes student responses to questions and selects items for the candidate that are of appropriate difficulty. Then, when a specified standard error of measurement is reached, the exam is terminated . . . [T]he psychometrically sound tailoring process in computer adaptive tests . . . provides for a more effective measure of language proficiency. (1991: 238–239)

The advantage was seen as primarily one of efficiency relative to paper-and-pencil tests, particularly because any individual examinee needed to complete only about one-third of the items. Moreover, Madsen reported that the international students who took the ESL tests tended to like the computer-delivered version of the test. Others seeking similar improvements and those interested in experimenting with CALT have developed similar testing projects for a variety of languages and purposes (e.g., Kaya-Carton, Carton, & Dandonoli, 1991; Burston & Monville-Burston, 1995; Brown & Iwashita, 1996; Young *et al.*, 1996; Laurier, 1999; Dunkel, 1999).

Alternatives to computer-adaptive testing

Interest in computer-adaptive testing (CAT) was growing by the mid 1980s, but at the same time it seemed evident that this was a narrow path to take in the exploration of CALT. In a seminal paper of this era, Canale (1986) raised questions concerning the effects of computer-adaptive reading tests on the critical needs in language testing because of the assumption of unidimensionality that their psychometric model relies on.

Such an assumption threatens to be trivializing and compromising in the following senses: First, it is overly reductionist and misleading to maintain that reading comprehension comprises only one major dimension, whatever that dimension might be . . . Second, and more generally, the assumption of unidimensionality threatens to compromise the value of CAT for educational achievement and diagnostic purposes. It is difficult to understand how CAT could serve useful achievement and diagnostic purposes if reading comprehension, for example, is assumed to be unidimensional and consequently neither influenced by instruction nor decomposable into meaningful subparts. (1986: 34–35)

Canale argued that CALT offered the opportunity to better understand multidimensional language constructs and improve the usefulness of testing for instruction, but that to realize these potentials researchers needed to look beyond testing methods constrained by a unidimensional psychometric model.

Some have argued that CALT applications could be constructed to resemble instructional activities, and that these assessments could record and analyze learners' performance to provide them with useful information about their knowledge and needs. Canale speculated on future assessments for reading comprehension by looking toward work in intelligent tutoring systems:

[W]ork on . . . 'intelligent tutoring systems' is promising for [CAT] of reading comprehension . . . Such research and images provide promising stepping stones if we are interested in moving toward more learner controlled, process-oriented and unintrusive assessment events in the language classroom. (1986: 38)

Additional suggestions about fruitful connections between instruction and assessment have been made periodically (Alderson, 1990, 1991; Corbel, 1993; Meunier, 1994; Scott & New, 1994). Alderson (1990), for example, suggested that the information gathered by the computer could encourage learners to develop their own strategies for evaluation. In fact, a number of the early CALL projects (Otto, 1989) included extensive evaluation and systematic feedback to learners. The French curriculum on the PLATO system at the University of Illinois, for example, kept records on learners' performance during each session of their work and over the course of the semester to provide them with summary information about their performance as they requested it (Marty, 1981). However, these capabilities have yet to be explored from an assessment perspective.

Computer-assisted SLA research

By the end of the 1980s, the concerns of many SLA researchers had evolved away from the idea that solely the input that learners receive through communicative activities would promote acquisition. Research through the decade had convinced many that learners need to notice and interact with linguistic input in order to acquire the target language (e.g., Schmidt & Frota, 1986; Long, 1985; Swain, 1985; Doughty & Pica, 1986). Moreover, this line of research supported empirical approaches to evaluating linguistic interaction and language development. Both of these developments in SLA research began to influence work in CASLA toward the end of the decade.

In an important paper in 1987, Doughty had laid out theoretical underpinnings from SLA with potential links to CALL. Shortly thereafter, she conducted a study using materials based on these theoretical principles, i.e., about the value of salient grammatical input. By constructing computer-assisted experimental materials that operationalized theoretically different learning conditions, Doughty (1991) compared the effects of explicitly salient L2 input with input which was not explicitly flagged to direct learners' attention. The findings, which supported theoretical predictions (e.g., learners receiving salient input performed better on grammatical post-tests than did the group receiving normal input), offered hope for the use of technology in the study of second language acquisition.

Other SLA research during this period used the computer for assessment of learners' strategies, thereby beginning to probe some of the methodological issues in assessment of processes of interest to SLA researchers such as monitoring input, advance preparation, and resourcing (Jamieson & Chapelle, 1987; Chapelle & Mizuno, 1989). These two areas – operationalization of learning conditions and assessment of learners' processes – were developed somewhat through the 1990s, but continue to hold untapped potential.

Local area networks

While research and development of CASLA for microcomputers continued, the widespread use of networked computers in the early 1990s expanded the characteristics of CALL activities. By the early 1990s, many teaching staff within higher education were connected to the Internet and had become participants in international electronic discussion lists, but the most tangible development for language learners was the adoption of Local Area Network (LAN) technology for computer labs.

Computer-assisted language learning

Prior to the LAN, CALL activities had for the most part been developed around computer–learner interactions – even if more than one learner participated in those interactions at a time (e.g., Piper, 1986). LAN activities, in contrast, were built around learner–learner interactions through networked computers. Technically speaking, computer-mediated communication has been in practice since the 1960s, when users of a single mainframe computer could exchange messages in both synchronous and asynchronous modes. Only with the development of LANs and the Internet, however, was this technology put into pedagogical use for teaching collaborative L1 writing, for providing practice in second languages, and for instructing deaf learners in 'written conversation' (Bruce, Peyton, & Batson, 1993). Warschauer (1995b) described uses of computer-mediated communication in and across second language classrooms, and many cases are given in Warschauer (1995a).

This teaching methodology provided a written record of learners' on-line discussion which could be examined from the perspectives of discourse analysis and SLA. Chun was among the first to publish results of such research based on an activity she constructed in which first- and second-year college learners of German in the US were to use the target language for functions associated with interpersonal communication (Chun, 1994). Through discourse analysis of the learners' electronic discussion, she identified the variety of interpersonal functions she had hoped the activity would engender, including some she believed might not typically be found in teacher-led classrooms: initiation of discussion through questions posed by students to the rest of the class, statements to the teacher which were not in response to questions, requests for clarification, and feedback from one learner to another. The LAN-based computer-assisted discussion methodology is examined in a volume containing case-studies and discussion of research edited by Swaffar, Romano, Markley, and Arens (1998).

Other CALL research continued as well. For example, a study combining methods in educational technology and computational linguistics investigated the effects of various types of response-contingent feedback to learners of Japanese who were studying the placement of syntactic particles. Nagata (1993) compared achievement of learners who received feedback that the computer had selected on the basis of an analysis of their response with those who had received only an indication of where they had made an error. The former group performed significantly better on both post-tests and end-of-semester tests, indicating that the computational linguistic methods had resulted in more effective feedback for learners to develop aspects of their syntax. Considerable experience and insight was gained in the use of wordprocessing for L2 writers during this period as well (Pennington, 1996).

Computer-assisted language testing

Developments in second language testing during this period were not directly related to the collaborative activities of LANs, but clearly this development in hardware configuration strengthened convictions that computers can and should be used for language testing. For example, testing centers could be envisaged as a server connected to computers in a single room. At the same time, many of the individual voices that had been calling for testing reform throughout the 1980s formed a noticeable chorus whose view was reflected in statements such as this one from the president of Educational Testing Service in the US: 'Testing is a field in the process of being recreated' (Cole, 1993: 72). The recreation, which was intended to include philosophical, social, and technical facets of assessment (including language assessment), was to have a particular impact on computer-assisted testing because computers were expected to play an essential role within new paradigms of testing. At least within the rhetoric of the leaders in assessment in the US, computer-assisted testing was expected to play an important role in testing practices.

More important than the short-term operational link between computers and testing, however, is the reconceptualization of fundamental issues which must be probed if computers are to contribute substantively to language testing. For example, when a writing test requires test takers to compose their essays at a computer keyboard, should the score obtained from the test be considered an indicator of writing ability in the same sense as the score on the paper-and-pencil test would be? When a computer program performs a detailed analysis of learners' linguistic responses to open-ended questions, what meaning can be attributed to the information provided by the program? Answers to both of these questions require an understanding of how test developers define the constructs they hope to measure and how tests are evaluated to determine the extent to which they are successful in measuring these constructs. In the early 1990s, some of these questions began to be probed (Jamieson *et al.*, 1993), but the depth and breadth of the issues raised by expanding computer-assisted testing beyond computer-adaptive testing had barely been suggested.

Computer-assisted SLA research

LANs expanded the possibilities for data collection in SLA research, which some researchers took advantage of, but some other researchers designed experiments on microcomputers which were also sufficient for small-scale data collection in laboratory settings. For example, DeKeyser (1995) developed a computer-assisted experiment to implement two learning conditions in a study of whether explicit-deductive or implicit-inductive learning worked better for simple categorical grammar rules and for linguistic prototypes. The computer introduced subjects to the rules or examples (depending on the condition) of an artificial language which included both categorical rules and prototypical patterns. The computer also controlled a speeded condition in which monitoring (in the sense of drawing on explicit knowledge) would not be expected. Results from a speeded judgement test, which did not allow time for learners to draw on explicit knowledge, provided evidence that the categorical rules had not been learned implicitly. Other computer-delivered tasks were devised for gathering data from which researchers made inferences about the interlanguage knowledge and processing strategies learners use while they are performing in classroom or classroom-like activities (Bland *et al.*, 1990; Hulstijn, 1993).

Also important during this period was SLA research drawing on computational linguistics to investigate how interlanguage grammars can be expressed formally with computer programs. Studying the developing grammars of learners of Dutch as a second language, Huiskens, Coppen and Jagtman (1991) found they had to modify the type of formalism computational linguists use for native-speaker grammars to express changes in the learners' grammars over time. The result is a grammar – expressed in a formalism interpretable by both computer and researcher – whose adequacy for accounting for the Dutch interlanguage data can be demonstrated empirically. Any of the data which the formalism will not identify correctly require the researcher to reconsider and modify the hypothesized rules of the learner's grammar. This method of expressing and testing interlanguage grammars makes explicit a number of methodological questions for interlanguage research (Jagtman, Coppen, & Bongaerts,

1991), and therefore holds promise even though this work was not used in interactive tasks.

The early 1990s saw substantive developments in all three areas – developments that would evolve throughout the decade. These developments were discussed regularly on the newly formed international discussion lists on the Internet. D. Douglas (1995) cited 1990 as a watershed year for language testing in part because of the formation of the Internet discussion list L-TEST, which has brought the international community of researchers and practitioners concerned with language testing into contact on a continuous basis. In this and other professional discussion groups, computer-related issues, which were once the concern of only a small fraction of the profession, began to be discussed 'in front of' everyone.

The Internet

By the middle of the 1990s, international connectivity was no longer confined to teaching staff in higher education because the instructional 'network' no longer was confined to the network of a LAN in a computer lab. The Internet by the mid 1990s began to affect most facets of professional life, including CASLA. Whereas the microcomputer of the early 1980s provided an affordable tool for teachers to explore, the Internet of the 1990s introduced universal access to CASLA materials and information as well as hybrid applications offering learners the best of both worlds (e.g., Burston, 1998). Some of the teacher education that had taken place in summer courses and workshops began to be conducted on a daily basis through discussion groups on the Internet. A new professional journal, *Language Learning & Technology*, published on the World Wide Web, began at the National Foreign Language Resource Center at the University of Hawai'i.

One immediately obvious effect on CASLA was that the resource-intensive activity of software development could be undertaken with the hope that efforts would have an impact on a large number of students through the Web. From the learners' perspective, interesting opportunities for autonomous language learning and self-assessment became widely available rather than being tied to particular institutions. CALL activities were no longer limited to interaction with the computer and with other students in the class, but included communication with learners in other parts of the world – either learners from specific classes chosen by instructors or self-selected participants who choose to spend time in computer-mediated communication for language learning (Paramskas, 1993; Warschauer, 1995a, 1995b).

Cummins and Sayers (1995) described potential benefits of Internet collaborations for SLA: communication can occur at a distance and asynchronously.

Distance . . . creates the possibility of collaboration with an unknown but knowable audience, principally through written communication. The inevitable cultural differences that exist between distant groups require clarity of written communication in disclosing local realities . . . asynchronicity allows second language learners the extra time they need to elaborate and polish written texts based on 'models' of native speakers of the target language, while seeking and relying heavily upon assistance from their local language and cultural resources in the form of teachers, peers and community members. (1995: 32–33)

Others have suggested the value of synchronous communications. An example of a synchronous CALL activity takes place in a chat room, or 'MOO,' on the Internet. Turbee (1995) described a MOO as follows:

MOO is a telnet-accessible text-based virtual environment in which synchronous communication takes place between 'players' logged on at the same time. MOO stands for 'MUD, Object Oriented.' A MUD is a multiple-user domain. The domain, or environment, is created by players who use MOO programming, which normally is in English, to write text that describes objects such as characters, rooms and things. The players may interact with and manipulate the objects, or they may simply 'talk' with each other in the created spaces. (1995: 233)

When the Internet became accessible to so many language learners, interested CALL users began constructing 'MOOs' where their learners could 'meet' and 'converse with' other speakers of the target language from around the world. Teachers' interest in Internet activities was revealed by indicators such as the popularity of Warschauer's book *E-mail for English Teaching* published in 1995. The activities described in this book obviously break through the walls of the traditional classroom to the extent that some have suggested a new pedagogy needs to be conceptualized if teachers and learners are to benefit from the resources of the Internet.

This is the position taken by many authors in a 1998 volume of papers from an Australian conference, *Language Learning through Social Computing* (Debski, Gassin, & Smith, 1997). The volume introduces the classroom practices and philosophical underpinnings of approaches to CALL which build on collaborative L2 teaching and learning. Similarly, in their introduction to the edited volume *Network-Based Language Teaching: Concepts and Practice*, Warschauer and Kern (2000) highlight the social and collaborative facets of CALL by drawing upon social constructionist philosophy to introduce the issues. A third edited volume in the late 1990s, *Computer-Enhanced Language Learning* (Egbert & Hanson-Smith, 1999), also reflects some of these perspectives while maintaining a more eclectic approach with chapters intended to cover a variety of conditions theorized to affect SLA, including sociocultural factors.

Regardless of how an Internet pedagogy is formulated, it must take into account the cross-cultural communication that is inevitable in most Internet activities. A few studies have identified some benefits through qualitative research investigating learners' experiences and attitudes. For example, Sanaoui and Lapkin (1992) found that electronic communication among English and French learners in grade 12 (aged 17–18) provided them with good language practice while increasing their appreciation for the target culture. Warschauer and Lepeintre (1997) described their observations of both positive and negative cross-cultural contact on an Internet list designed for EFL practice in which learners can exchange messages with other EFL learners throughout the world. Other discussion groups on the Internet take place in many different languages, thereby providing learners with convenient access to native and proficient speakers of the target language. Some depict technology as playing a central role in the language learning of the future precisely because of the cross-cultural experience it can provide learners through experiential learning (Cummins & Sayers, 1995; Debski, 1997), while others raise the equally important issue of the hegemony associated with technology for L2 teaching and testing (D. E. Murray, 2000). The Internet appears to be unique among tools of mass media and communication in both the cross-cultural opportunities it can provide and the strength with which it may privilege particular ideologies and practices (Hawisher & Self, 2000).

Questions about methodologies and implications of cross-cultural contact that have begun to be formulated for CALL will no doubt see their analogs in the future discussion of CALT and CASLR. As these issues take shape, it also seems safe to predict that the questions of evaluation will continue to be critical for the evolution of all three areas. How are applied linguists to evaluate the extent to which technology is being exploited in a manner that is beneficial to learners and to the profession? This fundamental question has been raised repeatedly throughout the past two decades, but primary attention has been devoted to practice (i.e., learning new technologies and developing new applications), and therefore evaluation issues are set aside. Even in Levy's (1997) substantial and thoughtful overview of CALL, the focus is on theory and practice, rather than methods of evaluating either. All of these areas – new technologies, theoretical guidance, and pedagogical practice – are critical to the use of CASLA, but as possibilities for technology, theory, and pedagogy expand, the need for evaluation has become more urgent.

The need is seen daily on professional discussion lists on the Internet. It is evident from ongoing discussion of the value of various perspectives for evaluation of CALL (Chapelle, 1997; 1998b; 1999a; Salaberry, 1999; Warschauer, 1998). Richard Tucker underscored the problem in his 1999 address at the annual CALICO symposium:

we must implement as soon as is practical a multifaceted and longitudinal research agenda to examine the value added to students who pursue some or all of their language education using innovative technologies. (2000: 217)

The issue is how to define 'value added' and how to assess the extent to which value has been added for learners who use CALL. Evaluation of CALT and CASLR has received even less attention. The next chapter begins to explore some potential bases for evaluation of all three areas through description of the academic areas that have influenced CASLA in the past. I consider the extent to which each might contribute to perspectives and methods for evaluation of CASLA.

2 The context and challenge for CASLA

The history of CASLA in the previous chapter revealed some of its interconnections with other academic areas, and in fact, developments in CASLA were precipitated by work in related fields. It is informative, therefore, to look more carefully at what these areas have to offer, particularly in terms of methods for evaluation. This chapter points out some of the important contributions of other areas for the technical infrastructure of CASLA as well as some general orientations to evaluation issues. At the same time, it argues that the specifics of evaluation for second language learning and assessment must be developed from relevant perspectives in applied linguistics.

Disciplines related to CASLA

In education, linguistics, and psychology, computer applications have been the subject of scholarly inquiry, thereby creating sub-disciplines directly relevant to CASLA such as 'educational technology' and 'computational linguistics.' Six such computer-related subdisciplines have made significant contributions to CASLA: educational technology, computer-supported collaborative learning, artificial intelligence, computational linguistics, corpus linguistics, and computer-assisted assessment.[1] Because these six have provided bases for CASLA, a brief examination of each will help to define CASLA from a historical, disciplinary perspective which reveals the origins of some current philosophies and practices.

---

[1] One might argue that the area of human–computer interaction (HCI) (e.g., Baecker & Buxton, 1987) provides an additional foundation for CASLA. Despite the logical relevance of work in this area of psychology, there is little if any evidence that CASLA has in fact been influenced by HCI research. See Levy (1997, Chapter 3) for a somewhat different characterization of the areas influencing CALL; discussion of the significance of HCI is included.

Educational technology

CALL has its roots in educational technology, a specialization within the study of education that has been active since the 1960s (Reiser, 1987; Saettler, 1990). By the early 1970s, a number of journals devoted to the topic had begun: *Programmed Learning and Educational Technology* (appeared in 1964), *Educational Technology* (appeared in 1966), *Journal of Educational Technology* (appeared in 1972), and *Journal of Computer-Based Instruction* (appeared in 1974). These pioneers in the field have been joined by others such as *Journal of Research in Educational Computing* (appeared in 1985), and *Machine-Mediated Learning* (appeared in 1991).

Researchers and practitioners in educational technology attempt to devise the best ways of using computer technology for instruction across subject areas and to design valid ways of evaluating its effectiveness. In the 1960s, both computer-assisted instruction and evaluation methods were strongly influenced by the 'systems approach' to instructional design (Dick & Carey, 1985; 1996), which encompasses a philosophy and broad range of practices for planning, developing, and implementing instruction, but which is known to many through the specific practices described by Skinner (1954; 1961) for programmed learning.[2] By the 1970s, researchers were experimenting with a variety of approaches for instructional materials, some of which were explicitly intended as alternatives to the philosophy and practice of the systems approach (Burton & Brown, 1982; Falbel, 1991; Mandinach & Linn, 1986; Papert, 1980), and much effort has been invested in articulating ideals of courseware design (e.g., Grabinger & Dunlap, 1996). Perspectives from educational technology on how to evaluate these learning activities have evolved over the years from the view that research should adopt an experimental or quasi-experimental design (Alderman, 1978; Kulik, Kulik, & Schwalb, 1986) to the perspective that such research is too narrowly focused and product-oriented (R. E. Clark, 1985; 1994; Papert, 1987). The debate on ideal research designs for investigating educational technology, which continues today, can be seen, for example, in a special issue of the journal *Educational Technology Research & Development* (volume 42 (2), 1994).

---

[2] Many of the practices consistent with the systems approach such as Skinner's programmed learning have a strong empiricist orientation because they define learning by breaking it up into its components, which are described as observable behaviors. The systems approach can also be coupled with cognitive approaches for the design and analysis of learning and instruction by defining components in cognitive terms (e.g. Gagne & Glasser, 1987).

Throughout this history, applied linguists have occasionally contributed to the educational technology literature with reports of CALL projects (e.g., Atkinson & Hansen, 1966; Hsu, Chapelle, & Thompson, 1993; Van Campen, 1981) but by the mid 1980s CALL had developed into a distinct professional community marked primarily by the success of professional organizations and journals devoted specifically to CALL: Computer-Assisted Language Instruction Consortium (CALICO) with *CALICO Journal* (first issue in 1983) in North America and EuroCALL along with two journals, *ReCALL* (first issue in 1990) and *Computer Assisted Language Learning: An International Journal* (first issue 1990) in Europe.[3] Despite the apparent independence of CALL, its actual practice and philosophies have remained closely tied to those of educational technology. At first, CALL developed within the philosophies of the systems approach to instructional design (Hart, 1981a), and by the 1970s research and development of diverse CALL activities was underway (see Hart, 1981a, and Chapelle & Jamieson, 1983, for a variety of examples), while explicit criticism of practices reflecting the systems approach began to appear (e.g., Sanders & Kenner, 1981). Criticisms were accompanied by suggestions parallel to those made by researchers in educational technology concerning how to develop alternative pedagogical approaches for second language learning (e.g., Underwood, 1984; Higgins & Johns, 1984; Johns, 1986; Paramskas, 1993).

With few exceptions (e.g., Doughty, 1987), discussion of CALL evaluation has also relied heavily on work in educational technology (e.g., Dunkel, 1991; Chapelle & Jamieson, 1991). The earliest CALL evaluation efforts were launched through larger projects in educational technology. For example, in the US, large-scale evaluations began in the 1960s when several universities with the help of federal funding initiated projects to investigate the success that could be achieved with computer-assisted instruction. Researchers in these programs were obligated to provide evidence about the effectiveness of the computer for teaching academic material in part to inform future funding for research and development. Numerous investigations were conducted with the objective of comparing the learning outcomes achieved through computer-assisted instruction with those obtained in traditional classrooms (e.g., Kulik, Kulik, & Schwalb, 1986). Influenced by this thinking, early CALL research attempted to demonstrate CALL's effectiveness using quasi-experimental research

---

[3] The first issue of *System*, a journal focusing on the use of technology in second language education, had appeared in Europe as a newsletter in 1973.

designs, which compared cognitive and affective outcomes of learners who participated in computer-based instruction with those who participated in regular classrooms (for summaries see Chapelle & Jamieson, 1989; 1991; Chapelle, Jamieson, & Park, 1996; Dunkel, 1991). From this work one can cite some studies in which CALL users performed better than learners who did not use CALL, others in which no differences were found, and even a few in which the control group performed better. Summaries of this work argue that results of this research do not warrant conclusions to be drawn about 'the computer' as a teaching method.

Problems with equating the computer to teaching method have been noted by CALL researchers, but the need for evaluation paradigms to rely on a more complex view of learning has been articulated most clearly by researchers in educational technology. In particular, R. E. Clark (e.g., 1985; 1994), the most public critic of instructional media research, explains that 'instructional methods [have] been confounded with media and that it is the methods which influence learning' (R. E. Clark, 1994: 22). Clark defines 'methods' as the 'structural' characteristics of tasks for learners which engender the processes and strategies necessary for learning; he contrasts methods with 'media,' a means of delivering methods to learners. His argument is that any 'method' produced in a media-assisted format can also be delivered by other means and therefore media may 'influence the cost or speed (efficiency) of learning but methods are causal in learning' (1994: 26). This argument is continually challenged on a number of grounds, yet most would agree that Clark succeeds in questioning the meaningfulness of any summary statement making claims about the overall effects of *the computer* on learning. Moreover, most would agree that what is needed rather than studies focused on the computer are studies which attempt to investigate the relevant task variables in computer-assisted learning environments. A second related problem of studies investigating computer effects, as Jonassen (1985) pointed out, is that they tend to ignore characteristics of individual learners. These problems of task and learner definition do not question the basic tenets of the treatment-outcome experimental design in educational research; they suggest instead that the paradigm has been poorly implemented.

Other educational technology researchers have attacked the research methods associated with logical positivism by criticizing outcomes-oriented research. They argue that studies focusing on quantified outcomes of a group of learners fail to document the many contextual factors influencing the process of learning. An important advocate for creative computer uses in education, Seymour Papert, asserted the need for research to examine the processes occurring within a classroom culture rather than the effects of a single technology (Papert, 1987). Other researchers, particularly those working within the social constructivist paradigm, echo this concern, arguing for example that 'the whole educational context that is created online . . . needs to be the focus of analysis' in research on computer use (Riel & Harasim, 1994: 92). Proponents of investigating contexts of computer use emphasize the significance of the processes through which linguistic interactions help to construct the meanings relevant to learning and they therefore support the use of qualitative research methods. In short, some evaluation perspectives that are relevant to CALL have originated in the field of educational technology.

Computer-supported collaborative learning

The area called 'computer-supported collaborative learning' (CSCL) may be considered a branch of educational technology, but work in this area appears to be motivated by some distinct philosophies and practices. In the introduction to a 1996 volume introducing educational theory associated with CSCL, Koschmann described what he considered a paradigm shift (in Kuhn's sense) relative to prior work in educational technology:

We are currently witnessing the emergence of a new paradigm in [educational technology] research; one that is based on different assumptions about the nature of learning and one that incorporates a new set of research practices. Although there is a noted lack of agreement among [other paradigms in educational technology] with respect to their theories and learning pedagogy, [they] approach learning and instruction as psychological matters (be they viewed behavioristically or cognitively) and, as such, are researchable by traditional methods of psychological experimentation. This newly emerging paradigm, on the other hand, is built upon the research traditions of those disciplines – anthropology, sociology, linguistics, communication science – that are devoted to understanding language, culture, and other aspects of the social setting. (1996: 10–11)

Researchers in this area refer to the emerging paradigm as 'a cultural constructivist approach' (Scott, Cole, & Engel, 1992). Constructivism encompasses a complex of philosophies and beliefs about the way that learning and experience are internalized and transferred. For example, most constructivists would argue that students' learning experience is critical to what they learn and how they are able to use it (Duffy & Jonassen, 1992). The cultural dimension includes the essential role the social environment plays in learning. The significance placed on the context of learning is reflected by their expression 'situated learning.'

The constructivist perspectives most closely associated with CSCL have roots in Vygotskyan cultural psychology (Wertsch, 1985). Vygotsky, who lived in the first half of the 20th century, has recently been rediscovered and reinterpreted by psychologists (e.g., Newman & Holzman, 1993) and some second language acquisition researchers (Lantolf & Appel, 1994). Vygotskyan psychology 'makes sense of "learning" by reference to the social structure of activity – rather than by reference to the mental structure of the individual' (Crook, 1994: 78). With respect to CASLA, the social structure of an activity can include the computer software with which a learner interacts in addition to other learners who collaborate in the same room or from remote locations through networked computers. A cultural constructivist approach hypothesizes that the experience crucial for individual cognitive development takes place through interaction with others, and therefore key evidence for the quality of a learning activity should be found in the discourse that occurs in the collaborative environment. Consistent with its philosophical foundations, research on computer-assisted collaboration takes the form of qualitative content analysis of collaborative discourse (e.g., Henri, 1992; Mason, 1992).

Some of the methodological approaches of CSCL, which overlap with those of second language classroom researchers, have been applied in collaborative CALL activities (Abraham & Liou, 1991; Esling, 1991; Mohan, 1992; Piper, 1986; Renie & Chanier, 1995), and more recently, with the introduction of Internet CALL activities, the idea of a new emerging paradigm based on social constructivist theory has been echoed in the CALL literature as well (Kemp, 1993; Debski, Gassin, & Smith, 1997; Warschauer, 1997b; Warschauer & Kern, 2000).

Artificial intelligence

Artificial intelligence (AI), which encompasses principles for the design of computer programs, combines perspectives from disciplines such as computer science, cognitive psychology, and linguistics (Charniak & McDermott, 1985). The particular area of AI which has played a significant role in the development of some types of instructional software is documented in edited volumes such as *Intelligent Tutoring Systems* (Sleeman & Brown, 1982a) and *Artificial Intelligence and Education. Volume 1: Learning Environments and Tutoring Systems* (Lawler & Yazdani, 1987). Sleeman and Brown (1982b) described the purpose and challenge of intelligent tutoring systems (ITS) research and development as follows:

These systems attempt to provide the problem-solving experience and motivation of 'discovery' learning with the effective guidance of tutorial interactions. These two objectives are often in conflict since, to tutor well, the system must constrain the student's instructional paths and exercises to those whose answers and likely mistakes can be completely specified ahead of time. To overcome these limitations, the system must have its *own* problem-solving expertise, its own diagnostic or student modelling capabilities and its own explanatory capabilities. In order to orchestrate these reasoning capabilities it must also have control or tutorial strategies specifying *when* to interrupt a student's problem-solving activity, *what* to say and *how* best to say it; all in order to provide the student with instructionally effective advice. (1982b: 1–2; emphasis in original)

These basic principles of ITSs are illustrated in Sleeman and Brown's volume through systems designed to teach subjects such as meteorology, algebra, elementary math, programming, and circuits. Computational recognition and production of natural language was an issue in their design only to the extent that it was necessary for the interface with the learner. For example, in the ITS on circuits, the system is designed to engage in an interactive dialog with the learner about the construction and operation of circuits and must therefore recognize learners' questions such as 'What is the current through R11? Across R9?' and respond with statements such as 'The current through R9 is 10 milliamps' (Brown, Burton, & de Kleer, 1982: 242).

Despite some negative appraisal of the feasibility and usefulness of ITS technology for CALL (e.g., Last, 1989; Higgins, 1988), discussion of such projects can be found throughout the history of CALL (e.g., Markosian & Ager, 1983; *Computers and the Humanities*, volume 23 (1), 1989; *CALICO Journal*, volume 9 (1), 1991) and more recently in the edited volumes *Intelligent Tutoring Systems for Foreign Language Learning* (Swartz & Yazdani, 1992) and *Intelligent Language Tutors: Theory Shaping Technology* (Holland, Kaplan, & Sams, 1995). In fact, a number of CALL developers work with AI approaches; however, in many cases 'AI' refers only to the language recognition component of the system rather than the full set of tutorial strategies that Sleeman and Brown explained. An example of an 'intelligent' CALL system which includes tutorial strategies is described by Chanier, Pengelly, Twidale, and Self (1992). This system was designed for learners of French (represented by 'L' in the following dialog) who are instructed to use the system (S) to discover the amount of their inheritance (according to conditions specified in a will) by querying the system about the family relationships of those mentioned in the will.

L: Qui sont les frères de Jean?   [Who are Jean's brothers?]
S: Robert et Tom.
L: Qui est marié à Tom?   [Who is married to Tom?]
S: Anne.
L: Est-ce que je le fils de Tom?   [Am I Tom's son?]
S: There is a problem in your last sentence.
    Would you accept this utterance (yes/no)?:
    Est-ce qu'il vivant?   [Is he living?]
L: yes.
S: OK, I think the problem is the following:
    Even if your utterance is comprehensible, there is a missing
    constituent of <the verb être>. (Chanier *et al.*, 1992: 146)

The tutorial strategy is illustrated by the program's attempt to discover whether or not the learner thinks that the verb *être* is unnecessary in questions formed with *Est-ce que* and to provide correction if necessary. Evaluation of such systems has focused on the success of the error identification and tutorial strategy in delivering appropriate material to the learner rather than on the learner's success in acquiring what was the focus of the interaction (Swartz, 1992).

Computational linguistics

Computational linguistics is sometimes viewed as one of the topics within AI but, in fact, this area does maintain a distinct academic community with an annual conference and the *Journal of Computational Linguistics*, which appeared in 1974 (as the *American Journal of Computational Linguistics*). It is useful to consider this area independently because of the specific relevance it holds for CASLA in providing natural language processing technologies. The area of computational linguistics investigates machine recognition and production of human language, including theoretical implications of a processing perspective toward linguistic description and the formal characteristics of computational grammars (Gazdar & Mellish, 1989; Winograd, 1983). Despite some progress in speech recognition, the best developed technologies within computational linguistics are those for recognizing written linguistic input to the computer and producing appropriate responses in an interactive mode within a defined topic domain. An example of such a 'conversation' comes from a classic early computational linguistics project, whose purpose was to identify precisely the information that the computer program (C) would have to include in order to carry on a conversation with a human (H) about colored blocks on a table. The following is an example of a segment from such a 'conversation:'

H: What does the box contain?
C: THE BLUE PYRAMID AND THE BLUE BLOCK.
H: What is the pyramid supported by?
C: THE BOX.
H: How many blocks are not in the box?
C: FOUR OF THEM. (Winograd, 1972: 9–10)

The idea of such a human–computer dialog within a limited domain captured the imagination of CALL researchers, who began to work on instructional software which offered learners interactive environments for conversing with the computer about topics such as two people in a room (Higgins & Johns, 1984), blocks similar to those in Winograd's research (Coleman, 1985), a spy adventure (Sanders & Sanders, 1995), a mystery house (Culley, Mulford, & Milbury-Steen, 1986), and provisioning a lifeboat (S. A. Douglas, 1995). Techniques from computational linguistics have contributed to other types of CASLA as well – in other forms of interactive instructional software for recognizing learners' input to the computer (Cook, 1988; Imlah & du Boulay, 1985; Levin, Evans, & Gates, 1991; Loritz, 1986; Sanders & Sanders, 1989) and in text analysis software for grammar checking (Liou, 1991; Hull *et al.*, 1987; Sanders & Sanders, 1987). In language testing, computational linguistics techniques can be used for evaluating learners' responses to open-ended questions (Henning *et al.*, 1993) and in second language research, for writing grammars which describe learners' interlanguage (Huiskens, Coppen, & Jagtman, 1991; Jagtman, Coppen, & Bongaerts, 1991).

Computational linguistics has proven useful for analysis of learners' language in CALL, and yet an important difference exists between the work of the majority of computational linguists and developers of CASLA. Computational linguists work primarily on recognition problems involving the language of proficient language users whereas language recognition in CASLA requires computer programs which can identify learner language. Pienemann (1992) described the problem as follows:

All interlanguage varieties of a given target language have certain crucial features in common: they share a lexicon, an as yet undetermined subset of the rule system of that target language, and a set of rules which are neither part of the source language nor of the target language. Thus many formal features of these developing systems are unknown to the researcher. (1992: 60–61)

His point is that, given the unpredictability of the grammatical forms that a learner may produce, it seems impossible to write a program that will recognize the learner's language. Yet, this is exactly the problem that CALL developers tackle when they write response analysis algorithms. Chanier, Pengelly, Twidale, and Self (1992) explain that the key to recognition of interlanguage forms is to restrict the subject domain of the input language, as Winograd (1972) showed for native language forms.

We have tried to place the learner in a problem-solving situation where the second language is being used for a purpose, but where the domain of discourse is sufficiently restricted so that a system could be developed to understand the meaning of the inputs [i.e., the learner's interlanguage forms] well enough to sustain a dialogue. (1992: 126)

This approach is an important contribution to the solution; however, in addition to these initial design considerations, a crucial need is the type of empirically based discourse analysis which others have noted might be useful for evaluation of computational linguistics (Luff, Gilbert, & Frohlich, 1990; Hirst, 1991). In other words, the question for CASLA is not whether or not the computational grammar is a good theoretical account of the language within a particular domain, but instead is whether or not the program is able to interact with the learner in a way that is useful relative to its purpose. Empirical evaluation of speech recognition software with learners (Coniam, 1996) has found that speech recognition of learner language by commercial programs (intended for proficient user language) falls short of what would be needed for pedagogical or assessment applications, but this work needs to inform improvements in software directed specifically toward learner language.

Corpus linguistics

The historical distinction between computational linguistics and corpus linguistics is less clear today than it was in the past and yet each makes unique contributions to CASLA. Computational linguists' primary interest has been on the nature of the grammars required to parse various constructions of human language whereas corpus linguists tend to focus on the results that can be obtained through observation of large databases comprised of texts. As Johansson (1991) pointed out,

we have seen encouraging signs that the gap is narrowing. On the one hand, corpus workers have shown that 'large-scale corpus-based linguistics can be the basis for deriving theoretically interesting insights' (Kallgren, 1990,

p. 99). On the other hand, there seems to be an increasing concern with data among computational linguists . . . (1991: 311)[4]

Despite overlap between the two areas, corpus linguistics has a distinct history documented in journals such as *Computers and the Humanities* (appeared in 1966), the *Association for Literary and Linguistic Computing Bulletin* (appeared in 1973), and most recently *Journal of Corpus Linguistics*. The history of corpus linguistics, however, is more typically recounted through the chronology of corpus development, beginning with the announcement of Randolph Quirk's Survey of English Usage Corpus in 1959 and the Brown corpus shortly thereafter (Leech, 1991). Since that time a number of corpora have been collected, and researchers are using them to work toward empirically based descriptions of varieties of languages (Altenberg, 1991; Garside, Leech, & Sampson, 1987; Biber, 1988; Aijmer & Altenberg, 1991; Kyto, Ihalainen, & Rissanen, 1988; Biber *et al.*, 1999).

From a theoretical perspective, this work provides valuable empirical data supporting probabilistic approaches to grammar (Sampson, 1987), which are useful in applied linguistics.[5] Moreover, this approach has increased linguists' awareness of the characteristics of different registers and their significance in the study of language. Results from corpus linguistics have demonstrated that

there are important and systematic differences among text varieties at all linguistic levels, and that any global characterizations of 'General English' should be regarded with caution . . . teachers of advanced students should focus on the English of particular varieties, in naturally-occurring discourse, rather than 'general' patterns that are culled from linguists' intuitions and do not accurately reflect the grammar of any variety. (Biber, Conrad, & Reppen, 1994: 179)

Some argue that the linguistic facts about language use can be helpful for developing dictionaries, syllabi and teaching materials, particularly in English for specific purposes curricula (Tribble, 1991), and may radically change the way that grammar is taught to L2 learners (Conrad, 2000). Others (e.g., Johns, 1986; Tribble & Jones, 1990) have proposed that ideally L2 learners can act as corpus linguists,

---

[4] This tendency, which Johansson noted in 1991, continued to such a degree that in 1993 two special issues of *Computational Linguistics* (volume 19, numbers 1 and 2) were devoted to using large corpora.

[5] A probabilistic approach to grammar is based on the observation that particular forms are more or less likely to occur depending on features of context and co-text. A probabilistic grammar predicts and investigates the probability of occurrence of combinations of words in texts.

investigating for themselves relevant facts about native speaker language use. In both of these cases, the corpora under investigation are comprised of native speaker language, but other L2 research applications of corpus linguistics rely on corpora comprised of learner language which the researcher wishes to describe (MacWhinney, 1995; Pienemann, 1992; Granger, 1998).

There are many implications for the study of corpora of native and non-native varieties of languages (Biber, Conrad, & Reppen, 1998); however, learners' interactive use of corpora is the central area for CASLA. This classroom methodology, referred to as 'data-driven' learning (e.g., Johns, 1986), 'attempts to cut out the middleman as far as possible and to give direct access to the data so that the learner can take part in building up his or her *own* profiles of meaning and uses' (Johns, 1994: 297). Given the significance of corpus linguistics for second language teaching and learning, it is not surprising that academics in this area began to meet regularly at a conference in 1994 at Lancaster. Collections of papers from this conference have been published (Wichmann *et al.*, 1997) and a special issue of *Language Learning & Technology* will feature corpora in second language teaching. At the turn of the century it seems evident that something like a 'corpus revolution' is changing dramatically the way that language is taught, even if the effects of these changes are felt gradually (Leech, 1997).

Computer-assisted assessment

Computer-assisted assessment refers to testing practices requiring a computer to assist in construction, delivery, response analysis and score reporting. CASLA, therefore, includes only a subset of computer-assisted assessment issues – those which involve computer-assisted test delivery and response analysis. The history of computer-assisted test delivery has been tied closely to developments in item-response theory (IRT), a psychometric theory and related practices which allow test developers to use item statistics such as item difficulty obtained from one test administration (e.g., a paper-and pencil administration) for selection of items in subsequent administrations (e.g., as other students take the test delivered individually by computer). Computer-adaptive tests based on IRT models have been used successfully in operational testing programs for increasing the efficiency of multiple-choice testing. In the past, computer-assisted response 'analysis' has primarily been used to perpetuate the testing philosophies and practices that developed in response to what Hunt called the 'paper and pencil technology,' which he defined as the practices that rely on the number 2 pencil and the computer scannable answer sheet to 'record the products of cognition' (Hunt, 1987: 13).

The paper and pencil technology is at its best when large numbers of fairly short questions are presented and when the respondent must choose from a fixed set of alternatives. The paper and pencil technology is not well suited to recording how the person chooses the answers, and is worse suited for situations in which free form responding is required. Perhaps, most important, the paper and pencil technology emphasizes counting the total number of correct items, or, in more recent applications [such as computer-adaptive testing], determining the most difficult item that a person can consistently answer correctly. (Hunt, 1987: 13)

Particularly in the US, where the paper-and-pencil technology has been so pervasive, test users and researchers alike question the validity of multiple-choice items as a sole means of assessment (e.g., Fredricksen, 1984). Concerns about construct validity (i.e., the defensibility of the inferences and uses made from test results) stem from the evidence that use of a single test method can result in systematic distortion of what the test is intended to measure; therefore, researchers are investigating the meaning of alternative response methods (e.g., Birenbaum & Tatsuoka, 1987; Bennett *et al.*, 1990; Bennett, 1993; Mislevy; 1993b; Traub, 1993). Other validity concerns are manifest in questions about the effects of selected response items on classroom instruction. The question, which is particularly pertinent to measuring cognitively complex abilities such as language (Linn, Baker, & Dunbar, 1991; Wiggins, 1993), is the extent to which such tests narrow the focus of instruction to include only the competencies which tests require learners to demonstrate. Such questions prompt proposals to integrate testing practices with instructional activities (Nitko, 1989). In computer-assisted assessment, these concerns have motivated exploration of how alternative item formats can be delivered and scored on a computer – explorations which have led innovators in this area to look to the design of computer-assisted instructional materials (Bejar & Braun, 1994; Glasser, Lesgold, and Lajoie, 1987).

Following trends in educational measurement, research and development in computer-assisted second language testing has made most progress in application of IRT to adaptive multiple-choice tests. At the same time, of course, language testing researchers have also questioned the sole use of multiple-choice testing for language assessment, raising issues of construct validity (Bachman & Palmer, 1982) and the consequences of testing (Canale, 1987). Drawing primarily from work in CALL, research and development in language testing explores computer delivery of test tasks other than multiple choice (Alderson, 1991) and investigates the use of computer-assisted response analysis (e.g., Chapelle, 1993; Henning *et al.*, 1993; Jamieson *et al.*, 1993; Reid, 1986). This preliminary work has shown that when language testing leaves behind the well-established technologies of the multiple-choice test, it must develop new test theory (e.g., Mislevy, 1993a; 1994) which must rely heavily on theory and practice in applied linguistics.

From related disciplines to CASLA

Given the goals of these related disciplines, it is not surprising that they have contributed to the development of theory and practice in CASLA. Particularly in developing technical capabilities, applied linguists working with CASLA will undoubtedly continue to draw on these disciplines. Despite important technical contributions, each area has an objective that is either much broader or pointing in a different direction altogether than those of CASLA. Table 2.1 summarizes the general goals of each of the related disciplines in contrast to corresponding goals of CASLA.

Like research and development in educational technology and computer-supported collaborative learning, the fundamental concern in CALL is to design successful learning activities. Developments in CALL, therefore, benefit from the authoring software, instructional practices, and methods of evaluation borrowed from these areas. However, as the past decades of research on instructed second language acquisition have demonstrated, unique issues arise in teaching an L2 and in evaluating the success of L2 learning. For example, an application of the systems approach from educational technology to CALL can result in materials which break up language into its component parts to teach each piece in a hierarchial fashion – a practice which runs contrary to accepted meaning-based approaches. No more successful were attempts to borrow directly the philosophy and instructional design alternatives to the systems approach, which had been designed for teaching mathematics to children. When this theoretical ideal was put into practice, the results produced less interesting activities for adult second language learners (see Higgins & Johns, 1984: 75–79) than they appeared to for children learning mathematics. Because of the unique character of SLA and the particular difficulties inherent in computer processing of natural language, design and evaluation of CALL through direct analogies with educational technology have not been successful.

Table 2.1. *Concerns of other disciplines and CASLA*

In . . .	The primary question is . . .	In CASLA, the corresponding concern is . . .
Educational technology	How can computers best be used to improve learning?	How can computers best be used to promote development of communicative L2 ability?[a]
Computer-supported collaborative learning	How can computer-assisted activities be designed to promote learning through collaboration?	How can collaborative computer-assisted language learning activities be designed to promote development of communicative L2 ability?
Artificial intelligence	How can rules of logic be implemented in computer programs to perform functions requiring knowledge-based analysis and judgement?	How can computer programs with capability for knowledge-based analysis and judgement be used to promote development of communicative L2 ability and to strengthen the validity of L2 assessment?
Computational linguistics	How can rules of language, and language processing be used to write computer programs to recognize and produce human language?	How can computer programs for language recognition and production promote development of communicative L2 ability and strengthen the validity of L2 assessment?
Corpus linguistics	What do descriptions and analyses of language from large corpora of texts reveal about the lexical patterns and grammatical structures that people use?	How can learners' use of corpora promote development of communicative L2 ability?
Computer-assisted assessment	How can computers be used to increase the validity of assessments?	How can computers be used to increase the validity of L2 assessments?

[a] Communicative L2 ability refers to a broad definition of communicative competence including control over both form and functions of the L2. The aspects of language ability entailed are most clearly laid out by Bachman (1990) and Bachman & Palmer (1996).

On the surface, the cultural constructivist perspective of CSCL may appear to solve the problem because of its concern with development and evaluation of learning through collaboration, which is almost always accomplished through the use of language. However, collaboration as it is used in many settings is not targeted toward language learning. As a consequence, discourse analysis methods for evaluation are not necessarily tuned toward identifying collaborative discourse that facilitates L2 acquisition. The key issue for development of CALL is how computer activities can best be constructed to promote development of L2 ability. There is no shortage of general-purpose authoring and computer-mediated communication software from which some types of CALL activities can be constructed. What is needed are theoretically and empirically based criteria for choosing among the potential design options and methods for evaluating their effectiveness for promoting learners' communicative L2 ability.

Although artificial intelligence and computational linguistics offer potentially useful software technologies, researchers in these areas are interested in developing computer programs rather than in developing learners' ability. As a consequence, research in these areas targets computer programs as end products and evaluates tools in terms of their quality for developing grammars (Shieber, 1985). Applied linguists hoping to use these technologies need to have criteria and methodologies for assessing their success in improving learners' L2 competence or increasing the validity of L2 measurement.

The goal of corpus linguistics, to identify and analyze the grammatical and lexical patterns that speakers and writers use, may pertain equally to the general study of linguistics and to the design of materials for pedagogy and assessment. However, the particular application of concern in this volume is the use of corpus methods as a tool for learners. From this perspective, the critical issue shifts from how adequate the linguistic description is to how effective the tool is in helping the learner to improve in the L2. Under what conditions are learners able to act as linguists, querying the appropriate corpora for useful data. What are the characteristics of the corpora that are useful to learners at various ability levels? When do learners need assistance in taking advantage of corpora? And what evidence should we accept as indicative that learners have used corpora successfully?

Research on computer-assisted assessment has contributed substantially to technical advances affecting computer-adaptive language testing. However, the results of such contributions are seen in tests which have many of the same characteristics as paper-and-pencil tests, even if they can be scored on the spot and require less time to take. There remains a need to think creatively about the possibilities that the computer allows for testing. To consider changes in testing, it is necessary to have some guiding principles or criteria that can be considered positive qualities of a test as well as methods for their evaluation.

Conclusion

Each of the areas outlined in this chapter has provided valuable contributions for aspects of the technical and conceptual infrastructure of CASLA as well as some general orientations to evaluation issues. Description of these areas helps to identify the origin of practices observed throughout the history of CASLA. Despite their contributions, each is limited in that it cannot make recommendations pertinent to the specifics of SLA. Therefore, progress requires methods for evaluating CASLA's quality for its intended purposes. The rest of the chapters in this book address this need by laying out principles and criteria for evaluation.

3 Computer-assisted language learning

One critic of research on computer-assisted learning described the reason for the lack of substantive progress in educational technology as follows:

Part of the difficulty, in my view, is that we tend to encourage students (and faculty) to begin with educational and instructional *solutions* and search for problems that can be solved by those solutions. Thus we begin with an enthusiasm for some medium . . . and search for a sufficient and visible context in which to establish evidence for our solution . . . If we begin by implicitly and explicitly attempting to validate a belief about the solutions to largely unexamined problems, we are less open to evidence that our intuitions might be very far off the mark. (R. E. Clark, 1994: 28; emphasis in original)

This situation, which may characterize CALL as well as it does computer-assisted learning in other areas, presents a problem for developing methodologies for CALL evaluation.[1] It continues to prompt some to conceptualize the evaluation of CALL from the perspective of gross comparisons between computer-using learners with those learning through other media (e.g., Adair-Hauck, Willingham-McLain, & Yongs, 2000; Nutta, 1998), an approach unlikely to shed light on the problem or solution. Moreover, as researchers such as Pedersen (1987) pointed out, comparisons of CALL versus classroom learning outcomes create an irony wherein the most precise and sophisticated modern tool is investigated through the most crude and outdated educational research methods.

This chapter applies current methods of evaluation to introduce principles for evaluating CALL as an instructional solution to the problem of instructed SLA. To articulate the problem, it therefore

---

[1] Brown and Duguid (2000) discuss the problem this type of 'tunnel vision' presents for society in domains other than education as well. Their point is that technology is a critical part of a web of constraints and resources that humans work with, and therefore people need to understand the nature of the technology as well as other factors.

begins by outlining theory concerning ideal cognitive and socio-affective conditions for instructed SLA. Basic principles underlying CALL evaluation are articulated including evaluation criteria drawn from theory and research on tasks for instructed SLA, one of which clarifies the importance of and the distinction between judgemental and empirical evaluation. Judgemental evaluation of CALL tasks is exemplified and research methods for conducting empirical evaluation are explained. Several CALL applications are evaluated to illustrate applications of these criteria.

The problem of instructed SLA

Evaluation of CALL as a solution to the problem of instructed SLA needs to begin with an understanding of, or at least hypotheses about, the conditions that ideally should be created for instructed SLA. Research on instructed SLA, including studies of conditions of instruction and of communication tasks (e.g., Long, 1996; Pica, 1994), addresses these issues. As Larsen-Freeman and Long (1991) pointed out, research on instructed SLA investigates how specifics of the environment influence SLA:

[This research] has potentially great practical importance for educators . . .
since input (and the structure of conversation) is something that can be
manipulated. Research findings are of interest to [second language]
materials writers, [second language] curriculum developers and classroom
teachers . . . (1991: 128)

Although the conditions and tasks made possible in CALL have not been a concern in this work, useful perspectives for examining CALL can be drawn from it. Egbert, Chao, and Hanson-Smith (1999), for example, propose conditions for optimal learning environments based on Spolsky's (1989) summary of conditions for successful SLA. Over ten years after Spolsky's presentation of these issues, additional research has added some useful detail to a theory of conditions in both the cognitive and socio-affective domains.

Cognitive conditions for SLA

Skehan (1998) reviews current work on cognitive conditions for SLA that can be implemented through task-based instruction, offering five guidelines for implementing effective task-based instruction:

1 Choose a range of target structures
2 Choose tasks which meet the utility condition
3 Select and sequence tasks to achieve balanced goal development

4 Maximize the chances of focus on form through attentional manipulation
5 Use cycles of accountability (1998: 132)

These suggestions summarize what can be gleaned from the current research base on instructional tasks and are therefore worth considering in an evaluation of CALL.

Range of target structures

The suggestion that a range of target structures be selected for learning materials stems from results of SLA research which indicate that learners will acquire particular structures or develop form–meaning connections when they are ready to. Instruction can help by speeding up the process, but is unlikely to change the sequence of development for particular structures. Given this finding, it may be pointless to attempt to keep a learner to a strict schedule of items to be acquired. At the same time, learners need to be exposed to language which is within their grasp. The research on sequences of development implies that language far beyond or beneath learners' abilities or needs is not useful for acquisition.

The utility condition

'Utility' refers to one category in a classification of L2 tasks proposed by Loschky and Bley-Vroman (1993) intended to distinguish among the degrees of likelihood that a particular structure will be used by learners as they perform a task. If a structure has 'utility' in a task, it would be a useful but not necessary structure for completing a task. Learners might choose the structure but they might circumlocute to express their meanings in a different way. Advocating the utility criterion for task selection is directly consistent with the previous principle. It puts the teacher in the position of creating conditions in which a range of target structures might be practiced rather than assuming that the teacher will select each structure one by one.

Balanced goal development

The goals Skehan associates with L2 tasks are three dimensions of language performance, fluency, accuracy, and complexity, which he defines as follows: 'fluency (often achieved through memorized and integrated language elements); accuracy (when learners try to use an interlanguage system of a particular level to produce correct, but possibility limited, language); and complexity (a willingness to take risks, to try out new forms even though they may not be completely correct)' (Skehan, 1998: 5). He sees acquisition as the learners' process of increasing in each of these areas, and therefore pedagogical tasks, he suggests, should be chosen to help learners develop in these ways. The 'balancing' of development among these areas should occur through the teachers' choice of tasks that alternatively provide opportunities for development of each.

Focus on form through attentional manipulation

Many researchers agree that learners need to notice and attend to linguistic form for acquisition (Schmidt, 1990; Robinson, 1995). Therefore, conditions directing learners' attention to linguistic form during tasks requiring meaningful language use are believed to be among the most important for learners' acquisition of target language structures. Learners' attention to form while they are engaging in meaningful tasks is called focus on form (Long, 1988).

Focus on form refers to how [the learner's] focal attentional resources are allocated. Although there are degrees of attention, and although attention to form and attention to meaning are not always mutually exclusive, during an otherwise meaning-focused classroom lesson, focus on form often consists of a shift of attention to linguistic code features – by the teacher and/or one or more students – triggered by perceived problems with comprehension or production. (Long & Robinson, 1998: 23; emphasis in original)

Doughty and Williams (1998) identify a number of ways that focus on form has been operationalized in L2 tasks, varying in how explicitly grammatical forms are selected and taught. The examples that best fit Long and Robinson's definition occur in communication tasks (Pica, Kanagy, & Falodun, 1993) in which learners' attention is on the meaning of the language, except for instances in which communication breakdowns occur. Communication breakdowns shift attention to the language until the breakdown is sufficiently resolved in a process referred to as *negotiation of meaning* (Long, 1985). In such cases, the grammatical patterns that receive attention are 'chosen' by the learners, who focus on those which cause problems. Such negotiations result in a communicative flow in which the normal interactional structure has been modified because of a request such as a repetition, clarification, or restatement of the original input. Larsen-Freeman and Long (1991) summarize this view of interactional modifications:

Modification of the interactional structure of conversation or of written discourse during reading . . . is a [good] candidate for a necessary (not sufficient) condition for acquisition. The role it plays in negotiation for meaning helps to make input comprehensible while still containing unknown linguistic elements, and, hence, potential intake for acquisition. (1991: 144)

Communication tasks are chosen on the basis of the meaning that learners are expected to practice, and no metalinguistic explanation is included as part of the task. However, meaning-based tasks can also be constructed in view of the grammatical forms that learners are expected to practice (i.e., structures are 'essential' in Loschky and Bley-Vroman's [1993] terms) and may include some metalinguistic explanation (Swain, 1998). Ideal methods for constructing conditions for SLA in tasks remain the topic of research, but sufficient evidence exists to suggest that it is worthwhile to attempt to get learners to focus on form during engagement in meaning-based tasks.

Attention to form can also occur when learners modify their linguistic output because of problems in getting a message across, for example (Pica *et al.*, 1996). Describing potentially valuable linguistic output, Swain (1985) suggested that 'comprehensible output' should aid learners' development when it plays a role in their conveying meaning by stretching their linguistic resources. Swain and Lapkin (1995) describe the hypothesis as follows:

[I]n producing the L2, a learner will on occasion become aware of (i.e., notice) a linguistic problem (brought to his/her attention either by external feedback (e.g., clarification requests) or internal feedback). Noticing a problem 'pushes' the learner to modify his/her output. In doing so, the learner may sometimes be forced into a more syntactic processing mode than might occur in comprehension. (1995: 373)

The hypothesis is that the syntactic mode of processing helps learners to internalize new forms and to improve in the accuracy of their existing grammatical knowledge.

In addition to negotiation of meaning and modification of output, Skehan identifies six task characteristics, although not all supported by research, which may help to manipulate attention in a way that directs learners' attention more or less to linguistic form: time pressure (e.g., Crookes, 1989), modality, support, surprise, control, and stakes. Adding to these the other ways in which attention can be drawn to language during the process of task completion, a number of possibilities exist as outlined in Table 3.1. These conditions cannot be used directly as a means for evaluating CALL tasks, but as a way of summarizing potential contributors to manipulation of learners' attention in learning tasks.

Table 3.1. *Conditions that may influence allocation of attention during L2 tasks*

Attention affected by...	Definition	Reason
Modified interaction	Interruption of a communication exchange due to a breakdown in comprehension and subsequent attempt to recover from breakdown.	Breakdown draws attention to unknown linguistic forms and recovery helps make unrecognized input comprehensible, and therefore makes it potential material for acquisition.
Modified output	Learners' correction of their own errors – either self-correction or correction prompted by something else.	Identification and correction of errors draws attention to linguistic form and accuracy.
Time pressure	An urgency in achieving communication caused by one's own anxiousness or external factors.	When no time pressure exists, attention to form is more likely.
Modality	Whether the language is spoken or written.	Written communication typically affords more opportunity for attention to form, whereas spoken language often occurs under time pressure to achieve fluency.
Support	Cues or information available to the learner to help in constructing meaning during task completion.	When learners have help with some aspects of the language, their attentional resources are more free to be devoted to form.
Surprise	Introduction of an unexpected element during task completion.	The surprise element might be expected to decrease attention to form because of the interruption of plans and need to focus on the surprise, but these hypotheses would depend on the nature of the surprise.
Control	Who makes decisions about the directions that the task is to take.	Control of various aspects of the task by the teacher or the learner may help to prompt focus on form, but research is needed to investigate questions about control.
Stakes	Learners' perception of the importance of accurate performance.	Tasks perceived as high stakes are likely to prompt more attention to form.

Cycles of accountability

Accountability refers to the learners' responsibility to keep track of what they are learning. However, learners cannot be expected to do this on their own; therefore, teachers have the responsibility of drawing learners' attention to the need to be aware of the language that they are acquiring in such a way that they can take stock of where they are and plan for their own development. The cycles imply that this process needs to be ongoing as learners work with a variety of tasks in somewhat unpredictable ways. Skehan's point is that since meaning-based tasks fail to proscribe the use of particular structures, learners have to take an active role in sorting out exactly what they are learning.

Socio-affective conditions for SLA

Another set of conditions that should be created for successful SLA are those affecting the social and affective aspects of learning. Work in this area has recently been synthesized to define a construct of 'willingness to communicate' (WTC), which is intended to articulate what it is that makes some learners willing to use their L2 while others are less so. MacIntyre, Clément, Dörnyei, and Noels (1998) define WTC as a 'situation-specific variable representing an intention to communicate at a specific time to a specific person' (1998: 559). As such, this construct provides a mechanism for conceptualizing the investment (Pierce, 1995) that prompts what van Lier (1996) refers to as authentic engagement in an activity. Moreover, by conceptualizing WTC as a situation-specific variable, these researchers open the possibility for classroom learning activities to interact with and influence the development of WTC.

They see a crucial goal of the learning process as developing learners' interest in seeking out opportunities for communication and their willingness to communicate in these situations. WTC is comprised of several layers of underlying predispositions, including (1) the desire to communicate with a particular person, (2) communicative self-confidence at that particular moment, (3) interpersonal motivation (the desire to control or affiliate with others), (4) intergroup motivation (related to the speakers' group affiliation), (5) self-confidence, (6) intergroup attitudes (e.g., integrativeness), (7) social situation (i.e., features of context affecting communication), (8) communicative competence, (9) intergroup climate, and (10) personality. The researchers' goal is to study learning contexts as they influence aspects of the WTC variable, but in the meantime the point is that ideal socio-affective conditions for learning should be constructed in view of the need to promote a positive disposition in these aspects of the learners.

Other factors

While these conditions for SLA offer the most solid basis for making decisions about task selection, they obviously do not account for all factors to be considered. First, the cognitive conditions do not take into account individual differences in cognitive characteristics of learners due to, for example, age or cognitive style. Second, task selection also needs to take into account factors of the learning situation such as the effects of task choice on teachers and learners, and others who may be involved with the task. A somewhat related third consideration is the need to take into account practical factors such as the available resources.

These three areas in addition to the cognitive and socio-affective conditions must be taken into account to inform the particulars of the evaluation criteria for CALL. However, before developing the specific criteria, a more general perspective toward evaluation needs to be laid out to clarify issues such as what CALL evaluation should consist of, what it applies to, and who conducts it. Unfortunately, the area of L2 materials evaluation offers no systematic guidance for formulating such principles. However, given the parallel needs of materials evaluation for L2 testing and for L2 instruction and the well-articulated perspectives for the former, principles for evaluation of the latter can be drawn by analogy.

Principles for CALL evaluation

CALL has always been viewed by some as an experiment requiring scrutiny and justification beyond what is expected of evaluation of other classroom activities. Today in many settings the experiment is over even though the results are inconclusive. Learners use computers for many different purposes and therefore teachers, classroom researchers and software developers need to be concerned about what kinds of CALL tasks may be beneficial. Given the need to make judgements about CALL, many teachers and CALL enthusiasts have developed guidelines, checklists, and evaluation rubrics for CALL materials as a means of setting some criteria for what can be considered good CALL. Whatever the merits of such evaluation systems for their particular contexts, three needs must be addressed to improve CALL evaluation. First, evaluation criteria should incor-

Table 3.2. *Summary of principles for evaluating CALL*

Principle	Implication
Evaluation of CALL is a situation-specific argument.	CALL developers need to be familiar with criteria for evaluation which should be applied relative to a particular context.
CALL should be evaluated through two perspectives: judgemental analysis of software and planned tasks, and empirical analysis of learners' performance.	Methodologies for both types of analyses are needed.
Criteria for CALL task quality should come from theory and research on instructed SLA.	CALL evaluators need to keep up with and make links to research on instructed SLA.
Criteria should be applied in view of the purpose of the task.	CALL tasks should have a clearly articulated purpose.
Language learning potential should be the central criterion in evaluation of CALL.	Language learning should be one aspect of the purpose of CALL tasks.

porate findings and theory-based speculation about ideal conditions for SLA such as those outlined above. Second, criteria should be accompanied by guidance as to how they should be used; in other words, a theory of evaluation needs to be articulated. Third, both criteria and theory need to apply not only to software, but also to the task that the teacher plans and that the learner carries out.

As a way of addressing these needs, a perspective is explained through five principles of evaluation developed by analogy to principles for evaluation of language assessments as described in Chapter 4. Even though the purpose of language testing is different than that of instructional tasks, at a general level, perspectives on evaluation of assessment tasks are also applicable to CALL tasks. Table 3.2 summarizes these principles.

Evaluation as an argument

Investigations of pedagogical L2 tasks (e.g., Doughty & Williams, 1998; Crookes & Gass, 1993a; 1993b; Skehan, 1998) demonstrate the complex of factors to be considered in designing appropriate tasks for learners. As a consequence, the outcome of task evaluation

Table 3.3. *Levels of analysis for CALL evaluation*

Level of analysis	Object of evaluation	Example question	Method of evaluation
1	CALL software	Does the software provide learners the opportunity for interactional modifications to negotiate meaning?	Judgemental
2	Teacher-planned CALL activities	Does the CALL activity designed by the teacher provide learners the opportunity to modify interaction for negotiation of meaning?	Judgemental
3	Learners' performance during CALL activities	Do learners actually interact and negotiate meaning while they are working in a chat room?	Empirical

for any L2 tasks including those for CALL cannot be a categorical decision about effectiveness. Instead, an evaluation has to result in an argument indicating in what ways a particular CALL task is appropriate for particular learners at a given time. In other words, CALL task appropriateness needs to be evaluated on the basis of evidence and rationales pertaining to task use in a particular setting. The idea of evaluation as a context-specific argument rather than a categorical judgement, of course, makes evaluation a complex issue, which needs to be addressed by all CALL users. Evaluation is not only the responsibility of CALL researchers because a justification needs to be an argument concerning the appropriateness of a CALL task for the learners involved at a particular point in time.

Judgemental and empirical analyses

CALL evaluation can denote several different types of inquiry, as outlined in Table 3.3, each with associated objects and methods. The first level of analysis refers to the software that is used for a CALL activity. CALL software is the target of many evaluation checklists that have been developed to help point teachers to its important features. Questions target features such as the following: How much control is the learner allowed? How interactive is the software? Are the quality and degree of feedback adequate? What kinds of records does the software keep? (Bradin, 1999: 174). A question at this level related to the conditions summarized in Table 3.1 would be: Does the software provide learners the opportunity for interactional modifications to negotiate meaning? These types of questions are addressed through judgemental analysis.

The second level of analysis is directed toward the teacher's planned activity. Any CALL activity that is assigned and used within a language class is influenced by the way in which the teacher introduces and structures it. As Jones (1986) aptly pointed out, 'It's not so much the program, more what you do with it'. These words are even more fitting today than they were in 1986 because so many CALL tasks are developed through the use of general-purpose software such as e-mail, electronic discussions, and materials on the Web not intended for language learning. The instructors' control or lack of control of such tasks is critical to the conditions the computer-assisted learning activity provides learners. An example of a question at this level would be the following: Does the computer-assisted learning activity designed by the teacher provide learners the opportunity to modify interaction for negotiation of meaning?

The third level of evaluation focuses on learners' performance, and is therefore conducted through examination of empirical data reflecting learners' use of CALL and learning outcomes. For example, to address the level 3 question, do learners actually interact and negotiate meaning while they are working in a chat room, data reflecting learners' interactions during their work need to be gathered and analyzed for instances of interactional modifications.

An evaluation argument should be constructed on the basis of both the judgemental and empirical analyses. These two methods provide different and complementary information both of which are relevant to CALL task evaluation (Chapelle, 1999a). The judgemental analysis should examine characteristics of the software and task in terms of criteria drawn from research on SLA. The empirical analyses address the same criteria but through data gathered to reveal the details of CALL use and learning outcomes.

Criteria from theory and research on SLA

Drawing from the theory and research on conditions for instructed SLA in addition to the other considerations mentioned above (e.g., individual differences), it is possible to chart some criteria for evaluating CALL. These are outlined in Table 3.4.

Table 3.4. *Criteria for CALL task appropriateness*

Language learning potential	The degree of opportunity present for beneficial focus on form.
Learner fit	The amount of opportunity for engagement with language under appropriate conditions given learner characteristics.
Meaning focus	The extent to which learners' attention is directed toward the meaning of the language.
Authenticity	The degree of correspondence between the CALL activity and target language activities of interest to learners out of the classroom.
Positive impact	The positive effects of the CALL activity on those who participate in it.
Practicality	The adequacy of resources to support the use of the CALL activity.

Language learning potential

Language learning potential refers to the extent to which the activity can be considered to be a language learning activity rather than simply an opportunity for language use. The difference between language learning and language use might best be characterized by the extent to which the task promotes beneficial focus on form. Given the importance of focus on language for language acquisition, characteristics among those Skehan identified as relevant for promoting focus on form – interactional modification, modification of output, time pressure, modality, support, surprise, control, and stakes – need to be considered in an argument for language learning potential. This list of conditions will no doubt change as additional research sheds light on these and other factors. Moreover, the complete meaning of language learning potential will develop as theory and research in SLA develop, but past research and theory-based predictions suggest that Skehan's list warrants serious consideration for the time being.

Learner fit

Whereas language learning potential captures the findings concerning general processes, *learner fit* takes into account the individual differences in linguistic ability level and non-linguistic characteristics.

Skehan suggests that the teacher choose tasks that will provide learners an opportunity to work with a range of target structures appropriate to their level. If the language of a CALL task is already known to the learner, the task presents no opportunity for development; language that is beyond the learners' grasp relative to their ability, is not useful either. Learner characteristics such as willingness to communicate, age, and learning style also come into play in task choice.

Meaning focus

The importance of meaning focus in language learning tasks may go without saying, but in order to underscore the dual goals of focus on form during completion of a meaning-focused task, *meaning focus* is included as one of the criteria. Meaning focus denotes that the learner's primary attention is directed toward the meaning of the language that is required to accomplish the task, the clearest example being communication tasks as defined by Pica, Kanagy, and Falodun (1993). Their primary defining feature is that they require learners to use the target language to accomplish something such as making a decision on an issue, or exchanging information to accomplish a goal. Such tasks differ from form-based tasks which might have learners filling in correct verb tenses in a written list of sentences, or changing declarative statements to yes/no questions in an oral drill. Meaning focus is not limited to oral communication tasks, but also can occur during tasks involving reading and writing when learners use the written language purposefully for constructing and interpreting meaning.

Authenticity

The criterion of *authenticity* indicates the need to develop learners' willingness to communicate but it also extends beyond the conditions believed important for acquisition. Authenticity refers to the degree of correspondence between an L2 learning task and tasks that the learner is likely to encounter outside the classroom. The choice of pedagogical tasks that learners see as relevant to their language use beyond the classroom should help to engage learners' interest and therefore their willingness to participate. Moreover, current theory of communicative language ability (Bachman, 1990; Bachman & Palmer, 1996) defines it as situation specific, implying that development of ability in language for particular purposes requires practice in using language for those purposes.

Positive impact

The *positive impact* of a CALL task refers to its effects beyond its language learning potential. The significance of this quality has been pointed out for assessment tasks (e.g., Bachman & Palmer, 1996), but it is equally important for learning tasks. Ideally classroom language learning tasks teach more than language; they should help learners develop their metacognitive strategies (Oxford, 1990) in a way that will allow them to develop their accountability for their learning in the classroom as well as to learn beyond the classroom. They should engage learners' interest in the target culture in a way that will help develop their willingness to seek out opportunities to communicate in the L2. They should help learners to gain pragmatic abilities that will serve in communications beyond the classroom. An argument concerning positive impact may be based on the impact on the learners and teachers who use a learning activity as well as on the educational system as a whole.

Practicality

Practicality refers to how easy it is for the learners and teachers to implement a CALL task within the particular constraints of a class or language program. Relevant constraints include the availability of hardware and software that are adequate for the planned activities. In addition, knowledgeable personnel need to be on hand to assist with unforeseen problems. Early experience with CALL showed that learners had to have adequate access to well-maintained software and hardware for CALL to be successful (Marty, 1981). This observation is equally valid today because even though learners use computers regardless of infrastructure provided by language programs, they cannot be expected to use computers for language learning without guidance, and guidance requires resources. Issues of practicality are closely tied to characteristics of institutional, social, and cultural practices in which some members have the power to make decisions about the amount and type of resources to be made available for CALL.

Criteria applied based on task purpose

These criteria for CALL appropriateness need to be applied in view of the purpose of a CALL task. Skehan's discussion of performance goals for tasks, including learners' fluency, accuracy, and complexity, might be augmented by comprehension goals and goals concerning pragmatic competence (Kasper, 1997). Moreover, tasks may have different purposes at various stages of instruction (Doughty & Williams, 1998). Whatever the goal of the CALL task, however, evaluation of the task requires that it have a stated purpose.

The centrality of language learning

Even though the importance of each of the six criteria may vary depending on the purpose of the task, language learning potential should be considered the most critical for CALL activities. Tasks not intended to promote language learning in more than an incidental way, may be good for other purposes, but it would be difficult to argue that they should play a central role in L2 teaching. CALL tasks can also be intended to work toward a number of objectives such as developing learners' social identity in the target culture, increasing their computer literacy, strengthening their cultural awareness, or developing strategies for language learning. These outcomes may be positive impacts of the CALL task, but in designing language learning tasks, the criteria of language learning potential should be considered the most important.

Judgemental evaluation of CALL

The criteria are intended to guide both judgemental and empirical analysis of CALL tasks. Table 3.5 contains questions that can be used to guide a judgemental evaluation of a CALL task planned by a teacher. They are intended to focus on both the aspects of the task defined by the software and those designed by the teacher.

These questions focus directly on individual tasks, but of course issues of sequencing and curriculum also need to be considered in task selection. For example, is the CALL task sequenced appropriately with other form-focus and meaning-focus tasks? Is the learner provided sufficient opportunity for learning and follow-up practice with the target forms? The judgemental analysis is intended to assess the appropriateness of a task for particular learners at a particular point in time and is therefore exemplified by examining activities relative to settings in which they were used. Five types of CALL activities that have been suggested and discussed over the past 20 years are looked at from the perspective of the judgemental analysis: computer-assisted classroom discussion, a microworld, text analysis, storyboard, and concordancing.

Table 3.5. *Questions for judgemental analysis of CALL*
appropriateness

Qualities	Questions
Language learning potential	Do task conditions present sufficient opportunity for beneficial focus on form?
Learner fit	Is the difficulty level of the targeted linguistic forms appropriate for the learners to increase their language ability? Is the task appropriate for learners with the characteristics of the intended learners?
Meaning focus	Is learners' attention directed primarily toward the meaning of the language?
Authenticity	Is there a strong correspondence between the CALL task and second language tasks of interest to learners outside the classroom? Will learners be able to see the connection between the CALL task and tasks outside the classroom?
Impact	Will learners learn more about the target language and about strategies for language learning through the use of the task? Will instructors observe sound second language pedagogical practices by using the task? Will both learners and teachers have a positive learning experience with technology through the use of the task?
Practicality	Are hardware, software, and personnel resources sufficient to allow the CALL task to succeed?

Computer-assisted classroom discussion

Kelm (1992) provides an example of a LAN-based computer-mediated communication (CMC) activity in a university-level, fourth-semester Brazilian Portuguese class held in the US. Students attended class three hours a week, and for one of those hours (each Friday), class was held in the microcomputer center of the university library. Before coming to class each Friday, they were assigned a particular Brazilian short story which was to serve as the topic for the computer-assisted classroom discussion (CACD). When the students arrived at the computer lab, they logged in and received a message from the instructor including three or four questions which he had selected to probe their comprehension of the story or to open discussion of topics raised in the story. After receiving the instructors' message, students were able to enter the electronic discussion by typing their comments at their computers. When an individual student had completed a message and was satisfied with it, he or she would send it to the rest of the class. Others did the same thing, each at his or her own pace. Based on his participation in the activity and the data he collected, Kelm expressed the following impression of the activity: 'From a pedagogical standpoint, one of the greatest advantages of CACD is the increased participation from all the members of the class' (Kelm, 1992: 443).

A logical analysis based on the criteria described above might result in the following observations. The synchronous CMC activity was intended to provide conditions in which learners would have some time for reflection while producing the target language within an otherwise fast-paced interaction. The fact that the meaning was expressed in written mode would be expected to provide opportunity for some focus on form, and the real-time interaction might make modified interaction, and modified output, possible. The language was intended to be the appropriate difficulty level for the learners because it was centered on the language of the story that they were reading for their class – a story which was presumably chosen to provide comprehensible but challenging language for the learners. On the other hand, individual differences may not have been considered as the task is designed to have all learners playing the same role.

The task was intended to have a meaning focus which was prompted by the instructor's questions about the content of the story the learners had read. However, in the early 1990s, when this task was used, it would have been difficult to argue that it was authentic relative to what learners would be doing outside the classroom; the learners would no doubt have seen the task as a classroom experiment rather than as preparatory for future language use. The task was intended to be fun and to provide learners with the opportunity to use the target language without the teacher-frontedness of many classroom activities – a change that was seen as having a positive impact by the instructor. The activity required a local area network, synchronous communication software, and a teacher who knew how to use it, which apparently were all available in this setting. Moreover, the fact that this activity was used each week meant that it was not necessary to spend a lot of time teaching students to use the software relative to the time they spent engaging in the learning activity.

Microworld

Chun and Brandl (1992) described a microworld activity designed for beginning learners of German: 'The functional goal of this situation is [for the learner] to locate objects in a room and to differentiate between stationary physical location vs. the action or motion involved in placing an object somewhere' (Chun & Brandl, 1992: 260). The task begins by asking the learner to imagine he or she is living in the year 2101 with a robot, who likes to keep the room neat, for a roommate. For the purposes of the task, the student is designated as an untidy person whose things are scattered all over the room. The robot cannot find anything, so he begins to ask questions such as 'Where did you put my fountain pen?' in the target language, German. The learner, who sees a picture of the messy dormitory room on the computer screen, is expected to answer the robot's questions by typing them on the computer screen in German. After the student provides a correct response (with reference to the picture), the computer replies in German, 'I found it. You put it on top of the TV,' for example. The goal and topic of this and other microworld activities are controlled by the program. If the learner asks the robot where his optical system was designed, or something else outside the defined topic, the computer will not be able to respond.

Conditions for language use in this activity allow for written production, with opportunity for interactional modifications and modified output. Focus on form would be expected to occur when the output could not be interpreted by the computer, which would then point to the error for the learner to correct. The activity is intended for beginning level learners of German, and in fact requires knowledge of a very limited range of language including declarative statements and interrogatives about locations, which would be expected to be appropriate for beginners. Aside from allowing learners to work at their own pace, it is not clear whether individual differences have been taken into account. The task is intended to focus learners' attention on meaning by constructing a scenario in which the computer and learner play roles as language users engaging in a dialogue. Despite the meaning focus of each question the computer addresses to the learner, the task does not have an overall communication goal, e.g., to find a particular number of items or to collaborate to make the room neat; therefore, the task relies on the learner to develop an agenda. The interaction with the computer using written language would not have been authentic relative to learners' language use outside the classroom in the early 1990s. It was not clear from the authors' description what the impact would be on learners and teachers, but one might speculate that if the software worked as planned and helped learners to identify errors in their output, the experience would be expected to seem worthwhile to them. In the setting the authors described, the required equipment and instructor knowledge were present.

Text analysis

Liou (1993) described the use of a grammar checking program in a first-year writing and grammar course for EFL majors at a university in Taiwan. The writing class took a process-oriented approach in which learners were required to write, participate in peer editing, receive comments from the instructor, and revise. The students were given a topic for their writing assignment, for example 'Some Career Tips for College Graduates,' and asked to complete a first draft on their own. The first draft was the object of discussion during the peer editing session which followed. Students were able to use the input from their peers as they pleased when they went to the computer lab to type their first draft that would be handed in. Teachers made general comments on content and organization at this point and identified grammatical problems without specifying the necessary corrections. The students had another opportunity to revise their papers on the computer and then they used the computer for grammar checking. Based on the suggestions provided by the computer program, the students were able to revise their papers again.

The use of the grammar checker in this activity should be expected to focus learners' attention on grammatical form and prompt them to modify their linguistic output. The written mode and absence of time pressure would also favor attention to grammar. It is not clear how an appropriate language level was targeted because learners were able to choose language within the broad range allowed by the topic selected by the instructor. Individual differences were not explicitly considered. Writing to the assigned topics was expected to have primarily a meaning focus, with attention to grammatical form during grammar checking and revision. The writing process described was similar to what learners might find outside the classroom, except for the type of grammatical feedback that they might have found in grammar checkers in commercial software in the early 1990s. Despite the quality of error correction afforded by the grammar checker developed specifically for this project versus what language users would find in general-purpose software, the learners would be expected to see the process of writing and revising with the use of a grammar checker as authentic relative to their future work with English. The impact of this activity on learners would include the experience they should gain in examining and evaluating their linguistic output for its grammatical correctness. However, the learners' enthusiasm for continuing to work with grammar checkers in the future would depend on the quality of the analysis provided to the learner by the software. The writing activity appeared to be constrained by some limited access to the computer equipment as the learners were scheduled carefully to proceed through the assigned steps of the composing process, using the computer equipment only as needed, but it is unknown whether this was by pedagogical design or practical necessity.

Storyboard

The storyboard activity Jones and Fortescue (1987) described was used by a group of students who sat together in front of a computer screen in a computer lab. 'The text is entirely obliterated, and the learners can see only the title (Superstition), a mass of blobs, a reference to various help features and an invitation to guess a word' (1987: 37). The activity is therefore a guessing game, which is set up as a storyboard containing a text on superstition. The learners work collaboratively through oral conversation to determine what, when, and how they will input words into the game. The conversation among the learners may or may not be conducted in the target language, and the learners are free to take their time producing the language used in the reconstruction.

The language of the task is likely to shift variously from the meaning of the text, the meanings associated with making guesses and arguing about gaming strategy to the forms of the language of the text. The task therefore offers some opportunity for attention to linguistic form, but the degree to which that opportunity is realized should vary depending on the learners and their game strategy. The difficulty level of the language in the storyboard activity described by Jones and Fortescue is not addressed, but one might assume that the text was chosen in view of learners' level, as these programs allow teachers to input their own texts for this reason. Individual differences are not considered except to assume that these learners would be of an age and disposition to like the guessing-game format. The discussion of game strategy would have a meaning focus, but conversation may not take place in the target language. The target language would be expected to be treated as an object throughout the task with attention occasionally to meaning as needed to help make guesses. Such word games exist outside the classroom, but most learners are unlikely to see this as an authentic target language activity that they are hoping to learn how to accomplish. The learners are expected to have fun working with the text in a group/game format. The task is intended to provide learner-centered groupwork which is expected to impact positively the classroom atmosphere and learning. The requirements of this activity did not stretch the resources of the classroom described, where computers were sufficient in number for each of the groups to work at one of them, and where the teacher and learners understood the operation of the software.

Concordancing

Johns (1994) illustrated the use of concordancing activities with international students in courses for English for academic purposes (EAP) at the University of Birmingham in England. He described the students, who had come from around the world to study a variety of academic subjects, as learners who 'respond to challenges to their intelligence; and most of them are accustomed to the idea of research and finding things out for themselves.' These students were reported to work successfully in pairs, learning about each other's countries and subject areas. A concordancer activity might begin spontaneously in class when a question of usage or function came up such as 'What is the difference between *therefore* and *hence*?' or 'Why aren't all *shoulds* real *shoulds*?' (Johns, 1994: 297). The teacher would respond that he does not know and that they can find out together. The student who asked the question might then turn to the computer, which was in the classroom for this purpose, choose a database of texts which are kept on the hard drive, and ask the concordancer to return all instances of *should*. The computer's output would include sentences with *should* that the learners would then attempt to classify with respect to their various meanings and contexts governing their meanings.

The language of the task is both the oral language the learners use to analyze and understand the particular grammatical forms they choose as well as the written language that serves as examples for them to analyze. The task is intended to focus learners' attention primarily on form in the example texts, although the questions investigated may arise during meaning-based activities. Other conditions conducive to attention to form would have been the use of language examples in written mode, and lack of time pressure, but it is not clear whether or not these conditions existed. This activity was tailored exactly to the learner's language level because it took up those grammatical questions that the learners raised in the English for academic purposes (EAP) course. The learner characteristics were considered to be matched with the activity because of the analytic, research-orientation of the learners in this class. The task of linguistic analysis was not intended to be like tasks that learners will engage in outside the classroom unless they choose to do so specifically for individualized language study, and therefore the learners may not be expected to see this task as authentic to their future language use.

The task is intended to develop not only the linguistic abilities of the learners but also their strategies for linguistic analysis, which are intended to serve their linguistic development beyond the scope of the EAP class. Instructors and learners are intended to have positive teaching and learning experiences with the concordancer because it is supposed to offer many relevant examples of linguistic form, thereby enriching the scope and flexibility of classroom materials. The scenario Johns offers requires a single computer, a concordancer program and some texts, which appear to have been available. Because of the unpredictability both of the types of queries that might be made to the concordancer and of the results, the possibility exists that the linguistic data to be analyzed may extend beyond the learners' and teachers' capacities for explaining them. If the activity causes too much of this type of unresolvable data, the effect could be negative because learners may see it as a waste of time.

Summary

Of the many possible CALL activities in use today, these represent only five examples. It should be noted that each, as it was described above, might be designed differently by a teacher who chose to use the software in a different way, or today when learners' experience with computers has expanded considerably. In other words, what was described here was the complete activity – which included the teachers' plans for the software. A summary of the analyses, included in Table 3.6, demonstrates that each activity in its context might be expected to have both positive and negative qualities. The analysis may provide a means for deciding whether or not to try a task in a class as well as a mechanism for identifying at the planning stage ways in which a task may be weak in order to attempt to improve it.

As the examples above demonstrated, the logical analysis of CALL tasks required a description of the complete task and context in which the software was used. As a consequence, the evaluation is necessarily context specific. As the second principle stated, the

Table 3.6. *Summary of the logical evaluation of CALL tasks*

Quality	Kelm's CACD	Chun and Brandl's Microworld	Liou's Grammar Checking	Jones and Fortescue's text reconstruction	Johns' concordancing
Language learning potential	Possible	Good	Good	Unknown	Good
Learner fit	Good	Good	Probably good	Probably good	Good
Meaning focus	All focus on meaning	Primarily meaning focus	Primarily meaning focus	Not clear	Not primarily meaning focus
Authenticity	Not authentic	Not authentic	Somewhat authentic	Not authentic	Not authentic
Impact	Positive	Unknown	Positive	Unknown	Positive
Practicality	Good	Good	Unknown	Good	Good

judgemental analysis provided in this chapter is only one part of the overall CALL task evaluation. Empirical evaluation is also needed to provide evidence of the extent to which the judgemental analysis accurately reflects how the learners work with the CALL task.

Empirical evaluation of CALL

Judgemental evaluation offers a methodology for making systematic hypotheses about the benefits to be attained through CALL tasks. As hypotheses, they stand in need of support through empirical data, because as L2 research has shown, 'students are often doing something very different from what [language teachers] assume they are doing' (Hosenfeld, 1976: 123). In other words, it is necessary to identify the observable data that provide evidence of CALL qualities.

Evidence for CALL qualities

The limitations of the study of learning outcomes have been well-rehearsed in the literature on educational technology (R. E. Clark, 1985; Papert, 1987) as well as in that on CALL (e.g., Doughty, 1987;

1992; Chapelle & Jamieson, 1989; 1991; Dunkel, 1991; Garrett, 1987). The arguments mirror those that have been put forward in other areas of L2 classroom research. Empirical research methods for evaluating L2 classroom tasks have to a large extent given up on evaluating language instruction solely through measurement of learning outcomes in favor of investigating classroom processes (Allwright, 1988; Allwright & Bailey, 1991; Chaudron, 1988; Cohen & Hosenfeld, 1981; Crookes & Gass, 1993a; 1993b; Day, 1986; Færch & Kasper, 1987; Gass & Madden, 1985; K. E. Johnson, 1995; Long, 1980; van Lier, 1988).

Despite the definitive move toward the study of learning processes over products, it would be difficult to argue that a research result showing language learning outcomes that can be attributed to particular features of instruction are irrelevant or uninteresting. In a sense, the study of learning outcomes is at the same time seductive and cause for suspicion. This tension can begin to be understood through examination of the qualities outlined above. What becomes apparent, is that some of the qualities (e.g., language learning potential) might best be studied by examining learning outcomes (as they are related to particular task features), whereas the study of learning outcomes would offer little or nothing to questions about task authenticity. In short, each of the qualities implies particular types of research questions and associated methods.

The methods that are suggested in this chapter are similar to those that have been used in other L2 classroom research. However, when applied to CALL, these methods are implemented somewhat differently, largely because the computer is able to record the language and some non-linguistic moves that the learner makes to provide a more detailed and readily available record of learners' behavior than can be gained through other forms of observation. These types of data prove useful for investigating some of the questions about appropriateness. However, the types of data the computer can collect is not the real issue. The issue is what kind of evidence is required to address a particular research question. Goodfellow and Laurillard (1994) demonstrate the irony of a perspective that begins with computer-gathered data:

The idea that data generated in the interaction between learners and CALL programs could provide us with information about language learning processes has created a lot of interest . . . The attraction is that the computer's ability to record complex processes accurately and unobtrusively means that we can use it to tell us exactly what learners do. However, whilst the general principle is clear, precisely what we should do with this information is not.

Table 3.7. *Questions for the empirical evaluation of CALL tasks*

Qualities	Questions
Language learning potential	What evidence suggests that the learner has acquired the target forms that were focused on during the CALL task? What evidence indicates that learners focused on form during the CALL task?
Learner fit	What evidence suggests that the targeted linguistic forms are at an appropriate level of difficulty for the learners? What evidence suggests that the task is appropriate to learners' individual characteristics (e.g., age, learning style, computer experience)?
Meaning focus	What evidence suggests that learners' construction of linguistic meaning aids language learning? What evidence indicates that learners use the language during the task for constructing and interpreting meaning?
Authenticity	What evidence suggests that learners' performance in the CALL task corresponds to what one would expect to see outside the CALL task? What evidence suggests that learners see the connection between the CALL task and tasks outside the classroom?
Impact	What evidence suggests that learners learn more about the target language and about strategies for language learning through the use of the task? What evidence suggests that instructors engage in sound second language pedagogical practices by using the task? What evidence suggests that learners and teachers had a positive experience with technology through the use of the task?
Practicality	What evidence suggests that hardware, software, and personnel resources prove to be sufficient to allow the CALL task to succeed?

Research questions about CALL need to be developed in view of the qualities about which evidence is sought. Table 3.7 outlines general research questions that would address each of the CALL qualities.

Language learning potential

Empirical research demonstrating the language learning potential of a CALL activity needs to show that learners have improved in their control of the aspects of the target language focused on in the activity. Rather than attempting to compare learning in CALL tasks to that of other classroom tasks, informative research on language learning potential has centered on particular aspects of CALL that are hypothesized to be beneficial – comparing the success of CALL tasks with and without the condition under investigation. To the extent that the conditions are carefully defined in such tasks, results can contribute to principles for designing CALL tasks with language learning potential. Even though this research is seldom described in terms of the conditions investigated by other SLA researchers, some studies can be interpreted in view of their contribution to these questions. The questions to be addressed are the following: What evidence suggests that the learner has acquired the target forms that were focused on during the CALL task? What evidence indicates that learners focused on form during the CALL task?

Focus on form

Given the theorized importance of salient input for acquisition (Sharwood-Smith, 1993), surprisingly little research has been conducted on the effects of CALL activities which focus learners' attention on particular linguistic forms in the L2 input, but one carefully conducted study yielded results that clearly favored highlighting linguistic form. Doughty (1991) compared the effects of two different types of explicitly salient L2 input with that which was not explicitly flagged to catch learners' attention. The input consisted of sentences containing relative clauses within reading passages which learners were instructed to read for comprehension. In other words, the primary attention during the task was to be meaning. In the two experimental groups, learners' attention was drawn to the relative clauses through highlighting on the computer screen as well as through either giving grammatical rules or providing meaningful restatement of the sentence. Both of the groups with the salient input performed better on grammatical post-tests than did the group receiving input with no highlighting; the group receiving the meaningful restatements of the target structure performed better in reading comprehension. These results provide evidence for the argument that CALL materials with carefully selected and highlighted target forms can offer superior language learning potential than those in which learners' attention is not directed to form.

In a study examining acquisition of vocabulary in CALL materials, researchers (Duquette, Renié, & Laurier, 1998) attempted to identify factors related to acquisition of particular lexical items. Following up on the overall finding of no significant differences in vocabulary gains between control and experimental groups, researchers identified particular words upon which learners in all groups had made significant gains. They concluded that 'a number of conditions must exist in a multimedia environment for there to be lexical gains. Words must occur frequently and be presented in specific contexts where images and text are closely linked before they are presented in animated form [as the multimedia materials did]' (1998: 23). They found the words that learners were most likely to improve on were those that were important to the story-line presented in the video, as well. This was a challenging study because it attempted to identify what was learned from existing materials, but it succeeded in identifying some of the critical characteristics of input that may help to focus learners' attention on unknown vocabulary and to remember it.

Other evidence concerning focus on form has been obtained through interviews with learners who have participated in CMC classroom discussion. Beauvois (1998) reports that L2 French learners reported the following when asked about their experience:

'In the lab, we do have our books there and . . . you can take the time to look up a word.'
'You have time . . . to think about how to conjugate the verb.' (1998: 105)

This is not to say that learners engage in such reflective processes naturally during CMC activities, but that it is possible to construct an activity in a way that some learners do.

Modified interaction

Modified interaction can be seen when an interruption of meaning making occurs due to a breakdown in comprehension or production. Such a breakdown can occur during face-to-face conversation, during the process of reading or listening, or in an on-line written conversation, for example. The modification refers to the interruption that disturbs the unproblematic flow in meaning making. In CALL materials, opportunities for interruption are often built in through interactive sequences and help options. Among the first studies to investigate whether interruptions in the input to learners would significantly affect their listening and retention of what was heard, Schrupp, Busch, and Mueller (1983) compared the value of different levels of interactivity in a CALL program. They found that the interactive video condition was the one in which the students remembered the content of the German material best. This is not to say that the language of the German video was acquired; however, comprehended target language material (intake) is at least a candidate for acquisition, and therefore this study provides some evidence for the value of interaction during listening.

Other studies investigating the value of modified interactions have examined the extent to which L2 vocabulary is more likely to be acquired when it is presented in conditions allowing for interaction. Interaction in these cases refers to the learners interrupting their reading to receive help with vocabulary by clicking on unknown words in the written input. Several studies have investigated the extent to which learners having access to various forms of on-line vocabulary help assists in their reading comprehension and vocabulary retention (e.g., Lyman-Hager *et al.*, 1993; Chun & Plass, 1996; Lomicka, 1998; Hegelheimer, 1998; Laufer & Hill, 2000). Overall, findings support the theoretically based suggestion that learners benefit from having provisions for the type of interactional modification supported by hypermedia glosses. At the same time, summary of this growing body of research is difficult because of the variety of issues investigated, including preferences for various types of glosses (e.g., L1, L2, text, audio, image), influences on reading comprehension, and vocabulary acquisition, and the variety of research methods employed, including experimental and within-group designs as well as interaction analysis and think-aloud procedures. Although the issue of interactional modifications with on-line linguistic input holds great potential for improving CALL, additional research is needed to clarify the relationship between the use of glosses and acquisition of vocabulary targeted by the learner through actual interactional modifications.

In an interactive listening task for learners of L2 French, Borrás and Lafayette (1994) investigated the effectiveness of optional L1 (English) subtitles as a means of modifying interaction. They compared performance on a speaking task of learners who had used the computer-assisted video materials with and without subtitle options. Learners who participated in the subtitle condition had the option of choosing to see English subtitles for the aurally presented French when they had difficulty in comprehending. The control group heard the video under exactly the same conditions but without the subtitle option. Results of the speaking task, which required all learners to address some questions about the content of the video, clearly favored the subtitle condition. The authors concluded 'the statistically significant difference found in this study in favor of the subtitle condition for higher oral communicative performance strongly suggests that when learning from "authentic video" in a multimedia environment, having the opportunity to see and control subtitles, as opposed to not having that opportunity, results in both better comprehension and subsequent better use of the foreign language' (Borrás & Lafayette, 1994: 70).

Each of these studies offers some support for materials that provide opportunities for modified interactions. However, results were less clear in a study that attempted to increase language-focused interactions by having learners work in pairs on Spanish interactive multimedia materials (Chang & Smith, 1991). The pairwork was intended to provide an opportunity for learners to question each other and discuss difficulties they encountered in comprehending the language of the video. Results indicated that the learners working in pairs did indeed discuss the meaning of the language of the video, primarily by attempting to translate to the L1 when they had difficulty. Overall, the learners who worked in the dyads scored equivalently on a test requiring recall of the story-line to those who had worked alone on the multimedia materials, even though the former scored significantly better on one type of question. One would expect the type of modified input received by the learners working in dyads to have had an effect similar to the subtitles in the study by Borrás and Lafayette, but apparently learners were not as effective at providing the needed modified input to each other as the systematically subtitled software was. This finding supports the value of continued research on how to best supply tutorial help to learners through software support materials, other learners (Klingner & Vaughn, 2000), or human tutors working on-line (Lamy & Goodfellow, 1999a).

Given the theoretical justification for tasks which require use of the target language for communicative language use along with a means for resolving communication breakdowns, these types of L2 tasks hold a unique promise for language teaching. While user-requested, on-line help is similar to the use of L1 captions in videos (e.g., Guillory, 1998), it is different in an important way: captions are presented uniformly and simultaneously with the L2 video allowing learners to follow the captions rather than the target language; user-requested help allows for the important process of attempting to understand, noticing problems in comprehension, and receiving help in resolving them. The latter is what is hypothesized to be beneficial.

Modified output

Conditions providing opportunities for learners to modify their output in CALL have not been studied extensively if output is to be understood as 'comprehensible output,' or language intended to convey meaning. The research that may be relevant in supporting the value of modified output has been focused on the type of feedback the learner receives after responding to a question or prompt from the computer.

A study by Robinson, Underwood, Rivers, Hernandez, Rudisill, and Enseñat (1985) compared the effectiveness of different kinds of feedback in CALL tasks consisting of learner–computer interactions. One comparison was made between 'student discovery strategies' feedback that identified the existence of an error but required the learner to identify the precise nature of the problem, and 'program disclosure' (1985: 160), which was operationalized with 'wrong, try again' types of feedback. Student discovery strategies were associated with greater learning gains. Another comparison was made among options for providing help after an error was produced: program-controlled help automatically offered the correct answer, student-controlled help offered a variety of options for the learner to choose after making an error, and a combination of learner- and program-controlled offered the learner the appropriate help relative to the error, but the learner had to choose to see it. The latter condition was most effective. These comparisons do not speak directly to the question of whether or not allowing the learner to modify their output when it contains errors is useful, but it does provide evidence for the value of identifying learners' errors in their output.

Another study also supports the strategy of pinpointing learners' errors as carefully as possible. Nagata (1993) found that learners of Japanese who received 'intelligent' feedback about their use of particles performed significantly better on both post-tests and end-of-semester tests than did those students who had received only an indication of where they had made an error. Intelligent feedback for a particle error in the learner's sentence would look like this: 'In your sentence, GAKUSEE is the "subject" of the passive (the one that is affected by the action), but it should be the "agent" of the passive (the one who performs the action and affects the subject). Use the particle NI to mark it.' The unintelligent feedback message for the same error would consist of 'NI is missing,' requiring the learner to remember or find out how, why, and where 'NI' was to be used in the sentence (Nagata, 1993: 335).

Unfortunately other studies of feedback through learner–computer interaction investigate structure tasks for which meaning clearly is not central, if it is relevant at all. Learners' output on such tasks cannot be considered 'comprehensible output.' It is not clear how hypotheses about noticing errors in comprehensible output apply to error correction during explicit grammar instruction in which the learners' attention is directed to the forms of the language. On the basis of the existing research, it also remains unclear whether it is the type of feedback or the quality of resulting modified output that should be seen as valuable. Additional research is needed to help assess the language learning potential of various types of feedback on comprehensible output in computer–learner interactions.

One study of learner–learner interactions in computer-mediated L2 tasks offers some hope for those designing tasks in which learners correct their comprehensible output. Based on investigation of the language of L2 Spanish learners in synchronous written communication of a chat, Pellettieri (2000) concluded that this medium supported tasks in which negotiation of meaning could occur.

> Learners involved in . . . chats negotiate over all aspects of the discourse, which in turn pushes learners to form-focused linguistic modifications. Additionally, learners provide and are provided corrective feedback, which was demonstrated to result in the incorporation of target-language forms into subsequent turns. (2000: 83)

At first, these results appear in sharp contrast to those of researchers who have studied the language of other internet chat rooms (e.g., Yates, 1996) and describe it as having characteristics of restricted registers including many non-standard forms (Murray, 2000). The difference can be explained by the types of pedagogical tasks that Pellettieri set for the Spanish learners. By drawing from knowledge about communication tasks in SLA, she was able to construct task demands that prompted learners to attend to language as needed.

Research methods

The most convincing way to demonstrate the language learning potential of a CALL activity is through the study of learning outcomes. In other words, if learners were to have acquired particular grammatical forms or vocabulary through a CALL task, then results of an assessment after learners have completed the task can provide some evidence for the language learning potential of the task. The evidence is much stronger, of course, if pretest data indicate that the learners did not know the target forms before beginning to work with CALL. Still stronger evidence is obtained if a contrasting group that did not use the CALL task or used the CALL task in another form failed to make similar gains. Any of these designs is strengthened if learners are shown to have retained what was learned at a later time. For example, Nagata (1993) prepared post-tests which 'followed the same format and content' as the CALL activities to be sure to assess what was taught (1993: 336), and then to assess longer-term retention of the target structures, '[t]hree weeks after the final experiment, the subjects took the final exam in which four questions were included as a retention test on the passive structures' (1993: 336). These research designs have provided tentative evidence for the language learning potential of some features of CALL tasks, but process-oriented designs might better be exploited for this purpose as well.

Interactional modifications are evident in a number of sequences of interactions in CALL tasks. The research described above presented learners with conditions in which they could *choose* to modify interactions. Evidence for learners actually choosing to modify appears in records of their interactions with the computer if they request modifications of linguistic input. In many CALL materials, such as an example called *Learn Language Now!* by Transparent Language, opportunities abound for the following type of exchange between computer and learner:

Computer   INT: Combien de types de vignes, de cépages cultivez-vous?
Learner   Clicks on *cépages*
Computer   Word Meaning ▾
                    varieties

This is the type of exchange which occurs during a task requiring comprehension of an aurally presented conversation between an interviewer and a vineyard owner in France. The learner can attempt comprehension of the aural language, request the written text of the conversation, and then make queries about the vocabulary and grammar by clicking on the appropriate parts of the text. The learner requests a definition for *cépages*, for example, by clicking on that word in the input text. The computer supplies a translation of the word, thereby making the meaning of the word known to the learner, at least for the moment.

Observation of such exchanges does not indicate that the learner has acquired the word, but it is evidence that the learner is engaging in a process of making unknown forms in the input comprehensible, which makes the input more likely to be acquired. The records of learners' use of such materials can reveal the extent to which they engaged in such interactional modifications, and therefore how useful the CALL task was for their potential acquisition. If learners listen to the conversation without asking for the written text or requesting any modified input, they may comprehend the language they hear, or not be interested enough to engage in interactional modifications. In either case, it would be difficult to argue that the CALL task held learning potential for those learners.

If normal interaction for reading a text on a screen is considered to consist of the learner's receiving input and requesting more input (i.e., scrolling down the page), this normal sequence is interrupted, or modified, when the learner clicks on a word to receive a definition. Modified interaction may also be apparent when the learner scrolls back to a previous sentence, or part of the interview, or when the learner interrupts reading altogether to seek additional grammatical information through the reference and search options. In the interview text, the lines appear in a relatively small window, as illustrated in Figure 3.1. When the learner modifies a strict linear pattern in moving through the text to go back beyond what is shown on the screen, there is evidence for modified interaction. This program provides an additional opportunity for gathering evidence about modifications because learners are able to click on words in each sentence as they read. The segment with the word is highlighted, giving the learner the option of hearing that segment aurally. A learner who uses this option of clicking produces evidence for the extent to which the linear progression through the text is interrupted. Of course, the concept of modified interaction would be different in a hypermedia document in which the message was not delivered in a linear text. The interactional modification of written or spoken input needs to be defined in view of the nature of the unproblematic flow of the CALL task.

MONSIEUR HURST: Je travaille sur huit hectares de vignes avec ma femme et nous avons une partie en propriété, la moitié, et puis l'autre moitié en location.
INT: Combien de types de vignes, de cépages cultivez-vous?
MONSIEUR HURST: Nous avons en Alsace les sept cépages de raisins, six blancs et un rouge. Nous avons le Sylvaner, le Pinot Blanc, le Muscat, le Riesling, le Pinot Gris, le Gewürztraminer et un seul cépage rouge, le Pinot Noir.

Figure 3.1 The text window displaying the interview in Turckheim et sa fête du vin *(from* Learn Language Now! *by Transparent Language)*[2]

---

[2] The translation of this screen to English would be as follows:

Mr Hurst: I work on eight hectares of vineyards with my wife and we own one part of it, half, and the other half we rent.
Int: How many types of varieties of grapes do you cultivate?
Mr Hurst: In Alsace, we have seven varieties of grapes, six white and one red. We have Sylvaner, Pinot Blanc, Muscat, Riesling, Pinot Gris, Gewürztraminer and one red variety, Pinot Noir.

The construct of modified interaction might also be productive in tasks requiring learners to construct linguistic output. In such cases, the unproblematic flow would be characterized by continuation of the writing process, for example. However, this flow is modified when learners interrupt themselves to request help. Bland, Noblitt, Armington, and Gay (1990) describe the process used by learners as they construct a text using *System-D*, which supports queries about the vocabulary and grammar of French while the learners are writing their French texts. Records of learners' use indicate that learners tend to interrupt their normal meaning-focused interaction (constructing a text) to focus on language.

Modified output can best be observed in sequences consisting of the learners' unsuccessful attempts at expression followed by their linguistic modification of the form perceived as problematic. Such cases provide evidence of the learners' partial knowledge, which then becomes the focus of attention. Swain and Lapkin (1995) suggest that it is not important *how* attention is drawn to learners' errors in their output. The learner may be the one to recognize a problem without external prompting. In such cases, the data would display the learners' original form, the process of correction (e.g., editing), and the learner's final form. These data would be like those used to infer 'self-monitoring' strategies that have been documented in CALL (Jamieson & Chapelle, 1987; Pellettieri, 2000). One can easily envisage the types of exchanges that would indicate modified output such as this hypothetical example from a tour-arranging task in a French class (Chapelle, 1998a).

Computer:	Qu'est-ce que vous voulez savoir du Québec?	[What do you want to know about Quebec?]
Learner:	Où peut-on fait du canoe?	[Where can you go canoeing?]
Learner:	Où peut-on fait du canotage?	[Where can you go canoeing?]
Computer:	Il faut corriger le verbe: Où peut-on <u>fait</u> du canotage?	[It's necessary to correct the verb: Where can you go canoeing?]
Learner:	Où peut-on faire du canotage?	[Where can you go canoeing?]

The example illustrates two cases of modified output, the first (the change from 'canoe' to 'canotage' was prompted by the learners' own reflection, whereas the correction of the form of the verb ('fait' to 'faire') is prompted by the computer. A program with the language recognition techniques capable of identifying errors in such tasks needs to be evaluated in part on the basis of evidence that the program is able to prompt modified output during completion of meaning-based tasks such as this.

The issue of control – the value of learners, teacher, or computer

Participant	Language	Function
Student 1	A quelle heure ouvira-t-il? Je pense que je voudrais une biere . . .	Imaginative/Social
Student 2	Bonjour, E. je voudrais une bière aussi mais il n'y a pas de vertu dans une bire virtuelle . . .	Imaginative/Social
Student 3	Bonjour D. Juis suis a Caen le 23 aout. Et vous? S.	Request?/Social
Student 4	Bonjour S. Moi aussi je serai Caen le vignt-troisime aot. Peut-tre on peut recontre . . .	Invitation?/Social

Figure 3.2 Social conversation through computer-mediated communication

programs having control over particular aspects of CALL tasks – has been an ongoing point of discussion for CALL enthusiasts for at least two decades. Unfortunately, systematic comparisons of features of control have not been reported in terms of learning outcomes, but recently some researchers have begun to look at process data which reveal some of the effects of degrees of teacher control.

One such study examined the language produced during CMC in tasks varying in the degree to which the instructor had specified a task assignment (Lamy & Goodfellow, 1999b). The task with little teacher intervention resulted in what Lamy and Goodfellow termed 'social conversation,' consisting of language that may not stretch the learners' capability and may therefore not hold potential for language learning. In the example they provide, shown in Figure 3.2, learners used their L2 French to discuss having a beer in a virtual bar in France. This finding is consistent with research on face-to-face oral L2 tasks (Pica, Kanagy, & Falodun, 1993): if no goal for the communication is specified, learners have no need to push their linguistic resources or to negotiate meaning. For example, even if some participating learners did not understand the expression Student 2 uses ('il n'y a pas de vertu'), the conversation could move, as it did, smoothly to a trip to Caen, losing the moment to push linguistic competence through discussion of that expression. In a task with no goal, there is no critical consequence for lack of communication.

Lamy and Goodfellow contrast this to 'reflective conversation' which focuses on language and language learning, which is prompted through the teacher's control. In their example, the teacher has provided a goal of working with vocabulary that the learners gather on their own. Learners also engage in computer-mediated discussion, but in this case, the data clearly show a language learning purpose in their conversation. The parallel observation in the L2 classroom has identified the 'language related episode' in classroom language. This is defined by Swain (1998) as instances when the learners talk about the target language. She argues that these sequences, which result from the particular task that the teacher designs, indicate the learner is focusing on language in a way that may be beneficial for acquisition.

Ironically, the majority of the research on classroom CMC has begun with the assumption that minimal teacher control is beneficial for acquisition. In fact, data from classroom CMC sessions that have been investigated demonstrate a greater quantity of learner participation than what is found in face-to-face communication (Kelm, 1992; Beauvois, 1992; Warschauer, 1997a; Kern, 1995; Ortega, 1997). This participation has been equated, perhaps inappropriately, with acquisition, but the finding of a high degree of learner participation associated with CMC discussions in which teachers exert little control may be positive in its own right.

Although examination of process data as they pertain to ideal conditions for acquisition is informative, the real challenge for research pertaining to conditions is to demonstrate whether or not learners' engagement in the conditions is related to acquisition. The product-oriented research has tended to assume that learners placed in a particular condition will participate as the condition allows. For example, learners provided with a text to read that contains hypertext word definitions are assumed to have clicked on the words they did not know while reading. In fact, such an assumption underlies acceptance of the research results described above. The real question is not whether the *provision for* interactional modifications increases acquisition, but whether the *use of* interactional modification increases acquisition of those forms for which interactional modifications are used.

In L2 classroom research, Swain (1998) has addressed the parallel issue by constructing assessments specifically for individual students to assess their knowledge of the linguistic elements *they chose to focus on* during task completion. Similarly, Hsu (1994) conducted a focused analysis of interactions between learners and the computer to identify their requests for modified input of segments of the story they listened to. The normal interaction in this part of the program consisted of learners' requests for continuation of a story with accompanying pictures on one computer screen after another. The researcher documented 'interactional modifications' evident from learners' requests for repetitions, written transcriptions, or written definitions for words in the input. She also recorded the specific linguistic input associated with each of the learners' requests. She then assessed outcomes through pre- and post-tests which had been constructed specifically for the research to include the lexical phrases in the input. She found significant relationships between interactional modifications and improvement in listening comprehension. Even though improved comprehension is only one facet of acquisition, and no delayed post-test results could argue that the effects lasted, this methodology, which is described further by Hegelheimer and Chapelle (2000), provides an example of how process and product data can be integrated to address questions about the effectiveness of engagement in particular conditions.

Learner fit

On a day-to-day basis, teachers implicitly assess how well learning materials fit their learners, but learner fit can also be assessed through more systematic research methods including observation of working processes, assessment of learning outcomes, and questioning learners about their opinions. Such systematic analysis can help to reveal the extent to which a CALL task engages learners in language at a useful level of difficulty in a way that is appropriate to their individual characteristics.

Level of linguistic difficulty

The empirical question about linguistic difficulty is what evidence suggests that the targeted linguistic forms are at an appropriate level of difficulty for the learners? One form of evidence about linguistic difficulty can be found in the type of process data described above – those that show the extent of use of interactional modifications. When learners use software that offers help options such as word definitions, their interaction with the materials can be examined to indicate whether they had sufficient interest and need to request definitions (e.g., Chapelle & Mizuno, 1989; Desmarais *et al.*, 1998). If learners read or listen to input without making use of the available help, it is possible that the material is either so easy that no help is needed or that the whole task is so difficult that they are unable to participate at all. If no evidence that learners used help appears in the record log of interactions, it may be that the level of difficulty is inappropriate. These observations of behaviors can be added to by introspective methods requiring learners to think aloud as they work. For example, Park's (1994) study investigating use of ESL multimedia

> Kang: Alda, est-ce que tes parents parle à toi en chinois et tu parle aux parents
> en anglais? Moi, mes parents ne me parle pas en anglais, mais je leur parle en
> anglais en meme temps. C'est un peu bizarre.
> Billy: Alda, est-ce que vous êtes chinoise? Si vous êtes chinoise, avez-vous
> célebré la nouvelle anneé chinoise hier? Avez-vous reçu beaucoup d'argent de
> votre famille?
> Kang: Alda, pourquoi 'tu n'aime pas trop' de traditions chinois? Que penses-tu
> a la NOUVELLE ANNEE de Chinois? (Kern, 1995: 458-459)

Figure 3.3 Computer-assisted classroom discussion in a second-year college French class in the US[3]

through think-aloud data (Ericsson & Simon, 1984) identified revealing thoughts such as 'I think I have a lot of vocabulary that I don't know' (1994: 147). This statement was made while the learner was clicking on one of the words in the input.

Researchers examining process data containing the language that learners produced in CMC tasks have evaluated its linguistic difficulty relative to learners' level of ability. For example, Kern (1995) examined the linguistic characteristics of his students' language in a computer-assisted classroom discussion on family heritage and customs. His analysis of the data concluded that 'students' language output [in the computer-assisted discussion] was of an overall greater level of sophistication than in oral discussion, in terms of the range of morphosyntactic features and in terms of the variety of discourse functions expressed' (1995: 470). He argued for the value of such a task for providing an opportunity to engage in language of an appropriate level of difficulty for his students' development. This argument pertains to the condition of written versus oral; many CMC enthusiasts have argued that the written language of CMC is beneficial for reflection on linguistic form during a meaning-based activity (e.g., Warschauer, 1997b).

Evidence for appropriate difficulty can also be gained through pretesting and post-testing of the language to be acquired during the CALL task. Language that is too difficult or too easy will not produce

---

[3] The English translation:

Kang: Alda, do your parents talk to you in Chinese and you speak to them in English? My parents don't speak to me in English, but I speak to them in English at the same time. It's a little strange.

Billy: Alda, are you Chinese? If you are Chinese, did you celebrate the Chinese new year yesterday? Did you receive a lot of money from your family?

Kang: Alda, why don't you like the Chinese traditions too much? What do you think of the Chinese new year?

any changes in learners' language knowledge; however, many other reasons for no pre-post differences may be possible as well.

Individual characteristics

What evidence suggests that a task is appropriate to learners' individual characteristics? This is a thorny question that has been addressed through assessment of outcomes and examination of learning processes, but which remains an important research issue for the future. Investigating cognitive style and task variables in materials teaching participial phrases, Abraham (1985) found that field-independent (i.e., analytic and independent) ESL learners performed better on post-tests when they had used a rule presentation (deductive) approach and field-dependent (i.e., holistic and dependent on others) learners performed better after using software presenting examples of the structure (inductive). These results are consistent with predictions that the analytic learners will prefer rules whereas the more holistic learners will prefer to learn through examples. In another study, Chapelle and Jamieson (1986) found field-independent ESL students tended to have a more negative attitude toward the CALL activities they investigated, while the field-dependent students had more positive attitudes. The CALL activities, which supplemented classroom activities throughout the semester in an intensive ESL program, provided structure and guidance for language that one might predict the field-dependent learners would welcome.

Other research has looked at factors such as motivation and gender (Meunier, 1996) and participation in CMC activities (Warschauer, 1997a). These results have proven interesting from the perspective of the willingness to communicate construct. Comparing the amount of participation in CMC versus oral classroom discussion, Warschauer (1997a) found that oral classroom discussion was characterized by uneven patterns of participation, presumably because of the normal differential levels of willingness to communicate on the part of the participants. The CMC discussion, in contrast, produced much more even patterns of participation. This and other studies of CMC in the L2 classroom (Beauvois, 1998; Markley, 1998) have shown the written non-face-to-face discussion of the CMC diminishes the effect of individual differences that may hamper communication in the classroom, thereby resulting in more comprehensible output produced by those who would otherwise produce little.

	(English translation)
ML: DB, Eu quero seu zapatos! Que cor!	ML: DB, I want your shoes (misspelled)! What color!
DB: DH, sua zapatas sao muitas bonitas, mas sua camisa e muita divertida	DB: DH, our shoes (misspelled) are very pretty but your shirt is lots of fun
DH: ML, os zapatos de DH o de DB?	DH: ML, DH's shoes (misspelled) or DB's?
PT: Que zapatos?	PT: What shoes (misspelled)?
CB: ML and DB, a palavra e 'sapatos' - nao 'zapatos'	CB: ML and DB, the word is 'sapatos' not 'zapatos'
DB: CB, Orlando falou que (spelling) nao e importante, nao e?	DB: CB, Orlando said that spelling isn't important, right?
ML: CB, Eu se a palavra por shoes e sapatos mais quero divirtir com a lingua. Como uma licensa de artista.	ML: CB, I know the word for shoes is *sapatos* but I want to have fun with the language, like poetic licence.
CB: DB, o que e a palavra para smartass?	CB: DB, what is the word for smart ass?
CB: ML, lingua nao e arte. e um trabalho.	CB: ML, language is not art. It is work.
DB: CB, nao briga com ML e mim. Todos sao amigos!	DB: CB, don't fight with ML and me. We're all friends!

Figure 3.4 A segment of the Portuguese text from computer-assisted classroom discussion (Kelm, 1992: 450)

Research methods

Research investigating both difficulty level and individual differences needs to be developed to better understand learner fit. Research investigating difficulty of the language of CMC needs to develop a clearer definition of the conditions of CMC tasks that may be related to difficulty. Commentary on this topic tends to attribute findings such as Kern's (beneficial linguistic complexity) to the written task condition; however, this single task characteristic is obviously not able to produce acceptable linguistic complexity in all cases, as evidence from other uses of electronic communication has demonstrated (D. E. Murray, 2000). The CMC task from the Portuguese class examined in the previous chapter was designed to keep the language at an appropriate level of difficulty through the instructor's designation of the topic from the material they were reading for class. As Figure 3.4 shows, however, the actual language of at least one segment of this session did not address this topic, and therefore may not have reached the beneficial level of complexity for these learners. This excerpt may have been an exception to what was beneficial language practice throughout, but the point is that the research needs to identify the characteristics of the CMC task that keep the learners engaged in beneficial communication.

The research on individual differences should be an important line of inquiry, particularly given the variety of task conditions that CALL can construct for individuals. Despite the need to understand differential effectiveness of learning conditions in CALL, research on individual differences has been plagued with both theoretical and methodological difficulties. Research on individual differences requires theory-based links to be drawn between specific individual variables and instructional task characteristics (Skehan, 1989). However, the best-developed theory of individual differences was developed around an aptitude construct, which implied that learners were categorically good or poor language learners even if the overall aptitude comprised different types of abilities. Recent work on L2 aptitude, in contrast, provides more hope for CALL with a situation-specific definition of willingness to communicate as well as a theory of learning differences that suggests that learners approach the process differently (through analysis or through memory) but that both paths can yield success (Skehan, 1998). On the basis of the theoretical differences among these learners' needs, Skehan suggests alternative paths for instruction such as the addition of a 'pre-task linguistic' stage for memory-oriented learners during which planning and preparation would be emphasized (1998: 272). These suggestions form the essential basis for development of CALL tasks which can be varied in ways that are intended to be appropriate for different kinds of learners, and their validity can be assessed through empirical evaluation.

The most fundamental methodological issue is assessment of individual differences. Even when hypotheses are made about relevant learner variables for CALL (e.g., Jamieson & Chapelle, 1988), uncertainty remains in the measurement of some individual difference variables (e.g., Chapelle & Green, 1992). What is the best way of assessing whether an individual is analytic or memory-based? The problem for establishing validity of individual difference measures is the same as that for language assessment (see Chapter 4), but additional work is needed to construct useful measures. CALL offers intriguing possibilities for assessment of individual differences through, as Hart (1981b) suggested, a 'bottom-up' approach which uses records of learners' task performance to assess their style (e.g., Curtin, Avner & Provenzano, 1981; Jamieson & Chapelle, 1987).

Again Skehan's (1998) approach, which is based on a processing perspective for SLA, appears most useful for the theoretical grounding needed to interpret individual difference process data obtained in CALL research. At the same time, exploratory empirical work has begun to examine the individual learning strategies learners use to navigate their language learning on-line (e.g., Park, 1994; Desmarais *et al.*, 1998).

Meaning focus

Empirical evidence for meaning focus is based on observation of learners' interactions and language in CALL tasks and their reports of how their attention is directed during the task. Meaning focus is analyzed on the basis of task performance alone rather than by comparison with tasks outside of class, which are often but not always meaning-focused. Examples of out-of class tasks that are not meaning-focused would be editing someone's job application letter, looking up words in a dictionary, or trying to guess a speaker's regional accent. Texts in which meaning focus is evident would include the one in Figure 3.3 in which learners are using the target language to discuss ethnic backgrounds and the celebration of holidays. Meaning focus is evident through the learners' development of coherence through a topic other than the form of the target language.

Effects of meaning-based instruction

The first question about meaning focus seeks evidence in CALL materials for the assumption that is largely accepted in the profession: What evidence suggests that learners constructing linguistic meaning aids in language learning? Several CALL studies have set out to investigate whether CALL tasks requiring learners to comprehend message meaning would be superior to those that learners could complete through manipulation of structure alone. Comparing 'meaningful' and 'non-meaningful' input in German grammar lessons, Schaeffer (1981) found that students who had to understand the meaning of the language to answer drill items correctly did better on both meaningful and structural post-tests than did students who practiced mechanically, without processing meaning. Meaning-oriented in the study was defined as requiring comprehension of sentence-level semantics, but even with this limited view of meaning, results favored this group.

Another study combined features of input and interaction to investigate six pedagogical and four answer-judging principles established on the basis of research in cognitive psychology and second language acquisition (Robinson *et al.*, 1985). Robinson and her colleagues developed experimental CALL tasks and compared them with lessons that did not reflect such principles. The hypothesis pertaining to meaning – that use of a context for 'introduction of discrete structural items [would] improve memory and subsequent learning of the items' (1985: 17) – was tested by providing an experimental group with a contextualized grammar task and a control group with a task containing semantically unrelated items. Drawing conclusions about this hypothesis along with several others, the researchers concluded that they had a 'high level of confidence that instructional treatments did significantly favor the experimental group' (1985: 35) on the post-test.

These two studies investigated the extent to which attention to meaning was important for acquisition of the target linguistic items through comparison of outcomes from meaningful and non-meaningful conditions. This design might be strengthened by demonstrating that learners in fact focused on meaning in the meaningful condition and not the other. The second question about meaning focus, what evidence indicates that learners use the language during the task for constructing and interpreting meaning, involves the analysis of what learners actually do while they are working on the CALL task as distinct from what the condition specified by the task design suggests that they should do.

Assessing engagement with meaning

The two examples of CMC discussion in Figures 3.3 and 3.4 provide evidence that learners are engaged in meaningful language use, discussing family customs in the first, and playfully discussing shoes in the second. The record of their language and analysis of the content themes that are developed through the target language provide good evidence for meaning focus in these two activities.

Data from another CALL task showing form-oriented target language use come from the oral language of German learners of EFL collaborating on story-writing on the topic of their choice, vampires. In this task, the computer is used to record in writing the language that they produced through oral collaboration rather than as a conduit for negotiation among participants. The researchers chose to examine only the oral language that the learners produced as they negotiated, as shown in Figure 3.5, rather than both the oral language of the collaboration and the writing on the screen. Their oral language includes very little of the target language, just one

> A: Nein, nicht *he*, sondern *Peter.*
> C: *And he rea-, and Peter realized.*
> B: *And Peter saw*
> C: Ja, guck mal! *Realized*
> B: Was heißt denn *realized?*
> C: 'Bemerken'
> A: Ja, das hatten – Ja, klar, schreib!
> B: Ja(?)
> A: *Realized.* Weil – die müssen ja so
>   wenig wie möglich Wörter wissen.

Figure 3.5 Conversation from German EFL learners' oral, face-to-face collaborative writing (Legenhausen & Wolff, 1992: 21)

word at a time in isolation, and it is used as the object of, rather than the means for, discussion. The textual cohesion, for example 'And' and 'Well,' either provide cohesion within the written text, or within the German of the oral text. With the English used as an object of discussion, it is not used to express meanings among the participants even if the written language constructed through the task on the computer screen would undoubtedly express meaning. Whatever the other qualities of this task, then, it would be difficult to argue that it was strong in meaning focus.

Learners' reports of their attention while working on a CALL task can add another dimension to the analysis. In a study of ESL learners' strategies while working on interactive multimedia software, Park (1994) identified clear instances in learners' reports of attending to meaning. For example, one participant, while listening to the video depicting shopping at a convenience store, reported that he was curious about the expression 'can't change anything larger than.' It was not the grammar that was a concern, but the cultural aspect of this expression, so he clicked on the help with culture, where he learned convenience stores in the US do not keep large bills on hand in case they are robbed. The learner reported: 'First I compared with the Korean situation and compared my knowledge of American culture and decide whether it makes sense or not . . . I didn't know this before, but when I read it makes sense with my background knowledge of American culture' (1994: 132). Other learner reports are clearly focused on language: 'Oh, so some verbs must follow a rule, which means, present progressive form . . . Yeah, in this part, we can see often in the TOEFL test' (1994: 138).

Authenticity

The two questions about authenticity seek evidence that (1) learners' performance in CALL tasks corresponds to what one would expect to see outside the CALL task, and (2) learners see the connection between the CALL task and tasks outside the classroom. Addressing the first question requires a comparison between the language that learners engage in during the CALL task and the language used in other situations of interest outside the classroom. Esling (1991) suggested examining the language of CALL activities in view of Brown and Yule's (1983) classification of discourse used for activities such as giving directions, telling a story, or expressing an opinion. Although Esling's point of comparison was the class of tasks performed in L2 classrooms, the idea of comparison from CALL to other tasks is similar to the authenticity analysis.

Comparing CALL with non-CALL activities

CALL research attempting such discourse analysis has examined learners' oral language as they worked on CALL programs (e.g., Abraham & Liou, 1991), and findings have been mixed. One study described the language of such activities as 'incoherent conversation where there is much clashing of participants and talking simultaneously' (Piper, 1986: 194). The researcher concluded that 'one obvious limitation of this range of language forms is the "here and now-ness" of the tasks, meaning that there is little use of any tense except the present simple' (1986: 197). In contrast, on the basis of a similar study, Mohan concluded that the conversation in which the computer was present was relatively 'context-embedded.' Through examination of the functional sequences in the texts documenting interaction among the learners, he also identified 'episodes of choice, decision-making or problem-solving' consisting of sequences of proposal, agreement, and supporting reasons – sequences which he interpreted as use of cognitively demanding language. In other words, Mohan interpreted the linguistic experience as positive for L2 development, presumably because these were the types of functions that learners would use beyond the classroom.

The CALL studies examining the language of classroom CMC have also typically chosen classroom language learning tasks as a point of comparison (Warschauer, 1997a; Kern, 1995). However, Chun (1994) suggested implications from her investigation of CMC in a first-year German class for learners' abilities beyond the classroom. Finding that learners used a variety of linguistic forms and functions, she concluded the following:

The types of sentences being written by students on the computer require not only comprehension of the preceding discourse but also coherent thought and use of cohesive linguistic references and expressions. These skills, which are important components of writing proficiency, are enhanced by CACD. In addition, since these types of sentences strongly resemble what would be said in spoken conversation, the hope is that the written competence gained from CACD can gradually be transferred to the students' speaking competence as well. (1994: 28–29)

Today interpretation of such an analysis would undoubtedly need to be recast somewhat, as the registers of language use outside the classroom have expanded beyond those involving face-to-face speaking and monologic writing. As language learners are increasingly preparing for a life of interaction with computers and with other people through computers (D. E. Murray, 1995), their 'electronic literacy' (Warschauer, 1999; Rassool, 1999) becomes an additional target. An argument about authenticity needs to address the question of the extent to which the CALL task affords the opportunity to use the target language in ways that learners will be called upon to do as language users, which today includes a variety of electronic communication.

Research methods

The study of CMC outside the L2 classroom has been developed over the past decade by researchers hoping to characterize the registers of language use in e-mail, chat rooms, electronic bulletin boards, and discussion lists, for example (Ferrara, Brunner, & Whittemore, 1991; Murray, 1991; Self & Meyer, 1991). Results from many CMC environments show features of simplified or reduced registers such as omission of subject pronouns, articles, and the copula, as well as use of contractions and abbreviations. Research has identified a large number of the words 'you' and 'I' in the texts, and a large number of WH and yes/no questions. This research begins to reveal the character of CMC, or 'interactive written discourse,' as a point of comparison for some CALL tasks.

It is therefore useful to have a means of register analysis which frames a description of registers in a way that captures the aspects of language use of interest to L2 researchers. In particular, the features of interest are those associated with the *input* that is provided to the learner, the learner's *output*, and the *interaction* between the learner and interlocutor. Each of these aspects of the language can be analyzed in greater detail through five descriptive categories: pragmatic function, linguistic characteristics, quantity, non-linguistic moves and forms, and medium (Chapelle, 1999a). The questions one would use to conduct an analysis of L2 input, output, and interaction are in Table 3.8. The descriptions of language from the CALL task and from the language of interest outside the classroom provide the data needed to make a comparison of the two – a comparison which speaks to the degree of authenticity of the CALL task relative to another identified context.

This methodology for systematic examination of CALL task authenticity demonstrates the complexity of the authenticity construct as well as the need for empirical research examining the extent to which the language engendered in CALL tasks is authentic relative to a particular register of interest. In other words, authenticity needs to be considered in a more-or-less fashion rather than as an all-or-nothing attribute of a task, and it needs to be considered relative to a context of interest rather than in absolute terms. Moreover, these methods of discourse analysis address only the first of the two questions about authenticity. The second question requires methods that produce evidence about learners' opinions concerning the value of the CALL task relative to what they need to be learning. Opinions can be gathered through introspective methods and questionnaire data.

Positive impact

Descriptions of CALL throughout the past 30 years abound with statements about the positive influence of CALL activities on language classrooms. One can pick up virtually any issue of any CALL journal from the past 15 years to find examples of enthusiastic CALL users' estimations of the experience of CALL as positive for their students. The current generation of CMC enthusiasts is no less euphoric about the impact of their CALL tasks, arguing that such activities offer the positive impact of changing classroom dynamics (Beauvois, 1992; Collombet-Sankey, 1997; Swaffar *et al.*, 1998). The impressions of CALL users are supported through examples from their students such as this e-mail message to the teacher in an EFL class in which learners were introduced to a variety of Internet activities:

I'm finding a new world with this class. Last week I told with people from Australia, New Zealand, USA and England. It was very interesting. I'm impressed how the world has become small with computers. (Paiva, 1999: 260)

Table 3.8. *Analytic categories for analysis of authenticity in L2 texts*

Aspect of discourse	Questions for analysis
Input to learner	What *functions* does the target language input perform in the task (e.g., give instructions; provide 'comprehensible input')? What are the *linguistic characteristics* of the input to learner (the features such as syntactic and morphological forms)? *How much* target language input does the learner receive? What *non-linguistic* moves and forms are used as input and what functions do they perform (e.g., give instructions; offer options)? Through what *medium* is the input transmitted (e.g., aural face-to-face; written on a computer screen)?
Output from learner	What *functions* does the target language output perform in the task (e.g., ask questions; display knowledge)? What are the *linguistic characteristics* of the output from learner (the features such as syntactic and morphological forms)? *How much* target language output does the learner produce? What *non-linguistic* moves and forms are used as output and what functions do they perform? Through what *medium* is the output transmitted (e.g., oral over the phone; written on paper)?
Interaction	What *functions* does the target language interaction perform in the task (e.g., negotiation of meaning; response to questions; signaling)? What are the *linguistic characteristics* of the interaction (e.g., the coherence and cohesion of text; its structure – openings, adjacency pairs, functional sequences; adaptations or modifications – with additional turns)? *How much* interaction does the learner engage in? What *non-linguistic* moves and forms are used to accomplish interaction and what functions do they perform (e.g., negotiation of meaning; response to questions; focus on form)? Through what *medium* is the output transmitted (e.g., oral over the phone; written on paper)?

Evidence such as this from learners as well as teachers' impressions are a valuable starting point for articulating a range of impact-related questions about CALL such as the following:

• What evidence suggests that learners learn more about the target language and about strategies for language learning through the use of the task?
• What evidence suggests that learners increase their literacy in language use through technology?
• What evidence suggests that instructors engage in sound second language pedagogical practices by using the task?
• What evidence suggests that learners and teachers had a positive experience with technology through the use of the task?

These questions and others that one might suggest concerning impact imply the need for qualitative approaches to investigating the use of CALL in context. A few studies using such methods have looked at some of the contextual factors associated with CALL. Examining adult ESL learners' use of hypermedia language learning software in an intensive English program in the US, Park (1994) identified factors in the language program and classroom contexts that shaped the learners' experiences with CALL, and in turn how her introduction of CALL influenced aspects of the program. Sanaoui and Lapkin's (1992) qualitative study revealed observations about the nature of the language that ESL and FSL learners in Canada produced and the quality of instructional experience learners and teachers perceived as they worked collaboratively with peers from the target language across a computer network. This type of work investigating the context of CALL use needs to extend throughout the global context of the Internet to examine the ways in which various CALL activities affect learning in different cultures (e.g., Hart & Daisley, 1994).

In this regard, critical perspectives on electronic literacy hold promise for building upon those of Bowers (1988; 1993) on educational technology, who pointed out the non-neutrality of educational technologies in the 1980s. The premise of Olson's 1987 paper 'Who computes?' has been repackaged into the expression 'digital divide,' but whereas Olson was referring primarily to access to technology associated with school learning, the digital divide refers to inequities in access to modern ways of life, which include the literacies developed primarily through communication on the Internet (Warschauer, 2000). Whereas careful researchers of the past decade qualified their results in view of the computer literacy of their participants (e.g., Hartman *et al.*, 1991), teachers and researchers today need to consider how and why some students are able to use technology and language to participate in modern life while others are not.

The question of who computes and how successfully they do so is clearly tied to communicative language ability as it is realized through electronic literacy, and therefore research needs to better define this domain. Fortunately, some researchers have begun to do so. Warschauer (1999) artfully links computer use in the ESL class-room to issues associated with the multiliteracies (including elec-tronic literacies) which all language users need in the 21st century, and he relates overall global economic trends to changes in English use and English learners' needs (Warschauer, 2000). With a similar interest in the future of literacies world-wide, Hawisher and Self (2000) have collected empirical studies of language use on the Web in a number of different countries, finding that typically English plays some role along with local languages in Web-based literacy experi-ences. Lam (2000) documents the development of ESL literacy on the Web through a case-study of a learner who uses English to develop a popular Web page and communicate with a transnational group of peers. These forward-looking studies begin to offer a glimpse of a complex future of language use and learning.

Practicality

Questions about practicality of CALL rely on evidence suggesting that hardware, software, and personnel resources prove to be suffi-cient to allow CALL to succeed. Assessing the adequacy of resources for all learners has become complex as resources extend beyond the language laboratory and as what is necessary seems to be a moving target. However, given the role of resources for the success of CALL, some formal mechanism needs to be in place to monitor adequacy, and an argument about CALL appropriateness should include a statement about sufficiency of resources.

Conclusion

This chapter outlined evaluation principles intended to address three needs for CALL evaluation. Criteria for evaluation were presented within a broader perspective of what the evaluation entails and what the results mean. The criteria developed in this chapter incorporate findings and theory-based speculation about ideal conditions for SLA, particularly Skehan's summary of cognitive conditions for SLA and the situation-specific construct of willingness to communicate.

The principles of evaluation and specific criteria apply not only to software, but also to the task that the teacher plans. Empirical research pertaining to the six ideal qualities for CALL was described by identifying general research questions concerning the qualities that are intended to guide formulation of specific questions that might be developed for a particular study. The types of evidence relevant to each of the qualities was outlined, demonstrating the utility of many perspectives toward second language classroom research.

Evidence concerning these qualities of a particular CALL task needs to be combined to form an evaluative argument about the appropriateness of a CALL task for particular learners at a given point in time. Integrated research is needed to examine the types of CALL activities such as those described above to seek evidence about CALL appropriateness in particular settings. From such research, implications can be drawn for specific contexts, and eventually research on particular types of activities might be generalized in a way that can inform general principles of CALL.

4 Computer-assisted language testing

In 1998 and 1999 three of the largest providers of educational tests[1]
introduced computer-based versions of proficiency tests for English
as a foreign language. At the same time, many institutions and
individuals began to offer Web-based tests for particular language
programs and classes. These two phenomena have added immeasur-
ably to the momentum of work in computer-assisted testing[2] that
began with a few research projects on computer-assisted language
testing (CALT). Despite the fact that computer-assisted testing in
large-scale programs is not without its problems, at the start of the
21st century, it seems clear that CALT is becoming a fact for all
language learners in educational settings, and therefore for all
teachers and applied linguists. As a growing number of people are
affected by CALT, many of them express the fear that computer
delivery may influence test performance.

The concern, which is echoed by SLA researchers about the results
of computer-assisted methods in research, is that the computer-
delivered methods are less valid than those requiring conventional

---

[1] The terms 'testing' and 'assessment' are used interchangeably here despite the fact that
some (e.g., Wiggins, 1993) would draw clear distinctions between the two. Tests and
testing can connote large-scale, impersonal, test use in which scores are compared with
group norms and used for institutional decision-making. Assessment is sometimes
intended to denote a range of test uses perceived to be beneficial to the learner because
results are used in support of learning. In fact, these distinctions are not clear-cut (e.g.,
Brown & Hudson, 1998), and current approaches to language testing seek to further
blur them. Moreover, despite the current fashion to prefer the term 'assessment,' 'testing'
is firmly rooted within our profession in the names of journals (*Language Testing*),
conferences (Language Testing Research Colloquium), and expressions such as computer
assisted language testing (CALT).

[2] Computers have been used for decades in all types of testing for managing item banks,
scoring multiple-choice responses, generating score reports, conducting statistical analysis,
and storing test takers' records (Baker, 1989). As technology develops, these and other
roles will continue to contribute to the efficiency of language testing (Burstein *et al.*,
1996). I will concentrate on computer uses resulting in second language learners
interacting with computer programs or with other people through computers.

means such as paper and pencil or face-to-face interview. However, to address this and other issues, a means for evaluating CALT is needed. This chapter begins by explaining the concern that test method may influence test performance in undesirable ways and then presents a practical method for evaluating the validity of computer-assisted tests which is based on the framework for test usefulness developed by Bachman and Palmer (1996). Examples of CALT are evaluated and empirical research methods for further investigation of CALT are presented.

Test method

The significance of test method as an influence on examinees' performance is well documented in the research on second language testing (e.g., Bachman, Lynch, & Mason, 1995; Bachman & Palmer, 1982; Chapelle & Abraham, 1990; Douglas & Selinker, 1993; Fulcher, 1996; Wigglesworth, 1997).[3] Results showing method influence are relevant to CALT because the computer can affect several aspects of the test method. On a computer-adaptive test, for example, the examinee might be presented multiple-choice questions which appear very similar to those that would appear on a paper-and-pencil test. Despite appearances, after the first few questions, each question is chosen on the basis of prior performance, a method that produces a test with few items that are easy relative to the examinee's ability level. Some examinees report that this method appears to create a test that is more difficult than the corresponding paper-and-pencil one would be. Moreover, because each question is scored as it is completed, the examinee does not have the option of skipping questions and returning to them later. The issue is whether or not these two features of the test method, or test task characteristics (Bachman & Palmer, 1996), influence the examinees' performance to the extent that computer-adaptive and pencil-and-paper versions of the 'same' test actually measure different abilities.

The issue of test method effects is most easily seen through the sociolinguists' perspective: that test-taking and performance-rating are communicative events which are influenced by the same contextual variables as language performance and evaluation in other settings. This view has been developed through critical perspectives

---

[3] The premise of sociolinguistics that language performance is affected by contextual factors has a measurement analogue – that test scores (i.e., the summary of performance) are affected by test methods (i.e., the contextual factors created by the test). In the measurement literature, this phenomenon is called 'test method effects.' See Bachman (1990) for an explanation.

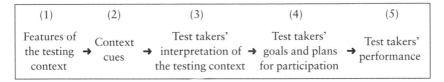

Figure 4.1 Factors involved in the relationship between a testing context and performance as outlined by D. Douglas (1998)

on assessment (Wiggins, 1993) and in empirical research. Emihovich (1990) explored the linguistic cues such as tone shifts and topic initiation, which were related to the roles and relationships of participants in an assessing interview. Finding that these context cues influenced children's linguistic behavior, she concluded that

[t]he experiment [or test] can be viewed as a communicative event in its own right, with all of the attendant rules and norms that are negotiated between [tester] and participant, or among the participants themselves as they carry out [test] tasks. (1990: 165–183)

In second language testing, D. Douglas (1998) theorizes the factors responsible for test method effects by hypothesizing a series of influences that begin with the test method, or task characteristics. His account, summarized in Figure 4.1, suggests that the *features of the testing context* (1), such as medium of the input, act as *context cues* (2) which signal test takers about the context, thereby affecting their *interpretation of the testing context* (3). This interpretation influences the *goals* (4) test takers set for their participation, which, in turn, influence their *plans* (4) for accomplishing the goals. The goals and plans affect test takers' *performance* (5), which is observed and scored. The set of associated influences is summarized in Figure 4.1, in which the arrows should be read as 'influence(s)' (e.g., the features of the testing context influence the context cues). Recognition of the influence of multiple test context variables on performance has prompted research attempting to identify the influences on test scores of test contexts such as those in which specific-topic language is used to simulate a particular language use context (D. Douglas, 2000).

The test method features (1) are specified in the test design; however, these may actually affect test performance in unpredictable ways because the context cues (2) they provide are open to the test takers' interpretation (3). For example, the test designer may include an explicit context cue through instructions directing test takers to read an entire passage before completing any cloze items; however, the test taker may not read the instructions, may disagree with them, or may simply forget during the process of test-taking. In any of these cases, the test taker may begin completing the items without reading the passage despite the efforts of the test designer. Because of the potential disjuncture between the designers' intended testing context and those that may come into play during test-taking, tests need to be examined from the perspective of both test design (1 in Figure 4.1) and test performance (5 in Figure 4.1). Principles of test validation address both of these perspectives.

Principles for validation in CALT

The concern about the test method characteristics in computer-assisted testing appears to pose a question of whether or not computer-assisted language testing is valid. Ironically, this frequently asked question cannot be answered categorically because validity does not refer to a test, or testing method. Validity applies to test interpretation and use in a particular situation. For example, a computer-assisted vocabulary test that selected the words a learner had focused on during an on-line reading task may be used validly for helping the student to identify words requiring additional study. However, if the instructor attempted to use test scores from the same test to assign marks or to certify overall proficiency, the validity of these uses should obviously be questioned.

Validity refers to the degree to which inferences from and uses of test scores can be justified. Validation is the process of investigating test score inferences and uses in order to yield data that contribute to their justification. Researchers in educational measurement develop and continuously revise a code of practice, or standards for valida-tion (American Educational Research Association, *et al.*, 1999), which are also considered a foundation for validation in second language testing. In order to move beyond the unanswerable question of whether or not CALT is valid, principles underlying this well-established code of practice need to be stated and applied to the evaluation of CALT.

Validity as an argument

The first principle concerns what validity means. Approximately 40 years ago, validity appeared to be thought of by many language testing researchers as an all-or-nothing characteristic of a test: 'Does a test measure what it is supposed to measure? If it does, it is valid' (Lado, 1961: 321). This view of validity is still reflected in questions

Table 4.1. *Principles of language test evaluation from educational measurement and language testing*

Principle	Implication
Validity is an argument about the appropriateness of test use.	Tests are not valid or invalid; a test use is more or less valid depending on the evidence that supports its use.
Specific validation criteria for evaluating language tests should be based on work in applied linguistics.	The specific practices of language test evaluation are best guided by theory and research in language testing.
Validation criteria must be applied in view of test purpose.	The purpose of a test must be clearly specified in order to consider questions about validity.
Construct validity is central in test evaluation.	The construct that the test is intended to measure must be clearly defined and other evaluative issues about a test should be secondary.
Tests need to be evaluated through both logical and empirical analyses.	Methodologies for examining the test method (1 in Figure 4.1) and the performance (5 in Figure 4.1) are needed.

about CALT such as 'Is a writing test valid if it requires test takers to compose an essay at the keyboard?' It would not be possible to answer this question without knowing what the test was intended to measure, and what scores were to be used for. Even so, the answer would not be a categorical yes or no. Instead, it would consist of an *argument* concerning the extent to which test interpretations and uses could be justified (Messick, 1989; Moss, 1992; Chapelle, 1999b). For example, a study showing that test takers' writing processes were similar on the test to those they used while writing in academic classes would provide one argument for the validity of test-based inferences about ability to write in academic classes.

Such a study would provide just one argument but validity is argued on the basis of a number of types of rationales and evidence, including results from research concerning what the test measures in addition to judgements about the influence of test use beyond the test setting. An example of the latter would be the argument that introducing a computer-assisted writing test as part of a large-scale test used for university admissions would encourage teaching of composing at the computer, with the assumption that this is a valuable skill for such students. The view of validity as a situation-specific argument is important for evaluation of CALT because it clarifies the need to evaluate CALT for a particular purpose and underscores the need for developers and users of CALT to understand the general principles of validation and the specific criteria that are used to evaluate language tests.

Criteria for evaluating language testing

Validation requires a definition of the types of evidence and rationales that can be drawn upon to develop an effective validity argument about a particular test. In educational measurement, these components of the validity argument are defined in general terms, but for evaluating a second language test, ideally one would like more specific guidance reflecting the values of applied linguists. Bachman and Palmer (1996) have applied the general principles of validity inquiry to second language testing by defining the specific types of arguments that they see as critical to evaluation of language tests. Substituting 'usefulness' for 'validity of score-based inferences and uses,' they outline six types of arguments that can serve as justification of the usefulness of a test for a particular purpose. These are defined in Table 4.2 (Bachman & Palmer, 1996, Chapter 2).

Evaluation of a language test is conducted by assessing the extent to which each of these qualities can be demonstrated in a particular context. Such a usefulness analysis begins from the assumption that the ideal is to maximize overall test usefulness. At the same time, it is recognized that no test will possess all of the qualities to an extreme degree because some tension will result from attempts to maximize all the qualities. For example, one might wish to maximize authenticity of a large-scale computer-assisted academic listening test by having test takers listen to two 50-minute lectures on video and respond to questions. A decision to include long lectures, however, would present problems for other qualities such as construct validity (because of the bias resulting from some learners having prior knowledge of the topic of one of the lectures), or practicality (because of the cost associated with a test lasting over 100 minutes). In other words, a decision to maximize authenticity should be made in view of all qualities contributing to usefulness, including construct validity and practicality. In conducting the usefulness analysis, the test user needs to justify the relative importance of the test qualities, and this must be done in view of the purpose of the test.

Table 4.2. *Qualities of test usefulness*

Quality	Definition
Reliability	The consistency of the performance reflected in scores
Construct validity	The appropriateness of the inferences made on the basis of test scores
Authenticity	The correspondence of characteristics of the testing activity to characteristics of relevant non-test contexts where language is used
Interactiveness	The expected extent of involvement of the test takers' knowledge and interest and of their communicative language strategies in accomplishing a test task
Positive impact	The positive consequences that a test can have on society and educational systems and on the individuals within the systems (i.e., learners and teachers)
Practicality	The adequacy of the available resources for the design, development, use and evaluation of the test

Validation criteria and test purpose

In both the vocabulary test for classroom diagnosis and the listening test used for decisions about university admissions, it is the purpose of the test that is fundamental to decisions about the relative importance of the usefulness qualities. One might argue, for example, that reliability would be of critical importance to the listening test whose results were to be used in decisions about who will and who will not be admitted to a university. On the other hand, in the diagnostic test whose results will guide learners' subsequent study of vocabulary, reliability might be considered less critical, although still an issue. Because the purpose of the test is pivotal to constructing a validity argument (Shepard, 1993), test users need a clear definition of what test purpose means.

Test purpose can be defined through the intended (1) *inferences* to be made from test scores, (2) *uses* made of those inferences, and (3) *impacts* of the test (Chapelle & Read, 1996). Inferences refer to the conclusions drawn about language ability (e.g., 'writing ability') on the basis of evidence from test performance (e.g., an essay). There are a number of ways in which inferences from language tests can be defined, including the areas of language knowledge (e.g., vocabulary) or 'skills' (e.g., listening comprehension) which one might infer on

Table 4.3. *Example components of a test purpose statement*

Component of test purpose	Example English for Agriculture test
Inference	Candidates' ability to speak about farming in English
Use	Selection of students for a short training program on farming in the US
Impact	Demonstration to students and their sponsoring agency the level of their field-specific language ability, and help to focus content in training program on spoken English for Agriculture

the basis of language test performance; researchers explore how test purpose influences the way inferences are described (Chalhoub-Deville, 1997; Dunkel, Henning, & Chaudron, 1993), and in turn relate test inferences to test specifications (Alderson, 2000). Language test use consists of two primary types: assessment for decision-making about learners in an educational context, and assessment for research on SLA, the latter of which discussed in Chapter 5. Educational assessments can be further defined. For example, some tests can be used for decisions about learners' readiness for something like an academic program, placement within levels of an instructional program, success in a language class, and instructional needs (Bachman, 1990).

A test's intended impacts refer to the effects that the test designer intends it to have on its users, whom Bachman & Palmer (1996) define as consisting of individuals (e.g., students and teachers), language classes and programs, as well as society. The intended impact of a weekly assessment in a language class, for example, might be to help students organize and stay up-to-date on what is covered in the course. In making decisions about the design of large-scale tests, test developers today consider the potential test effects on instruction. An example of a test purpose statement for a test designed for selecting candidates for a training program on farming in the US is shown in Table 4.3. The test purpose statement would be the following: The test is intended to measure candidates' ability to speak about farming in English (inference) in order to select students for a short training program on farming in the US (use) and to demonstrate to students and their sponsoring agency the level of their field-specific language ability to help focus training (impact).

Articulation of test purpose is particularly critical for computer-assisted language tests because of the apparent potential of the computer to record and report a variety of detailed information about test takers. The idea is that a single testing session might yield a single score to be used for making a placement decision, for example, as well as diagnostic profiles for providing feedback to the student and teacher. J. L. D. Clark (1989) pointed out, however, that the synthesis of test purposes into a single test poses more than a technical challenge: different test purposes are associated with different means of test construction and analysis, and therefore multipurpose tests will require new conceptual approaches to testing.

The centrality of construct validity

The foundation of test purpose which is used to structure the validity argument is the inference to be made on the basis of test performance. The fundamental role of inference in test purpose gives construct validity a central place among the usefulness arguments. In a sense, this brings the definition back to Lado's 'Does a test measure what it is supposed to measure? If it does, it is valid' (Lado, 1961: 321). However, today's definition of construct validity is different in three important ways. First, as mentioned above, Lado's definition appears to treat validity as an all-or-nothing characteristic of a test. The current conception of construct validity would be the extent to which test-based inferences can be justified; this implies that inferences will be justified to some degree rather than in an all-or-nothing fashion Second, Lado's appears to be intended as an overarching definition of validity, whereas currently, construct validity is considered one form of validity argument, even if it is the central one. While other validity arguments are seen as related to construct validity, they are treated as conceptually distinct, as well. In short, relative to today's standards, Lado's definition for validity was a narrow one, referring to test-based inferences, whereas test usefulness, a way of portraying 'validity of test inferences and uses,' encompasses the appropriateness of test inferences, uses, and impacts – all of which rest on construct validity.

Logical and empirical analyses

In addition to criteria to be used in a validity argument, Bachman & Palmer (1996) articulate heuristics for evaluating tests throughout their development and use. Concerns about test usefulness need to be raised continuously; however, conceptually, the analyses can be divided into two stages: logical and empirical evaluation of test usefulness. These two perspectives on evaluation correspond to Douglas' perspective on test design and test performance outlined in Figure 4.1 above: logical analysis is conducted on the test design, which specifies the features of the test context, and empirical analysis applies to test performance.

Logical test analysis is the responsibility of anyone who is constructing, choosing or developing a test, whereas empirical test analysis has typically fallen within the domain of the language testing researcher. Logical test usefulness analysis is conducted on a test instrument by addressing questions about the test design that pertain to each of the six qualities of test usefulness: reliability, construct validity, authenticity, interactiveness, positive impact, and practicality. Questions about *reliability* address how the test design minimizes irrelevant, or unmotivated, variation[4] between forms of a test, and between items of a test, in order to obtain the most consistent indication possible of the learners' ability. Factors such as instructions, and consistency of the input to the test taker, their response, and scoring procedure all influence judgements about reliability. Questions about *construct validity* concern the clarity of the inference to be made, the expected knowledge of the test takers, and the relevance of the test tasks and the scoring procedure to the inference. Construct validity requires that inferences be well defined, the knowledge of the participants be adequate so as not to bias performance, and the test tasks and scoring be consistent with the inference to be made.

Authenticity is evaluated by judgements about the extent to which the characteristics of the test tasks reflect tasks in the setting where the test taker's ability is of interest.[5] *Interactiveness* is evaluated by assessing the extent to which task features engage participants' knowledge, communicative language strategies, and interest in the test tasks. The questions for assessing construct validity, authenticity, and interactiveness are often included in a content analysis consisting of experts' judgements of what they believe a test measures –

[4] Irrelevant or unmotivated variation refers to any factors affecting test performance which cannot be justified on the basis of the construct definition. For example, on a computer-assisted reading test, motivated variation in performance would be caused by test takers' vocabulary knowledge (if this is part of the definition of 'reading ability'). Unmotivated variation might result from a learner's dexterity in using a mouse to navigate a hypermedia environment, *if* this ability is not included in the construct definition. The former would be a source of reliability while the latter would be a source of unreliability. Analysis of reliability, therefore, is tied to construct definition.

[5] Recent work (e.g., McNamara, 1996; Douglas & Myers, 2000) also points toward the importance of evaluation criteria in the test setting corresponding to those used in the target language use (TLU) setting (Bachman & Palmer, 1996).

judgements about the 'content relevance, representativeness, and technical quality' of the test material (Messick, 1995: 6). A number of studies illustrate approaches to and problems with content analysis of language tests (e.g., Bachman *et al.*, 1988; Alderson, 1993), but these important questions have not been applied systematically to computer-assisted language tests.

Questions about *impact* address the extent to which the test can be expected to yield positive outcomes for testing which affect students, language classes and programs, and society. Judgements about impact present a different dimension for a validity argument than the other forms because they involve hypotheses and research directed beyond the test inferences to the ways in which the test affects people involved with it. The scope of such effects is the topic of discussion (e.g., Alderson and Wall, 1993; Bailey, 1996; Wall, 1997). *Practicality* is assessed through a calculation of the feasibility of implementing the test design given the available resources. The expense associated with design, development, and delivery of CALT makes practicality a particularly important aspect of usefulness for CALT.

On the basis of the logical usefulness analysis, the test designer or user gains an indication of the test's strengths and weaknesses from a design perspective, which provides a basis for considering modification or adoption. Bachman and Palmer (1996, Chapter 7) provide a list of 42 questions which should be consulted during test design for considering the qualities of test usefulness. This logical analysis is intended as a first step in test evaluation, which is followed by empirical analyses conducted during test-taking and after the test has been given.

Test usefulness applied to CALT

Although there are very few CALT projects described thoroughly in the applied linguistics literature, it is possible to present four examples to illustrate some of the issues CALT raises in the logical usefulness analysis as well as to demonstrate the process of usefulness analysis.

A computer-adaptive reading test

The purpose of the computer-adaptive reading test described by Madsen (1991) was to make inferences about learners' ESL reading comprehension to be used for decisions about placement into an intensive ESL program. It was intended to provide a short, convenient testing procedure for students, accurate placement for the benefit of both teachers and students, and a model computer-adaptive language testing project for the profession.

The test tasks contained a series of multiple-choice reading items, each of which consisted of a 1–3-sentence stem and four alternatives from which the examinee was instructed to choose the best response. The language of each item was not related to that of the previous one to ensure that the items were independent from one another. Because each item was evaluated immediately after it was completed, examinees were not allowed to return to previously completed items. The total time it took to complete the test differed from one examinee to the next, as did the number of items each responded to, and therefore no time limit was imposed on test completion. Testing took place in the ESL program's computer lab, which was also used for instruction. Each item was scored as correct or incorrect and the total, which was reported as a single score, was derived on the basis of the difficulty of items that the test taker could consistently respond to correctly.

Evaluating the usefulness of this test requires examination of its design in view of each of the six qualities. According to Madsen (1991: 245), the intensive English directors who were going to use the test placed priority on the reliability and practicality primarily in terms of time spent in test-taking and scoring. Beginning with a judgemental analysis of reliability, the scores the test produces would be expected to be reliable based on principles of item construction and selection. For example, the linguistic input for each item is very short and is therefore unlikely to engage the learner's topical knowledge extensively. The short items provide the opportunity to include a wide variety of topics, thereby avoiding bias due to topic knowledge. Without the influence of topic, consistency among items and test forms is likely. For construct validation, however, one might question the extent to which reading 1–3-sentence prompts should be considered to reflect the construct of reading comprehension.

The 1–3-sentence reading items also present a problem for authenticity because presumably authenticity is evaluated from the perspective of academic reading. The test may possess some degree of interactiveness because communicative language strategies may be required for comprehension of the input sentences, but interactiveness would not be strong because the shortness of the input would engage little of the test taker's knowledge or interest. The test's impact might be considered by noting that it should be expected to produce the reliable information required and therefore get students into appropriate classes. However, at the same time, it may mislead teachers and students about the reading ability they should be teaching and learning. Provided the researchers were appropriately funded and the

Table 4.4. *Summary of logical usefulness analysis for computer-adaptive reading test*

Quality	Positive attributes	Negative attributes
Reliability	No unmotivated variation between items or forms. An appropriate number and difficulty of items is administered to each examinee to obtain good reliability.	
Construct validity	Little possibility for topical bias.	No measurement of textual knowledge.
Authenticity		One-to-three-sentence inputs are unlike most academic reading.
Interactiveness	Communicative language strategies may be required to some extent.	Little topical knowledge or interest in the test items is likely to be engaged.
Impact	Teachers may succeed in getting information about ability. Equipment obtained and maintained for the testing program might be available for instruction as well. The profession can learn from an operational example of computer-adaptive language testing.	Teachers and learners may practice reading comprehension by working with 1–3 sentences at a time.
Practicality	Adequate funding and infrastructure for testing was available at Brigham Young University.	

program had the necessary computer equipment, as was the case at Brigham Young University, the test would score high on practicality. Students were able to take the test on their own in the computer lab, and the results were made available immediately. A summary of the usefulness analysis appears in Table 4.4.

This analysis was conducted for the particular CAT described by Madsen and therefore cannot be applied in general to any computer-adaptive language test. As the papers in Chalhoub-Deville's 1999 collection demonstrate, other computer-adaptive tests would be evaluated differently. For example, the computer-adaptive placement test for French as a second language described by Laurier (1999) contains a variety of item types that would be likely to be judged more favorably with respect to authenticity. The five types of test tasks include the following:

1 Short paragraph reading tasks which are based on approximately 30-word paragraphs that can be encountered in daily life (instructions on a label, excerpts from a film review, statements of a problem . . .).
2 Sociolinguistic judgements which consist of selecting the most appropriate French statement in a given situation . . .
3 'Fill-in-the-gap' sentences where the student must select the word that fits best in the blank; approximately half the items are related to lexical knowledge and half to the application of grammar rules.
4 Listening comprehension based on two-minute 'semi-authentic' passages (radio advertisement, answering machine message, short dialogue . . .); each passage is followed by three questions. (1999: 124)

The differences between this and the computer-adaptive reading test are evident in both the constructs measured and the variety of item types. Moreover, 'adaptivity' may be conceptualized in a variety of ways in future computer-adaptive tests. In short, the term *adaptivity* can be used to denote a range of possible tests.

A computer-assisted EFL listening test

The second example is an ESL listening test which was used in research investigating the feasibility of operationalizing a computer-based version of the TOEFL. The purpose of the operational computer-based TOEFL for which this test method was intended as a trial is to make inferences about learners' ESL listening comprehension for decisions about admissions into North American universities. The test is intended to improve the process of selecting non-native speakers, thereby increasing the likelihood of success for those chosen. Moreover, the computer-assisted format is intended to positively impact English instruction through task characteristics that simulate listening in the academic setting. The paper-and-pencil version of the TOEFL's listening comprehension section provides aural input using audio-tape with no non-linguistic visuals. The computer-assisted TOEFL used the technology to provide visual, non-linguistic input (i.e., still photographs, diagrams, and pictures) along with the aural input that learners were required to comprehend (Taylor *et al.*, 1999). The visual display included for the 'mini-lectures' consists of a series of photographs and drawings illustrating, for example, the person who is speaking, the objects he or she is referring to, and a blackboard where key terms from the lecture are written. The visual input is intended to increase the similarity of the test input to what ESL students will encounter in academic settings – the domain of interest to test users wanting an estimate of test takers' ability.

The test is administered in centers equipped with computers, where examinees have 60 minutes to complete the whole test (of which the listening section was just one part). The questions required test takers to respond to multiple-choice questions in addition to three other response types: '(a) click on a picture or letter where the letter may be placed on a diagram, chart or picture; (b) select two answers; and (c) match or order information presented in a lecture or academic discussion' (Taylor *et al.*, 1999: 245). The score is the number of correct responses. Table 4.5 provides a summary of the logical usefulness analysis for this test.

This example with its positive and negative attributes represents just one of the possible types of computer-assisted listening tests. Dunkel (1999) described a listening proficiency test of Hausa constructed as a computer-adaptive test which tested examinees' ability to perform four listener functions (identification/recognition, orientation, main idea comprehension, and detailed comprehension) in short utterances, mini-dialogues, and short monologues. Coniam (1996; 1998) reported results of research on two types of computer-assisted dictation tests, one requiring examinees to fill in one part of a dialogue as they listened to it, and the other requiring completion of a passage in a partial dictation. These tests offer unique features not present in linear selected response listening tests, such as allowing learners to modify responses on the basis of the computer's evaluation of correctness. Results of a usefulness analysis for each of these would reveal their own positive and negative points.

A computer-assisted writing test

The third example comes from a writing test for native speakers of English which was one part of a new academic skills assessment battery that was investigated in a pilot project. Such writing tests are also being developed for L2 testing, but this example offers an early prototype examining some issues of computer delivery. The project described by Powers, Fowles, Farnum, and Ramsey (1994) included the test which was intended to address questions about administering a computer-assisted writing test in the US to college graduates who

Table 4.5. *Summary of usefulness analysis for computer-assisted listening test*

Quality	Positive attributes	Negative attributes
Reliability	All items are selected response. High quality, learner-controlled audio and video for each test taker at each administration.	Several different response types are required to answer questions. Topical knowledge may produce unmotivated variation from one set of questions to another. This test has a small number (20) of items.
Construct validity	The construct of academic listening is clearly reflected in test tasks.	Differential topical knowledge among examinees may influence overall performance.
Authenticity	Input to learners simulates classroom lectures and academic discussions. Questions vary in their response type.	Length of lectures and timing of questions is unlike those features in most classroom lecture settings.
Interactiveness	Lectures and long academic discussions should prompt engagement of components of language knowledge, communication strategies, and topical knowledge for listening comprehension.	Topics will not be uniformly interesting to all test takers.
Impact	The test should prompt practice in listening to lectures and work with multimedia in ESL classes.	Tests are so expensive that some examinees may not be able to take them and, therefore, may not be able to apply to North American universities.
Practicality	Test providers have obtained services to deliver tests successfully.	Services are expensive for the testing program and for examinees.

were familiar with using computers. Because many writers are now accustomed to composing at a computer keyboard, the test design attempted to create a test that was authentic for these test takers.

The purpose of the test is to make inferences about learners' English writing ability to be used as one component of assessment of achievement in academic skills for teachers in the US. The test is intended to allow examinees to write in a medium they feel comfortable with and to provide valid information about achievement. The research project was also to provide information to inform future developments in computer-assisted assessment of writing. The test gives the examinees 50 minutes to write an essay on a single topic, which the authors describe as falling within the domain of 'personal experience' and 'general interest.' The essays were scored based on judgements of human raters on a holistic scale from 1 to 6. The raters had been trained to consider expression, organization, style, support of ideas, as well as grammar and mechanics. The score was reported as a single number referring to level of performance. The usefulness analysis is summarized in Table 4.6.

A reading test with computer-assisted response analysis

The fourth example is from a research project investigating a response analysis program for recognition of test takers' linguistic output. The use of such technologies would expand the types of items that could be practically and reliably included in large-scale testing programs in which machine scoring is necessary. Despite the apparent advantage to the approach, there have been few investigations of computer-assisted response analysis reported. Those that have are exploratory (Chapelle, 1993; Coniam, 1998; Holland, 1994), some taking an important first step of trying to gain an understanding of the test takers' output likely to appear in response to various types of tasks (Kud, Krupka, & Rau, 1994; Bennett, Ward, Rock, & LaHart, 1990; Bennett, 1993; Mislevy, 1993b). The example is an ESL reading test which evaluates learners' linguistic output comprised of short phrases and sentences produced in response to open-ended questions about reading passages (Henning *et al.*, 1993).

The purpose of the test if it were to be adopted for operational use would be to make inferences about learners' ESL reading comprehension to be used for decisions about admissions into North American universities. The test would be intended to improve measurement of reading comprehension over selected response formats currently used by the TOEFL program, thereby improving selection of students to North American universities; the project was also to provide data concerning the feasibility and effects of computer-assisted scoring. The examinees were requested to read eight passages, each on a different academic topic, and to respond to 120 open-ended questions,

Table 4.6. *Summary of usefulness analysis for computer-assisted writing test*

Quality	Positive attributes	Negative attributes
Reliability	Raters were trained for holistic scoring, and two raters judge each essay.	A single essay test relying on raters' judgements is fragile.
Construct validity	Examinees produce a complete text which should provide an opportunity to demonstrate textual competence. General and personal topics are intended not to bias individuals based on topical knowledge.	Differential experience composing at the keyboard may affect performance.
Authenticity	Composing at the keyboard may simulate processes used for academic writing by some students.	Time-pressured keyboard composing on an unplanned topic is unlike much academic writing.
Interactiveness	Essay-writing should prompt engagement of components of language knowledge, communication strategies and topical knowledge.	
Impact	The format should prompt practice composing at the keyboard in academic programs.	
Practicality	Test providers have obtained services to deliver tests successfully.	Services are expensive for the testing program and for examinees.

returning to the passage as needed. Examinees were given 90 minutes to complete the test and responses were scored to give examinees partial credit for partially correct responses. Results were reported as a single score representing a sum of the item values. The analysis reported in Table 4.7 considers the potential usefulness of the test.

Table 4.7. *Summary of usefulness analysis for ESL reading comprehension test with open-ended comprehension questions*

Quality	Positive attributes	Negative attributes
Reliability	Large number of items. Partial-credit scoring should provide more precise measurement (and larger variance). Constructed responses provide less opportunity for construct-irrelevant guessing.	Topical knowledge may produce unmotivated variation from one set of questions to another.
Construct validity	Construct of academic reading reflected in test tasks. Open-ended responses are less likely than multiple-choice to be affected by systematic test-taking strategies.	Differential topical knowledge among examinees may influence overall performance.
Authenticity	Input to learners simulates academic reading. Questions simulate some academic study questions and exam questions.	Length of readings and timing of questions is unlike most academic reading settings.
Interactiveness	Reading and open-ended response should prompt engagement of components of language knowledge, communication strategies, and topical knowledge.	
Impact	Questions should prompt the study of reading for comprehension, restatement, and summary of information. Test writers should have to better understand what constitutes partial knowledge.	Tests may be so expensive that some examinees may not be able to take them and therefore, may not be able to apply to North American universities.
Practicality	Computational analysis of responses makes open-ended questions a possibility in operational testing programs, where they had been considered impossible.	It may be too expensive to prepare the partial-credit scoring for items on a regular basis. Within the constraints of the operational TOEFL, 90 minutes cannot be devoted to reading assessment.

Summary

These examples of CALT and the logical analysis of their usefulness demonstrate that CALT issues do not center around the technology alone. Instead, the capabilities of the technology need to be evaluated within the complete usefulness framework to make judgements about the relative usefulness of the test as a whole for a particular purpose. If the sum of the technology issues is identified for these examples, some positive and negative effects of the technology can be identified, as shown in Table 4.8. Included in the table are only those qualities that are associated uniquely with technology in these examples as well as a few other points that have been raised by examples not covered here.

Despite the utility of summarizing some potential benefits and limitations of computer-assisted approaches, each potential needs to be considered in view of the test purpose and all of the usefulness qualities – not just those associated with technology. The usefulness analysis demonstrates that questions about technology in testing cannot be answered independently; in other words, the question of whether or not CALT is valid is not answerable.

Empirical evaluation of CALT

It is one thing to speculate that a computer-assisted test will or will not have positive characteristics in view of a particular purpose but it is another matter to demonstrate that the results of testing behave according to speculation. The discussion of empirical validation of CALT is framed in terms of the same principles of test usefulness used to conduct judgemental analysis. The empirical methods for investigating test usefulness are summarized in Table 4.9. The difference between these definitions and the ones outlined in Table 4.2 is that the latter refer to judgements made about aspects of the test on the basis of examination of the test design. For example, a logical examination of reliability requires a judgement about the extent to which the test will reflect unmotivated variance; the corresponding empirical question examines the actual amount of unmotivated variance reflected in test scores. Logical analysis of authenticity entails a judgement about the correspondences between the test tasks and those outside the testing situation, whereas empirical evaluation requires investigation of the language and processes the examinees actually engage in during test-taking, and comparison with the language and processes beyond the test setting.

Table 4.8. *Positive and negative aspects of technology for example projects*

Quality	Positive attributes	Negative attributes
Reliability	Partial-credit scoring implemented by computer should provide more precise measurement (and larger variance).	
Construct validity	Constructs of academic reading, listening, and on-line composing can be reflected in computer-assisted test tasks. Open-ended responses are less likely than multiple-choice to be affected by systematic test-taking strategies.	Constraints placed on computer-adaptive testing can proscribe test tasks making them poor measures of textual competence.
Authenticity	Computer-assisted test tasks simulate some academic tasks.	Computer-assisted test tasks are dissimilar to those that are completed through other media in academic settings.
Interactiveness	Multimedia input may offer opportunities for good interactiveness.	Short items sometimes used on computer-adaptive tests may limit interactiveness.
Impact	Anticipation of CALT should prompt computer work in L2 classes, which may help L2 learners gain important skills. Language programs may be prompted to make computers available to learners and teachers.	Tests may be so expensive that some examinees may not be able to take them
Practicality	Computational analysis of responses makes open-ended questions a possibility of an operational testing program. Internet-delivered tests add flexibility of time and place for test delivery.	It may be too expensive to prepare the partial-credit scoring for items on a regular basis. Internet-delivered tests can raise problems for test security in high-stakes testing.

Table 4.9. *Empirical methods for test usefulness arguments*

Reliability	Estimation of the correspondences of learners' performance with the hypothesized structure of language abilities.
Construct validity	A variety of empirical evidence indicating that test results reflect the construct as it is defined.
Authenticity	Comparison of learners' strategies and language during test-taking with those in non-test settings.
Interactiveness	Analysis of the test-taking processes.
Impact	Studies of the effects of a test on learners and other factors in the educational setting.
Practicality	Assessment of actual costs and benefits.

Reliability

Reliability is investigated through statistical methods that assess the extent to which item performance data fit a psychometric model, the mathematical expression of the components of a construct and their relationships (Bachman, 1990). Figure 4.2 illustrates the place of the psychometric model relative to the aspects of testing. The one-headed arrows are read as 'inform' or 'influence.' The test design informs the test's construct theory, which in turn should influence the choice of the appropriate psychometric model. For example, if a construct of vocabulary size is defined along *one* dimension (word frequency), the construct definition would imply the choice of a *uni*dimensional psychometric model as a basis for examining the internal structure of the performance data. The construct theory also influences the design of the test tasks, which in turn influence the resulting test performance. The double-headed arrow indicates that the performance data are tested against the psychometric model to determine the extent to which they fit. Appropriate psychometric models for representing constructs in second language testing have been the source of much discussion over the past 15 years, the depth and breadth of which are too much to summarize here. However, because one aspect, the use of unidimensional models, has been critical for computer-adaptive testing, this issue must be considered.

The question for test usefulness is expressed by the double-headed arrow: To what extent are the performance data consistent with the psychometric model that corresponds to the construct theory? Computer-adaptive language tests have typically been constructed

Test design	$\rightarrow$	Construct theory	$\rightarrow$	Psychometric model
		$\uparrow\downarrow$		$\updownarrow$
		Test tasks	$\rightarrow$	Test performance

Figure 4.2 The relationship of the psychometric model to other aspects of testing

under the assumption that test performance can be modeled unidimensionally. When the psychometric model is unidimensional (Henning, Hudson, & Turner, 1985), existing methods can be used to investigate the data fit, including classical true-score reliability methods and some item-response theory (IRT) methods (see Bachman, 1990, Chapter 6). Multidimensional psychometric models in which the multiple dimensions can be hypothesized to correspond to substantive dimensions of the construct are a continuing topic of research (Ackerman, 1994; Embretson, 1985; Mislevy, 1994; 1995). Multidimensional models would be appropriate if vocabulary were to be defined, for example, in terms of not only size, but also knowledge of derivational morphology, and each of those dimensions was expected to be evident from the way performance was summarized. Because multidimensional models are more a subject of research than a tool in practice, they have not played a role in constructing computer-adaptive language tests. The fact that computer-adaptive language tests are designed and interpreted in terms of a unidimensional psychometric model continues to be a source of concern for researchers, as it was over a decade ago for Canale (1986).

Concern has been raised on the basis of the relationship of a unidimensional model to both the empirical performance data and the construct theory. Concerns from the data side are raised through empirical investigation of the dimensionality of language test data, which can be accomplished through a number of procedures related to factor analysis, as illustrated in studies by Choi and Bachman (1992) and by Blais and Laurier (1993). Both studies found that different methods for assessing the unidimensionality of data produced different results, making the decision of whether the test data should be treated as unidimensional a matter of judgement. Choi and Bachman concluded: 'the dimensionality of a given test is difficult to assess, and is a matter of degree, so that the question is not whether a test is unidimensional or not, but rather the degree to which it departs from unidimensionality' (Choi & Bachman, 1992) and, one might add, what the consequences are of its departure when test development and score interpretation assume unidimensionality.

These critical points rest at the nexus of construct validation and practical test development issues for computer-adaptive language tests because test developers may be inclined to assume unidimensionality without testing this assumption.

The construct theoretical concern is the one raised most clearly in language testing by Canale's (1986) paper, 'The promise and threat of computerized adaptive assessment of reading comprehension.' His discussion of 'the threat' took up the problem of developing a construct theory of reading comprehension which was constrained by the need for the theory to adhere to the unidimensional model. He argued that such a constraint would 'require us to trivialize our theories of reading comprehension' because 'current computer implementations of item response theory require the construct measured to be unidimensional, i.e., be assumed largely to involve only one major factor or underlying trait' (1986: 33). Another theoretical concern about these models is raised by the assumption they entail about the independence of items. As described previously, the computer-adaptive reading test consisted of 'readings' 1–3 sentences in length in order to meet the item independence assumption of the psychometric model. By having such short 'readings,' test designers were able to adhere to the independence requirement because each item required comprehension of a unique segment. From the perspective of construct theory, this practical constraint on the amount of linguistic input that test takers receive precludes their engagement of textual knowledge, and therefore fails to reflect a current understanding of reading comprehension (Chalhoub-Deville, Alcaya, & Lozier, 1996). Swain makes this point more generally with respect to the inherent incompatibility between the independence requirement of psychometric models and the positive test qualities of authenticity and interactiveness (Swain, 1993).

Research has been directed toward seeking compromises to the independence requirement,[6] but the unidimensionality assumption is more difficult. Henning (1992) asserted that concerns about dimensionality from a theoretical standpoint fail to distinguish

---

[6] Tests containing questions about a single passage fail to meet the statistical requirement of independence, and therefore a different approach to adaptivity must be explored. Fortunately, research investigating how to handle related groups of items on a computer-adaptive test has proposed some solutions involving what is known as a 'testlet.' 'A testlet is a group of items related to a single content area that is developed as a unit and contains a fixed number of predetermined paths that an examinee may follow' (Wainer & Kiely, 1987: 190). If empirical investigation of the relationships among items on the tests finds that the theoretically expected dependencies occur in the data, the items within a passage cannot be treated as independent, and therefore the testlet solution is needed.

psychometric unidimensionality from psychological unidimensionality: He argued that psychometric models assuming '"psychometric" unidimensionality can be applied in the analysis of test data that satisfy those "psychometric" assumptions, even when the psychological reality underlying those data is multidimensional in nature' (1992: 10). Despite the usefulness of the unidimensional psychometric model for some test purposes, the thought of a new generation of computer-assisted testing incapable of any broader assessment than the previous generation of paper-and-pencil tests is disappointing at best (Bejar, 1985; Bejar & Braun, 1994). Those looking to computer-assisted testing methods in the future hope their efforts will pay off with tests that elicit, gather, and evaluate information that extends beyond current unidimensional models. So, rather than confining efforts to seeking an acceptable degree of unidimensionality in data so as to warrant use of a unidimensional model, researchers might look toward ways of best using the computer to detect construct-relevant multiple dimensions of language performance. One way of approaching this may be through a better understanding of process-oriented performance data – data that provide evidence for the cognitive information processing models of cognitive psychologists (Snow & Lohman, 1989). These are in the domain of empirical task analysis, one form of construct validation.

Construct validity

Construct validity studies require the researcher to hypothesize that test performance (i.e., typically summarized by a test score) should be used to infer a particular aspect of language ability (i.e., a construct), and then to conduct research to reveal the extent to which that hypothesis is justified (Embretson, 1983; Messick, 1989). Several different forms of product- and process-oriented research (summarized in Table 4.10) can be used to provide empirical construct validity evidence. These methods have not been used extensively to investigate CALT but the existing examples along with examples of other language tests illustrate methods for future construct validation for CALT.

Relationships

One type of construct validity evidence comes from correlational research investigating relationships of test scores with other tests and behaviors. The hypotheses investigated in these validity studies specify the anticipated relationships of the test under investigation

Table 4.10. *Construct validation methods for CALT*

Research method	Definition
Relationships	Correlations with other tests and behaviors compared with theoretically predicted levels of covariance among tests and behavior in other contexts.
Experimental studies	Investigation of changes in test performance which accompany systematic changes in tests and examinees.
Empirical task product analysis	Investigation of factors affecting item-level performance (usually as measured by item difficulty) to provide statistical evidence relevant to researchers' understanding of what a test measures.
Empirical task process analysis	Documentation and analysis (through qualitative methods) of the language performance or the metacognitive and communication strategies that learners use as they complete test tasks.

with other tests or quantifiable performances. An important paradigm for systematizing theoretical predictions of correlations is the multitrait-multimethod (MTMM) research design which has been used for language testing research (e.g., Bachman and Palmer, 1982; Stevenson, 1981). The MTMM design requires that tests of several different constructs be chosen so that each construct is measured using more than one method, and then evidence for validity is found if the correlations among the tests of the same construct are stronger than correlations among tests of different constructs. Hypotheses about the strengths of relationships (i.e., divergent and convergent correlations) among tests can be made on the basis of other theoretical criteria as well, such as content analyses of tests (Chapelle & Abraham, 1990). Questions about the extent to which computer delivery influences test performance could be addressed in a carefully designed study including computer and non-computer delivery of tests intended to measure the same constructs in addition to both types of tests intended to measure different constructs.

The significance of correlational studies is that the researcher has to make theory-based hypotheses about relationships between two tests or between a test and other behaviors. The goal is to produce empirical evidence that two sets of scores are related to the degree predicted on the basis of the inferences they are intended to make. To conduct such research, the inference – defined as part of test purpose – is used along with the actual scores derived from the evaluation procedure. Two types of correlational studies have been used to investigate the construct validity of CALT.[7]

The first example is a study of the computer-based TOEFL (Taylor *et al.*, 1999). The intended inference from the computer-delivered TOEFL is academic English proficiency, the same inference intended from the paper-and-pencil TOEFL. The hypothesis was that if students took both computer-delivered and paper-and-pencil TOEFL, the two sets of scores would be highly correlated because the two tests would measure the same thing. In fact, the correlation, which was not corrected for attenuation, was .84, leading the researchers to conclude that use of the different media did not significantly affect the inferences that could be drawn from test scores. If the two sets of scores had not been highly correlated, the researchers would have concluded that the features of the method unique to the two tests such as the medium were responsible for the differences in scores. It is important to note that the correlation gives no indication of which was a better measure of academic language proficiency; it was only an indicator of the similarity of the inferences that can be made from the two tests. The interpretation of one test as better than the other must be based on other criteria.

A second more focused type of correlational study identified facets of the test method more precisely than computer delivery. Several studies have attempted to isolate the influence of features of evaluation – in particular, computer-assisted scoring method – on observed scores. One study investigating the use of a text analysis program, Writer's Workbench, for evaluation of ESL learners' essays found that the quantitative Writer's Workbench measures – consisting of essay length, average word length, Kincaid readability, percent of complex sentences, and percent of content words – correlated positively with holistic scores on ESL compositions (Reid, 1986). However, the correlations ranged only from .57 for essay length to .15 for percent of content words. If the holistic score is considered to provide a good indicator of writing ability (the intended inference), the magnitude of the correlations with the Writer's Workbench scoring method would argue against the construct validity of this computer-assisted scoring method as a measure of writing ability in this case.

Other correlational studies have found computer-assisted scoring

---

[7] These types of studies may be seen more as investigations of reliability, the assumption being that the two test forms or scoring methods create parallel forms of a test. The perspective here is that the medium and the scoring method are expected to influence scores and therefore the assumption is that they represent variation in the test method.

methods to appear more promising when they are developed specifically for a particular test. In a study conducted on the reading test with constructed responses described previously, correlations were calculated between scores from a multiple-choice version of the test and scores obtained from two different scoring methods for the open-ended items. One method for scoring the open-ended items yielded dichotomous scores, and the second yielded polytomous scores. Correlations indicated that the dichotomously scored open-ended items produced higher disattenuated correlations with the multiple-choice test (r=.99) than the polytomously scored, open-ended items did (r=.89). This indicates that only when open-ended items were polytomously scored was the resulting test score somewhat different from the score produced from the multiple-choice items. Again, other criteria need to be brought to bear on the question of which is the better reading test, but the correlations show that this feature of evaluation made some difference in what was measured.

Another study of scoring method investigated the degree of correlation between scores awarded by human raters and those awarded by a computer program which had been designed to make the same evaluations as the human raters (Jamieson *et al.*, 1993). The linguistic output evaluated in this study consisted of students' notes taken while completing a reading passage and their recall protocols of the passage.

First, the reading was presented paragraph by paragraph on the top half of the computer screen. Students were encouraged to type notes which appeared on the bottom half of the screen. After the students waited at least one day, they reviewed their notes and typed everything they could remember about the reading passage. (1993: 308)

The researchers wanted to award high scores when complete information about what had been in the reading passage was present in the students' notes and recalls. Low scores were to be awarded when the information was incomplete, and when the students' notes and recalls contained the less important information from the passage. Students expressed the information in the passage using the same words as those in the reading or using different language to express the same meanings. It was therefore necessary to construct the computer program to recognize linguistic variations of the ideas from the passage, and to award a number of points depending on the importance of the idea unit. Results indicated strong correlations between the two evaluation methods.

Other correlational studies such as this one which estimated the degree of similarity between scores obtained by computer and human raters in addition to other types of comparisons between the two evaluation methods have been conducted in second language testing (Molholt & Presler, 1986) and in other areas (Bennett, Rock, Braun, Frye, Spohrer, & Soloway, 1990; Birenbaum & Tatsuoka, 1987) but more work in this area is needed to provide one form of evidence concerning the extent to which the two scoring methods can be used to obtain a measure of the same construct.

Experimental studies

Experimental or quasi-experimental research investigates the extent to which differences among groups' test performance are consistent with predictions. Such research is based on construct theory that makes predictions about systematic differences expected across groups of test takers, time, instruction, or test task characteristics. The experimental construct validity study is similar to a correlational study in that the goal is to discover the extent to which particular features affect performance relative to theory-based predictions, but in an experimental study, test scores are not obtained from a single group of test takers. Instead, sets of scores are obtained from test takers systematically assigned to groups and can be compared in a number of different ways, including their difficulty level, reliability, and distributions. The study of how differences in test task characteristics influence performance can be framed in terms of generalizability (Bachman, 1997) – the study of the extent to which performance on one test task can be expected to generalize to other tasks. This type of evidence has been particularly important as test developers attempt to design tests with fewer but more complex test tasks (McNamara, 1996), and is therefore important for efforts attempting to expand computer-assisted testing beyond selected response tasks. Hypotheses about bias resulting from language test tasks delivered on the computer can also be tested by comparing scores of test takers with varying degrees of prior experience with computers.

One such study was conducted to investigate the effects of L2 test takers' prior experience with computers on their performance on a computer-delivered version of the TOEFL (Taylor *et al.*, 1999). The test takers in the study were designated as either familiar with computers or unfamiliar with computers on the basis of their responses to a questionnaire asking them to estimate their knowledge and amount of use of various computer applications. The scores of the two groups were then compared (while scores on the paper-and-pencil version of the TOEFL were used as a covariate) to determine the extent to which computer familiarity affected performance on the computer-delivered test. The researchers concluded that after they had adjusted for language ability (as measured by the paper-and-pencil TOEFL), there was no meaningful difference between performance of computer-familiar and computer-unfamiliar participants on the computer-delivered test when all had first taken a tutorial on how to use the computer.

An exploratory group-difference study investigated how test taker characteristics influenced the features of their writing that were identified by a computer program. Frase, Faletti, Ginther, and Grant (1999) gathered essay exam data from a group of native speakers and from ESL learners from three different language backgrounds. The only feature that systematically differed among the performances of the groups was the language background of the test takers; other task characteristics, such as topic and timing, remained the same across groups. The researchers used a text analysis program to identify linguistic features of the test takers' writing that were quantifiably different between the native speakers and the distinct groups of ESL learners. The linguistic features investigated included, for example, vocabulary size, 'directness,' 'expressiveness,' and 'academic stance.' This exploratory comparison of group performance identified a number of the significant features of writing that the computer program was able to recognize.

An experimental construct validity study was also used to compare open-ended and multiple-choice response types on the reading comprehension test described previously. The version of the test with open-ended, computer-scored questions was investigated in part through comparison of its reliability with its multiple-choice counterpart. The differences between the multiple-choice and open-ended forms are illustrated as follows:

Multiple choice:
According to the passage, mistletoe seeds travel from place to place by:

(1) clinging to birds' beaks
(2) sticking to berries
(3) spreading over loose bark
(4) blowing to nearby branches

Open-ended:

How do the mistletoe plants spread from tree to tree? (Henning *et al.*, 1993: 124–125)

Comparisons of internal consistency reliabilities between the two forms indicated higher reliabilities for the form with the open-ended responses when they were scored to reflect partial correctness (.83) than for the multiple-choice items (.74). An additional hypothesis was tested about the evaluation method: that the reliabilities of the scores from the open-ended questions would be the same whether they were scored on a dichotomous or a polytomous scale. It was found that if the open-ended items were scored dichotomously, the test's reliability was lower (.69) than that of the multiple-choice test. This showed that a partial-credit scoring procedure requiring a computer-assisted output recognition and scoring algorithm produced a demonstrable improvement in reliability over the test with dichotomously scored or non-linguistic responses.

Comparing effects of different forms of input to the test takers, another experimental construct validity study investigated ESL test takers' performance on an academic listening test (Shin, 1995). It was hypothesized that the academic listening test could maximize authenticity and interactiveness if input were presented in video (with audio) form rather than in audio alone. Additionally, it was hypothesized that the input presented through audio alone would prove more difficult for listening comprehension than the video. The two forms of the test were given to two different groups of students who were assessed by other means to be equivalent in their academic listening ability. Comparisons between group mean scores supported the hypothesis that the audio alone was more difficult. In fact, the audio was so difficult that the resulting distribution was positively skewed (i.e., there were a lot of low scores) whereas the video version produced a near normal distribution, which was desirable because the test was intended for norm-referenced use.

Empirical task product analysis

Empirical item or task product analysis investigates the extent to which hypothesized knowledge and processes appear to be responsible for learners' performance on each test task. Such studies require hypotheses about the inferences to be made by the test as a whole, but in addition, it is necessary to specify the construct developmentally, or in terms of levels of ability (Carroll, 1989). For example, the construct of L2 vocabulary size would include a developmental hypothesis that beginners know few high frequency L2 words, and that the number increases developmentally so that advanced learners know a lot of words including both high and lower frequency words, as shown in Table 4.11.

The developmental definition is used to make hypotheses about learners' performance on test tasks on the basis of the frequency of

Table 4.11. *Example showing a developmental hypothesis associated with a construct definition*

Construct	Construct definition	Developmentally defined hypothesis based on the construct definition
L2 vocabulary size	How many L2 words the learner knows	Beginner knows few words and these are frequent in L2. ↕ Advanced learner knows many L2 words, both frequent and infrequent ones.

the vocabulary in each, and 'performance' in such studies has been operationally summarized through empirical task difficulties, as Carroll (1989) described. In a construct validity study of a vocabulary test, researchers would investigate the linguistic feature of the input, 'vocabulary frequency,' to discover the extent to which it has the theorized impact on item difficulty, as Perkins and Linnville (1987) did. This is done by coding each test task for 'vocabulary frequency' so that those with frequent words in the input would get a high score (meaning the item is predicted to be easy), and tasks with infrequent words would get a low score (meaning it is predicted to be difficult). The vocabulary frequency score for each item would then be correlated with the difficulty of each task, which is operationalized as the percentage of examinees who got the item correct (i.e., a high item difficulty means that a lot of people got it correct; it is an easy item). If the items with high frequency words are the ones that a lot of people get correct (i.e., high item difficulty) and the ones with low frequency words are the ones that a lot of people get incorrect (i.e., low item difficulty), there will be a positive correlation between the vocabulary frequency of the input and item difficulty. Given the developmental definition of vocabulary size – which is expressed in terms of vocabulary frequency – this positive correlation would provide evidence for the construct validity of the test for making inferences about vocabulary size. If there were no correlation between frequency and difficulty, one would conclude that other factors were responsible for performance, and therefore the construct validity of the proposed inferences would not be supported.

This example illustrates the principle of prediction of item performance (operationalized through difficulty) as a construct validation strategy. Constructs measured in language tests are sometimes operationally defined through a single variable such as one expressed through a readability formula (Linacre, 1999), but more often through many test task features that are expected to jointly contribute to performance. A good example of the latter is Kirsch and Mosenthal's (1988; 1990) test of 'document literacy.' Documents are defined as consisting of written materials such as forms, charts, and labels, which one might read in order to subscribe to a magazine, find which bus to take, or determine the appropriate dosage of medicine, respectively. Defining 'document literacy' as the ability to read documents to be able to do something, they were concerned with language ability which would not include complex syntax, vocabulary, rhetorical organization and a variety of illocutionary and sociolinguistic knowledge. On the basis of their construct definition, the variables they hypothesized to be related to task difficulty were the linguistic characteristics of the documents to be comprehended and the specific pragmatic function of the instructions of the tasks that learners were asked to perform, as well as the processes that the learners were expected to engage in as they completed the task. Variables within each of these general categories were significant predictors of difficulty, which means that these factors influenced test takers' performance and, to the extent that they represent the construct theory of document literacy well, this finding provides one source of evidence for the construct validity of the test.

Identification of test task features related to performance is a useful method to improve understanding of test design, and therefore this method appears to hold potential for the study of CALT. However, to use difficulty prediction for learning more about variables unique to computer-assisted testing, it is necessary to expand the task features expected to account for performance (e.g., Nissan, DeVincenzi, & Tang, 1996) by identifying features expected to be relevant to the difficulty of the construct the test is intended to measure. For example, if a construct theory of listening comprehension predicts that input accompanied by visual cues makes listening easier than input with no visual input (e.g., a conversation on the phone would be more difficult than the same one face-to-face), then a test would need to include some items with visual input and others without. The empirical item difficulties would need to be investigated to discover the extent to which visual support predicted easy items. Unfortunately, research on video in L2 listening indicates that the presence of visual information does not have a systematic effect across situations and individuals so more context-specific theories of listening are needed (Gruba, 1999).

Another potential feature of interest might be the level of interaction built into reading test tasks. If a construct definition of reading includes knowledge of vocabulary, it would predict that tasks in which learners are given access to vocabulary definitions would be easier than those in which no such interactions were possible, and this prediction could be tested empirically through analysis of data from a computer-based test including both with and without interaction types of items. Despite the usefulness of the approach, this type of validity inquiry places difficult demands on construct definition (because of the need for a developmental hypothesis associated with construct definition) and inventiveness in test design. For the time being, it remains an analytic approach awaiting clearly motivated research into CALT.

Empirical task process analysis

Qualitative analyses attempt to document the strategies and language that learners use as they complete test tasks to discover the extent to which observed processes are consistent with those specified in the construct definition. Empirical task analysis is carried out using two approaches corresponding to the two ways of describing task processes.

If task processes are to be described in terms of the metacognitive and communicative strategies called on during test-taking, the research methods are likely to be qualitative introspective methods requiring test takers to explain their thought processes during or immediately after test-taking (Grotjahn, 1986; 1987). A number of studies have been conducted to evaluate this type of hypothesis on tests of listening and reading, as well as cloze tests and cloze-like tests (Cohen, 1984; Buck, 1991; Yi'an, 1998; Feldmann & Stemmer, 1987). Findings from this research, as Cohen (1998) summarizes, indicate that test responses were often the result of elaborate meta-cognitive strategies, rather than the communicative strategies that one would hope would affect performance on a language test, and that this is the case particularly on multiple-choice tests. This mismatch between the intended construct and the process affecting performance may be cause for questioning the construct validity of the tests investigated.

If task processes are to be described in terms of the language that learners produce during the test task, the methods are likely to include discourse analysis of learners' output. In such cases, discourse analysis is used to compare the linguistic and pragmatic character-istics of the language that learners produce in a test with what is implied from the construct definition. For example, in a discourse analytic construct validation study of an EFL speaking test, Lazerton (1996) focused description of the learners' linguistic output on the pragmatic role it performed in each of the questions she investigated. Her objective was to investigate the degree to which the pragmatic role of the learners' output was consistent with that intended by the test developers. Her finding that it tended to be consistent was used as one argument for the validity of the speaking test.

These are not the only perspectives relevant to empirical task process analysis; one might look at other aspects of language, learners' retrospective judgements about their strategies (Purpura, 1996), timing during task completion, or evolving goals throughout test-taking, for example. It should be evident that the range of process-oriented approaches that can be applied to questions of construct validation are similar to methods used in SLA research. The difference between qualitative research directed at construct validation and other SLA research is that the former sets out with hypotheses about – or at least evaluates the data against – a construct definition which implies the language and strategies that would ideally be discovered through the research.

Process approaches to construct validation for CALT offer intriguing possibilities but no results. At this point, one can look only to examples from other research in language testing in addition to some computer-assisted assessment research in other areas (Gitomer, Steinberg, & Mislevy, 1995). A look in both directions makes it evident that process approaches to validation are a natural for CALT because of the ways in which the computer can control, manipulate, and document the test-taking process. At the same time, process approaches to validation raise some of the thorniest measurement issues (Mislevy, 1996; Nichols, 1994) because the field of educational measurement has tended to focus on the products of performance rather than on the processes, and perhaps with good reason. Most test researchers and users would agree that the complexity inherent in a processing perspective toward language ability far exceeds that which is needed for most uses of test scores. Despite the propensity of testing researchers to stick to product-oriented construct definitions, investigation of test-taking processes *is* one of the ways of investigating construct validity – a method which requires joint perspectives from SLA research and language testing.

Authenticity and interactiveness

Authenticity and *interactiveness* can be investigated through the methods outlined above for empirical process-oriented task analysis.

The study of authenticity focuses on the degree of match between performance on the test and performance in the context of interest, the target language use context (Bachman & Palmer, 1996). For example, computer-assisted reading tests provide opportunities for constructing tasks which require learners to identify and highlight information in the text, or to select and rearrange information from a text. The question for an empirical authenticity study is to what extent test takers' processes in working on such tests are similar to those they use in reading in the L2. Research on interactiveness is intended to find evidence that test takers use communicative language strategies as specified in the construct definition of what the test is intended to measure. The study of authenticity and interactiveness needs to take into account the ways in which examinees will be using their target language through many forms of electronic communication that have become an integral part of most target language use contexts (Rassool, 1999).

Impact

Impact is investigated by seeking evidence for the influence of a test on those involved with it such as learners and teachers. Empirical methodologies for investigating impact are a topic of exploration in language testing. Alderson and Hamp-Lyons (1996), for example, attempted to identify some of the impacts of the TOEFL on teaching and learning within an intensive English program in the US. Through classroom observations, interviews with teachers, students, and administrators, and examination of classroom materials, they uncovered a complex set of relationships among teaching practices, teachers' styles, learners' wishes (and teachers' perceptions of those wishes), and administrative decisions. The form and content of the TOEFL did play a role within this complex of factors, but the role was not direct or clear-cut. Qualitative research such as this is needed to identify the intended and unintended impacts of introducing CALT. Without such data, one can only speculate, as the logical analysis is intended to do, on the extent to which CALT affects learners positively or negatively. Quantitative data on computer familiarity by potential examinees are also useful for examining impact. One might expect that the introduction of computer-assisted testing will impact more strongly areas in which examinees are not accustomed to using computers. For example, a survey of potential TOEFL candidates found that in 1997, 5.9% of respondents indicated that they had never used a computer, but in Africa the number was 24.5% (Taylor, Jamieson, & Eignor, 2000).

Practicality

Practicality is assessed through analysis of actual costs and resources required for the testing process. The cost of testing is usually considered as a business or administrative decision, rather than as a quality of the test itself. However, CALT can require significant resources for development and delivery, and, as a consequence, cost issues need to be considered throughout the process, and weighed against long-term practical benefits of ease of delivery and efficiency of data handling.

Conclusion

The possibilities offered by CALT need to be evaluated in view of the broader context of language testing. In educational measurement, evaluation of tests refers to their validation, and in language testing the principles of validation have been interpreted by Bachman and Palmer to provide criteria for evaluating test usefulness. This chapter applied Bachman and Palmer's principles to CALT from the perspective of a test designer or someone who is selecting a test for a language program and then from the perspective of the language testing researcher who is conducting empirical investigations of CALT.

Validation theory, including the usefulness analysis, has proven indispensable for organizing research in language testing by providing a common set of terms, concepts, and procedures familiar to those who conduct and read research on language testing. These methods will prove equally indispensable for research on CALT if it is to move beyond current testing practices to offer tests that draw on the computers' capabilities. However, the few examples of CALT research and development to date demonstrate that much territory remains to be explored if CALT is going to add substantively to language testing research and practice. In short, examination of CALT in 2000 demonstrates that many of the questions Canale raised in 1986 about how to improve both theory and practice in language testing through the use of computers still remain. After all the progress language testing researchers have made in understanding communicative language ability and test task characteristics, it is disheartening at best to read papers on testing which make technology-driven claims such as 'reading aloud is a good indicator of overall ability in English' (Coniam, 1996: 20). Hopefully, future work will aim to improve language testing through technology by building on the fruitful work of the past.

5 Computer-assisted SLA research

Computer-assisted SLA research ideally complements research and development of CALL and CALT by offering results pertaining to questions about instruction and assessment. A computer-assisted second language research (CASLR) task is defined as one in which learners are expected to work on the target language interactively with a computer program or with other people through the medium of the computer. Such tasks may appear to the learners to be a regular part of instruction or testing, or they may be explicitly introduced to learners as research tasks. One type of CASLR is to *gather evidence about the effects of instructional conditions of learning,* as illustrated in a study by de Graaff (1997a), who compared the effects of implicit and explicit instruction by operationalizing each condition through CALL. A second type of CASLR is used for assessment, i.e., to *make inferences about aspects of learners' language ability and learning* (e.g., vocabulary, metacognitive strategies). Such tasks fall within the purview of assessment and are therefore discussed in the terms introduced in Chapter 4. One example of a CASLR task used for assessment was designed by Hulstijn (1993) to assess learners' vocabulary look-up strategies during reading. In both assessment and learning condition CASLR, past work exemplifies research methods and points to future research.

Investigating conditions for SLA

Doughty (1992) offers a comprehensive perspective on the use of technology in studies investigating learning conditions:

Research designs should address issues relevant to understanding the process of second language acquisition. [Her] experiment . . . incorporated a theoretically-motivated instructional design, and though not the object of investigation, computer applications nevertheless were significant in all phases of the research: *design* and development of the experimental instrument, *description* of the data gathered, and *discovery* of the significance of the findings. (Doughty, 1992: 129; emphasis in original)

Doughty's characterization of the three facets of her computer-assisted SLA research – design, description, discovery – helps to define the domain. *Design* refers to the CASLR tasks intended for students' language learning. The process of computer-assisted data *description* relies on a computer program to assist in identifying, tabulating, and organizing SLA data which were gathered through a computer-assisted research task or through other means. The best-known software packages intended specifically for linguistic data are CHILDES (MacWhinney, 1995) and COALA (Pienemann, 1992) for creating, tagging, and searching a database of learner language, and COMOLA, for writing computational L2 grammars which describe a given set of data (Jagtman, 1994). *Discovery* refers to the use of the computer for statistical analysis of data (Davidson, 1996). Discussion of CASLR here is limited to the first of these three.

A CASLR task may appear to the learners to be a regular part of instruction or it may be introduced as a research task. In the former case, learners work on a task while the computer collects data on their performance; in the latter case, the researcher may also gather data such as learners' introspective comments. By definition, CASLR tasks might be exactly the same as the instructional tasks described in Chapter 3. In practice, however, CASLR has tended to be conducted in laboratories, sometimes with participants who were not studying the language, and sometimes with an artificial language as the object of instruction.

CASLR for investigating instructional conditions

The examples of CASLR to date offer a glimpse into some of the possibilities for investigating conditions. DeKeyser (1995) investigated whether explicit-deductive or implicit-inductive learning worked better for simple categorical grammar rules and for linguistic prototypes. He constructed an artificial language which included both categorical rules and prototypical patterns and he taught it to the subjects by introducing them to rules or examples, depending on the condition. Each sentence of the artificial language was displayed with a picture which illustrated its meaning. The computer was used to control the instructional conditions and to document 'developing knowledge under speeded conditions, that is, where monitoring (in the sense of drawing on explicit knowledge) is difficult.' Use of the speeded judgement tests, which did not allow time for learners to draw on explicit knowledge, throughout the learning sessions allowed the researcher to conclude that the categorical rules had not been learned implicitly.

In another study using an artificial language, DeKeyser (1997) investigated the hypothesis that explicitly learned morphosyntactic rules (i.e., gender and case marking) would become gradually automatized through practice. Instruction was provided through approximately 22 hours of CALL materials he produced, and different conditions for practice (e.g., with and without production) were also carried out on the computer. The computer provided a vehicle for collection of longitudinal data which allowed the researcher to document the learners' gradual automation of learned material over the time of the experiment. The carefully controlled instructional conditions and testing procedures yielded data indicating that automation was 'skill-specific,' e.g., that practice in comprehension did not transfer to atomization in production.

Constructing CALL materials to resemble those of a self-study course, de Graaff (1997b) controlled the instructional treatments in his comparison of implicit and explicit instruction throughout a course that lasted approximately 15 hours. Learners received all instruction in an artificial language from the computer-based materials which were produced in two forms – with and without explicit instruction on the grammatical forms that they were supposed to be learning. Learners in the implicit condition were given equal exposure to the target language forms as those in the explicit condition. The only difference for the former was that the input they received contained no explicit explanation of grammar. The controlled instructional treatment gives one confidence in the results, which indicated that the explicit instruction was associated with significantly higher scores on the post-tests for the four grammatical structures of the artificial language.

Such research can also be conducted using natural languages, as illustrated by Robinson's (1996) laboratory-like experiment using English grammar rules. Four conditions of instruction were constructed through the methods of presentation to the learners in each of the four groups: an *implicit* condition requiring learners to memorize sentences containing the relevant grammatical structures, an *incidental* condition instructing learners to read input sentences for meaning, a *rule-search* condition asking learners to identify the rules that were illustrated by the input sentences, and an *instructed* condition providing learners with explicit rules about the target grammatical points. Each of the conditions was presented in computer-assisted format, as was the achievement test following the instruction. The instructed condition was found to produce superior results for learning both 'easy' (e.g., subject + verb + location) and 'hard' (e.g., compound sentence with two contrasting locations) grammatical rules.

These types of studies, which use CASLR to control instructional conditions, are proving to be a reliable source of data about instructed SLA. The selection of participants, control of conditions, and testing that can be done in an experiment exceeds that which is possible in the language classroom, and therefore results may form a more stable basis for theory. To date, the conditions investigated have focused narrowly on types of presentation to learners, but as work in this area continues, one might hope to see conditions about interaction tested as well. As Larsen-Freeman & Long (1991) pointed out years ago, there is a need to pursue an 'applied research agenda to identify and assess the outcomes of psycholinguistically relevant instructional design features.' Given hypotheses about the role of interaction in SLA, relevant instructional design might include opportunities for learners to interact with the input, as well.

Other conditions for SLA

The majority of the laboratory CASLR studies to date have been concerned with comparisons between various forms of implicit and explicit instruction (Hulstijn, 1997), but given the ongoing work on conditions of instruction, such as that described by Skehan (1998), these are only a starting point. In a special issue of *Studies in Second Language Acquisition* featuring such research, Hulstijn (1997) made a distinction between two types of studies: laboratory studies 'pertinent to theories of SLA' and 'applied studies such as investigations into computer-assisted language learning' (Hulstijn, 1997: 133). Both types are among a growing body of research (e.g., VanPatten & Cadierno, 1993) which investigates theory-based predictions of the effects of specific psycholinguistic conditions on learning outcomes. As some of the research reported in Chapter 3 demonstrated, the distinction need not be so clear-cut when theoretically motivated studies are carried out in classrooms.

A good example of the promise of such research is an investigation of acquisition of aspect in the past tense in French by Ayoun (forthcoming). Materials were developed on the basis of theory and research results in SLA suggesting that a 'recast' (a corrected restatement of a learner's utterance) should be more effective as feedback for learners than models or grammatical explanations. She found some support for this hypothesis through results obtained when groups of learners were provided with CALL materials designed to operationalize one of the three conditions. Results are of interest theoretically because materials were constructed to test hypotheses and pedagogically because they were obtained through the use of the type of CALL materials that students can use in a French class.

In a description of ongoing research, Hulstijn (2000) described several CASLR studies stemming from laboratory research, but with clear links to classroom instruction. One study attempts to teach learners to increase their automaticity of lexical access through CALL materials (i.e., 'computer games', p. 37) with the intention of increasing success in reading comprehension. A second compares incidental acquisition of words looked up during reading and during writing, both of which were perceived as instructional tasks by learners. A series of prior studies of electronic dictionary use has informed development of instructional strategies for helping learners to use the electronic dictionary effectively. Hultstijn's (2000) description of these projects underscores the natural synergy developed through the interplay between CASLR and theoretical knowledge of SLA: 'theories and methods influence each other. New theories may lead to the search for and invention of new methods and tools, whereas new tools and methods may give rise to new theoretical thinking,' (2000: 39) and one might add, to more effective instructional practice, as well.

Evaluation of learning condition CASLR

CASLR used for implementing instructional conditions needs to be interpreted and evaluated in a way that can improve this research method. Hulstijn (1997) raises several concerns and recommendations in his overview of laboratory research on instructional conditions. Those issues particularly relevant to CASLR are the following: (1) the quality of operationalization of the learning condition, (2) the participation of the learners in the condition, and (3) the generalizability of results. The set of criteria for CASLR summarized in Table 5.1 borrow these three criteria but add others identified in classroom research.

Operationalization of learning conditions

The concern for operationalization, as Hulstijn pointed out, is that the researcher has correctly constructed the operational conditions theorized to produce particular effects and that the learners actually participate as intended in those conditions. The two aspects of the operationalization correspond to the logical and empirical analyses of the CALL tasks as described in Chapter 3.

Table 5.1. *Criteria for CALL research tasks*

Quality	Definition
Operationalization of the learning condition	The degree to which the theoretically defined learning condition is produced in the CASLR task and the degree to which subjects participate in the learning condition.
Generalizability	The degree of correspondence between the learning conditions in the experimental CASLR tasks and the learning conditions outside the research setting to which results are intended to generalize.
Difficulty level	Opportunity for engagement with language whose level of difficulty and conditions of use offer a possibility for learners to increase their language ability.
Impact	The positive effects of the CASLR tasks on participants, researchers, and the profession.
Practicality	The adequacy of resources to support the use of the CASLR task.

At one level, one can judge on the basis of logical analysis the extent to which CASLR creates the conditions that are the focus of the research. Hulstijn (1997) points out the need for a detailed explanation of the conditions of instruction in this type of research. Examples of both CASLR and CALL illustrate that some relevant design features of interest can be incorporated into computer applications; however, micro-level design features such as presentation of an 'incidental' condition, or provision of opportunities for interactional modification, need to be considered in view of the degree to which the complete task represents the theorized ideal of a good SLA task. To some degree, this evaluation can be accomplished through comparison of the features of the task and those for which hypotheses have been made; however, such comparisons are not always clear-cut. Computer-based materials offer a different range of options for investigating features of instructional design; it is therefore necessary to justify rationally the psycholinguistic and sociolinguistic conditions believed to be operationalized by particular design features.

At the other level, the quality of a learning condition depends on the extent to which learners actually took part in the conditions available during instruction. For example, the validity of results from research on a task presenting explicit instruction depends on the extent to which learners engaged in the instruction. When learners are presented with instructions to use a rule-search strategy, relevant data would include evidence that the learners had searched for rules. Hulstijn (1997) suggests that the experimental treatment be ended with a retrospective interview or questionnaire to assess the extent to which learners participate. Another means of producing relevant evidence for some conditions is through computer-documented data indicating the processes through which learners complete a task. DeKeyser (1995) was able to make a number of relevant observations about the results of his study through examination of data pertaining to the actual working processes of the learners. He noted, for example, that records of learners' progress through the teaching materials as well as the retrospective data obtained from subjects' explanation of their strategies indicated that the intended 'implicit/explicit distinction was sometimes overridden by their learning strategies' (DeKeyser, 1995: 398).

In an investigation of learners' acquisition of indirect speech in Spanish through multimedia materials, Collentine (2000) recorded the behaviors hypothesized to promote learning: audio events (requests for audio segments), digital-video events (interaction with video segments), substantive written answers (the number of responses given to consciousness-raising questions), exemplar contemplation time (the time spent on screens containing examples), and incorrect answers. Records of learners' engagement with each of these features were used as independent variables in the research rather than the condition that learners are assigned to being used as the variable, as is the case in experimental research.

Generalizability

Generalizability, also called external or ecological validity, refers to the extent to which results can be considered relevant to contexts beyond the research setting. Concerns about generalizability are raised about laboratory SLA studies because they trade the authenticity of the learning environment for the control of the laboratory design in which learners' prior knowledge and the conditions of their learning are carefully monitored. The most extreme controls are evident in laboratory studies of artificial languages, about which N. C. Ellis (1995a) wrote:

It will become clear that the experimental rigour of artificial grammar studies does not come free. It is won at the cost of ecological validity. Artificial languages are usually devoid of referential or social meaning; they are usually learned over short periods of an hour or two; unlike SLA, there is little role of transfer from L1 in their acquisition; and they are learned as experimental tasks rather than in naturalistic situations as a means to communicate. (1995a: 125)

Given the effects of the learners' perception of the task and individual strategies on their performance, a primary concern of SLA researchers should be establishing the scope over which research results of a given study can be generalized. Aside from the quantitative concern that more data or subjects should result in greater confidence about generalizing results, a qualitative issue must be raised concerning the degree of similarity between the experimental setting and the context to which research results are to generalize. As DeKeyser points out, 'learning a miniature linguistic system in a laboratory is very different from classroom language learning' (1995: 398). But how different? In what ways different? And from which language classrooms?

De Graaff's (1995b) instructional materials were intentionally developed to resemble CALL used for individualized instruction, and Hulstijn summarizes three studies of artificial languages as follows:

The studies of Yang & Givón, DeKeyser, and de Graaff show that it is possible to motivate individuals to devote themselves to the learning of an artificial language during several weeks in a setting resembling 'real' second or foreign language instruction. (1997: 140)

Evaluation of generalizability therefore relies on the authenticity of the research task *relative to* the other tasks to which generalization might be made. A judgemental analysis of the correspondence between a laboratory L2 task and other tasks can be undertaken using the analysis for authenticity of CALL materials outlined in Chapter 3. This approach to analysis of authenticity attempts to formalize what *different from* or *similar to* mean by identifying features that can be used to describe aspects of L2 tasks. Such an analysis might also be useful in applying results of laboratory research to the design and subsequent research of CALL materials. The authenticity analysis would help to heed Hulstijn's warning that 'without additional research in real L2 learning environments, one should be extremely cautious in drawing immediate conclusions from laboratory studies to language pedagogy' (Hulstijn, 1997: 132).

Difficulty level

In SLA research, difficulty level needs to be evaluated on two dimensions: the difficulty of the language for the learner, and the difficulty of the conditions for performance. The analysis of linguistic difficulty relative to participants should justify the choice of linguistic items to be taught in the CASLR task. There is a need to demonstrate that learners do not already have control over the target linguistic forms. The desire to control learners' prior knowledge of the targeted linguistic items is an important justification for the use of artificial languages in CASLR. However, as the research by Doughty (1991) illustrated, aspects of natural language can also be chosen in a way that ensures that the participants' prior knowledge does not pose a threat to the validity of the research. In her study of relative clause acquisition, she chose to teach types of relative clauses that were more difficult on the hierarchy of difficulty established in prior research, and she pretested learners to assess their knowledge of relative clauses. Choice of target forms and pretesting are controls available to laboratory researchers that are often not available in classrooms.

Approaching task difficulty from a processing perspective, Skehan (1998) defines pedagogical L2 tasks in terms of particular conditions that psycholinguistic theory hypothesizes affect task difficulty:

Processing-based analyses of tasks are concerned with their information-processing load, and effectively focus on the difficulty of the task. The assumption is that more demanding tasks consume more attentional resources simply for task transaction, with the result that less attention is available for focus on form. As a result, the scope of the 'residual' benefit from the task is reduced . . . So one goal in researching tasks is to establish task characteristics which influence difficulty. (1998: 97)

This type of research has investigated conditions such as the distribution, type, organization, and familiarity of information, types of goals, relationship and knowledge of participants, and task familiarity. In controlled settings, conditions such as these have been shown to influence task difficulty in addition to affecting the language of participants during the task and in some cases, learning outcomes as well. Skehan's summary is based on research investigating learners' oral language in face-to-face communication during tasks in which meaning is the primary focus. There remains much scope for applying the premises of task condition research to computer-assisted research tasks requiring either or both oral and written language.

Impact and practicality

Impact and practicality are aspects of research tasks that are sometimes overlooked because of overriding concerns for obtaining results at whatever cost. However, to the extent that researchers look toward developing knowledge that can influence classroom teaching, they should also attend to developing expertise in future language teachers and informing development of computer-based materials that will implement that knowledge in classrooms. The projects described by Hulstijn (2000) illustrate progress in research that straddles the domains of both research and instruction. It is therefore no coincidence that the practical issues figure as an important part of his description of that work: 'use of computer technology, of course, comes at a considerable price, both in terms of financial costs and in terms of logistics' (2000: 37). To accomplish the research in a classroom setting, sufficient hardware and software is needed for students at different schools (where incompatibilities made use of the school's equipment impossible). Laptops had to be transported from one school to the next, software suitable for the research had to be developed because none existed, mechanisms for data transfer and backups were needed. In short, the researchers faced the same set of challenges that confront commercial testing programs attempting to deliver tests in locations where computers are not available.

Summary

Early attempts at constructing CASLR have demonstrated their potential for investigating specific conditions for instructed SLA, particularly those about implicit versus explicit instruction. Results have overwhelmingly favored explicit learning conditions in these settings; however, researchers have cautioned that results from laboratory settings may have limited generalizability to L2 classrooms. Generalizability is therefore one of the criteria for evaluation of these research tasks. Others are quality of operationalization of learning conditions, difficulty level, impact, and practicality. These criteria help to point to fruitful directions for CASLR tasks, including links with classroom CALL.

Computer-assisted research tasks for assessment

Over the past several years, the relationship between assessment and SLA research has begun to be better understood. The formerly distinct areas within applied linguistics – language testing and SLA research – are beginning to be integrated in ways that are crucial for the development of CASLA. An important first step is the recognition that SLA researchers assess language ability, a fact that has sometimes been obscured by the different terminology used by researchers in each area. Bachman and Cohen (1998) help to clarify some of the fundamental issues by distinguishing between 'language' and 'language ability.'

We would argue that it is not language per se that is measured or acquired, but language ability. That is, even though we speak of language acquisition and language testing, what we are primarily interested in, in both cases, is not the system of language itself, but rather the learner's capacity for acquiring and using a language system . . . We would further argue that both LT and SLA researchers make inferences or assumptions about the nature of language ability in their research, and that a clear definition of this construct is thus essential to both LT and SLA research. (1998: 4)

CASLR tasks designed for assessment are used to draw *inferences* about aspects of learners' language ability, which can be defined as language knowledge and strategies (Bachman, 1990; Bachman & Palmer, 1996). The inferential process used in SLA assessment is the same as that used in language testing: observed performance on a carefully designed task is summarized and treated as *evidence* for particular underlying capacities of the learner about which the user wants to make an inference. The capacities investigated through research uses of assessments are similar in principle to those of interest in other language tests in that they are unobservable learner capacities that are assumed to be responsible for performance on the assessment task.

Recent discussion in SLA research at least implicitly recognizes that measures used in SLA research are governed by the same principles as other language tests. Researchers refer to measures as a means for drawing inferences about learners and discuss validity. The concept of measurement as inference is put clearly in some of the papers in the volume that resulted from the 1991 Second Language Research Forum conference and was edited by Tarone, Gass, and Cohen (1994). For example, in describing their grammaticality judgement and imitation tasks, Munnich, Flynn, and Martohardjono (1994) noted that 'experimental methods used to evaluate developing language ability only provide *indirect* measures of learner's competence' (p. 228 [emphasis mine]). In other words, learners' ability is inferred on the basis of their performance on the measures. Also, noting the inferential nature of measurement, Bley-Vroman and Chaudron (1994: 245) introduced their validation study of an SLA measure as follows: 'the connection between the data collection technique and a subject's behavior independent of the data collection context is always one that should concern the researcher.' In other words, the subject's performance in situations outside the testing context are inferred on the basis of their performance on the measure.

Examples of CASLR for assessment

The measurement concepts of inference and evidence are critical for examining examples of computer-assisted assessment in SLA research. Table 5.2 summarizes the examples in terms of the inference, type of task, and evidence derived from aspects of observable language and behavior. Only two examples assess aspects of language knowledge, whereas the others use CASLR to assess learner strategies.

Language knowledge

In a study investigating learners' developing linguistic knowledge, learners were instructed to use specially designed software for writing their essays in French (Bland *et al.*, 1990). The software included a bilingual dictionary that the learners were invited to query in either English or French and it had procedures for recording their queries to the dictionary. The data documented longitudinal observation of learners' queries to the dictionary, which the researchers interpreted as indicators of learners' stages of lexical development. Based on these data, the researchers suggested that as the learner developed, the words requested became less tied to English – closer to the L2 concepts and were sometimes even L2 words. The lowest level queries, 'token matching,' were very English-bound: English inflected words, English phrases, and lexical representations for grammatical concepts (e.g., 'none'). Words in the second level, 'type matching,' were English base forms (i.e., no inflections) and grammatical concepts (e.g., negation, pronouns). The third level, 'relexicalization,' were words representing English circumlocutions and French words. This method of vocabulary assessment is potentially interesting because it was conducted unobtrusively as learners worked on pedagogical tasks of consequence in their language class.

Using a set of Web-based tasks in a research setting, Ayoun (2000) assessed L2 learners' knowledge of several features of French syntax (e.g., dative alteration, distinctions in verb tense and aspect). Four types of tasks were administered to learners, three requiring various forms of learners' judgements and a fourth requiring translation. Findings were interpreted in view of Universal Grammar parameter setting hypotheses, but they also indicated significant differences across the four tasks, revealing a clear hierarchy of difficulty, with the translation task the most difficult and the three judgement tasks each with distinct levels of difficulty.

Table 5.2. *Examples of research assessing learners' knowledge and strategies with CASLR tasks*

Inference	Type of task	Evidence	Reference
Level of lexical development	Write compositions as routine class assignments	Learners' linguistic output – requests made to an on-line bilingual dictionary	Bland, *et al.* (1990)
Grammatical knowledge	Judgement and production tasks	Learners' responses to judgement queries and translations	Ayoun (2000)
Lexical strategies in reading	Read and answer questions for research	Learners' linguistic output – requests made to an on-line dictionary	Hulstijn (1993)
Resourcing (metacognitive strategy)	Construct and edit sentences for instruction	Learners' non-linguistic output – requests made to on-line reference materials	Chapelle & Mizuno (1989)
Exploration (metacognitive strategy)	Construct and edit sentences for instruction	Learners' choices and linguistic editing	Hsu, Chapelle & Thompson (1993)
Automaticity of access to grammar	Complete grammar exercise for instruction	Requests or non-requests for help	Doughty & Fought (1984)
Inferencing and hypothesis-testing	Complete grammar exercise for instruction	Requests for rules versus examples	Doughty & Fought (1984)
Advance preparation (metacognitive strategy)	Complete dictation exercise (listen and write) for instruction	Elapsed time prior to learners' linguistic response	Jamieson & Chapelle (1987)
Monitoring output (metacognitive strategy)	Complete dictation exercise (listen and write) for instruction	Learners' linguistic editing prior to computers' evaluation of responses	Jamieson & Chapelle (1987)
Monitoring input (metacognitive strategy)	Complete dictation exercise (listen and write) for instruction	Requests for repetition of input	Jamieson & Chapelle (1987)
Automaticity of grammatical knowledge	Judge grammaticality of input for research	Elapsed time prior to learners' response	Hagen (1994)
Automaticity of processing meaning	Judge truth of propositions relative to world knowledge	Elapsed time prior to learners' response	Hulstijn (2000)

Strategies and processes

Investigating vocabulary strategies, Hulstijn (1993) documented learners' use of an on-line dictionary, which they could consult while completing an exercise consisting of a reading passage followed by questions about the meaning of the text. The resulting data, documenting the words which the students had looked up in the dictionary and the time that each was looked up, were used as evidence of learners' vocabulary strategies during reading. Another study investigating similar strategies in a different task (Chapelle & Mizuno, 1989) posed the research question in terms of the learners' 'resourcing,' defined by O'Malley, Chamot, Stewner-Manzanares, Kupper, and Russo (1985) as a cognitive strategy: the learners' use of reference materials for obtaining information about the second language. Consistent with this definition, the researchers collected data on all students' requests for help as they worked on a task requiring them to construct and edit sentences. The program provided them with help only at their request; they could ask for help with vocabulary, grammar, or the semantic facts pertaining to the sentences in the exercises.

Using the same sentence constructing and editing task, Hsu, Chapelle and Thompson (1993) assessed another strategy, exploration, which was defined in the CALL literature as the use of software to experiment and test hypotheses about the target language (Higgins & Johns, 1984). Exploration was operationalized in two ways: the number of sentences students constructed after having completed the number required by their assignment and the number of times they edited an answer after receiving a message that it was correct – which the software allowed but did not require them to do. The most salient finding from these three strategy studies was the large individual variation in strategy use among the learners, leaving causes for the variation a question for future work.

Doughty and Fought (1984; reported in Doughty, 1987) also documented learners' help requests but interpreted them differently. Learners' requests for help while they were working on grammar items were used as an indicator of students' 'controlled access of explicitly learned knowledge' and 'attempts to complete tasks without any help from the program [were interpreted to] reflect automatic access to implicit knowledge in memory' (Doughty, 1987: 151). Other strategies indicated by choices of particular types of help in software were 'hypothesis-testing' and 'inferencing based on L1.' Doughty and Fought operationalized the definitions of these strategies as the type of grammar help requested by students while they worked on grammar lessons. When students consulted help consisting of examples, they were considered to be displaying evidence of 'hypothesis-testing.' When they chose grammar help consisting of formal rules or the correct answer, students were considered to be 'inferencing [about syntactic forms in the L2] based on L1.'

Another strategy assessed while learners were working on instruction is 'advance preparation,' a metacognitive strategy defined as 'planning for and rehearsing linguistic components necessary to carry out an upcoming language task' (O'Malley *et al.*, 1985: 33). Using ESL dictation tasks over the course of a six-week period, students listened to words (on the 'spelling' task) and individual sentences (on the 'dictation' task) and then typed what they had heard. Assuming that the time the student spent after hearing the input and before responding was spent planning for performance, the researchers inferred advance preparation on the basis of the amount of time elapsed between the end of the input and the time that the student pressed the first key to begin to answer. An indicator of the degree to which each student used advance preparation was obtained by having the computer store the time it took to respond to each item, and calculating the mean 'time-to-begin' by dividing each student's total by the total number of items he or she had completed (Jamieson & Chapelle, 1987).

Other strategies were also assessed in the same task (Jamieson & Chapelle, 1987). Students were able to edit the response they had typed by deleting, inserting, and changing characters or words before it was evaluated by the computer. This behavior, documented in the records kept by the computer, was considered an indicator of monitoring output, in the sense described by Krashen (1982), Bialystok (1981), and O'Malley, Chamot, Stewner-Manzanares, Kupper, and Russo (1985). The number of times a student edited was divided by the total number of items the student completed to obtain the average number of times a student edited in the completed items. Another strategy assessed during this task was 'monitoring input,' as defined by Bialystok (1981): reflecting on the formal aspects of a message as it is comprehended. The dictation tasks allowed learners to listen to the input as many times as they wanted to before attempting to type it. The demands of the task required students to focus on formal aspects of the input. Therefore, when students had not comprehended a sentence or word the first time it was presented and they requested to hear it one or more times, those requests were used as evidence for monitoring input.

A final example illustrates how the computer was used to assess the degree of automaticity of learners' second language processing.

Automaticity in language processing is hypothesized to be indicative of language knowledge efficiently stored for expedient retrieval; as an aspect of the target language is better learned, restructuring of knowledge occurs, making access more automatic and therefore quicker (McLaughlin, 1987; 1990). In an experiment designed to investigate the degree to which subjects responded to a grammaticality judgement task using implicit or explicit grammatical knowledge, Hagen (1994) used a computer program to present items to subjects and to time their responses. Crucial to the interpretation of time-to-respond in this case was the learners' understanding that they were to respond as quickly as they could – a task demand the researcher had to make clear to the subjects. Hulstijn (2000) describes ongoing research in which response times will be used as an indicator of speed of semantic processing, which is to be investigated as a predictor of reading comprehension in a longitudinal study. The use of the computer on such experiments makes possible assessment of automaticity through response times in addition to response accuracy that is typically assessed (e.g., DeKeyser, 1997).

This collection of individual efforts to improve assessment in SLA research through the use of the computer is at the stage where CALL was in the 1960s. No consistent conceptual groundwork has been laid for constructing, using, or evaluating the unique potentials offered, and in fact the issues have not even been explored. Examination of the past work is a first step. However, learning from and building upon this research requires an evaluative perspective that can examine the quality of assessment methods and probe issues that must be clarified to improve upon them.

Evaluation of CASLR for assessment

Evaluation of new forms of assessments such as those used in CASLR requires reexamination of the tenets of measurement theory. In SLA research, this means that the characteristics of constructs assessed need to be made explicit (Bachman & Cohen, 1998). A construct is defined as a meaningful interpretation of the learners' performance; it is what is inferred on the basis of observed evidence. When performance such as the amount of time the learner waits before responding to a question is interpreted as an advanced preparation strategy, *advanced preparation* is a construct. When learners' queries to an on-line dictionary are interpreted as a level of vocabulary ability, *vocabulary ability* is a construct. Since evaluation of assessments in SLA research draws upon the same principles of validation that were outlined in Chapter 4, the quality of the assessments can be evaluated first through the logical usefulness analysis, and then through empirical evidence.

A logical usefulness analysis

An example of a logical usefulness analysis for a CASLR task is developed through examination of the task used to assess advance preparation in the study by Jamieson and Chapelle (1987). Each of the six qualities of usefulness is examined in terms of the researchers' judgement about the task to be used for assessment of the advance preparation strategy (Table 5.3).

The reliability of the indicators obtained for advance preparation was expected to be adequate because the construct was hypothesized to be consistent across time, and the task itself was not expected to introduce unmotivated variance because of its consistency. The construct validity of the advance preparation assessment is supported by the clear construct definition of advance preparation and the apparent appropriateness of the measure. The researchers justified the use of the measure as follows:

[A]dvance preparation was inferred by the amount of time it took for the student to press the first key of his or her answer. O'Malley et al. (1985) defined advance preparation as a metacognitive strategy that means 'planning for and rehearsing linguistic components necessary for an upcoming language task.' (p. 33). The student behavior of consistently waiting before answering may indicate the degree to which he or she was engaging in preparation to answer. (Jamieson & Chapelle, 1987: 531)

Authenticity needs to be considered from two perspectives. The task was authentic with respect to other language learning tasks that the learners were exposed to because it *was* one such task. The students routinely practiced their listening by completing dictation tasks. On the other hand, relative to the language and tasks outside the classroom, the tasks consisting of word or sentence-length dictations were not authentic. The interactiveness would be evaluated as low because there was little integration among the aspects of language knowledge and strategies while completing the task due to the short independent items comprising the dictation.

The impact of the assessment on the students was minimal because it was carried out unobtrusively. Potential impact on the profession was assessed to be positive in the early 1980s when the data were collected because the research was intended to chart new and useful territory in computer-assisted SLA research. The practicality of the assessment was assessed very positively at the time and place where it occurred because the infrastructure was in place to implement the

Table 5.3. *Summary of a usefulness analysis for assessment of advance preparation*

Quality	Judgement
Reliability	The construct is hypothesized to be consistent over time and the task is not expected to introduce any construct unmotivated variance.
Construct validity	The construct is clearly defined and the procedure for assessing the construct appears appropriate.
Authenticity	The activity was authentic relative to learners' normal class assignments, but not relative to language use outside the classroom.
Interactiveness	The activity requires little interaction among aspects of language knowledge and strategies, and only narrow aspects of language knowledge (e.g., phonology, syntax).
Impact	The assessment was unobtrusive and conducted during normal class work; it did not produce a score which would affect their grades. Therefore, it would be expected to have little impact on students and teachers. It would affect the SLA profession to the extent that the research is read, and drawn upon, in subsequent work.
Practicality	Given the technology and personnel resources, the assessment was very practical at the time and location where it was conducted.

data collection in a program where the learners were already using the necessary materials.

Empirical usefulness analysis

Since the corresponding empirical usefulness analysis is constructed retrospectively, data for all aspects of usefulness were not gathered, so only data about reliability and construct validity are discussed. The reliability was estimated as the degree of internal consistency of the assessment. A sufficient degree of consistency was found in strategy use over a six-week period to provide evidence that a construct was being assessed through the observed data. 'Mean working-style scores from six randomly selected weeks were treated like 6-item scales on which . . . reliability estimates were made' ($\alpha = .72$ and .82 on the two activities; Jamieson & Chapelle, 1987: 535). Construct validity was supported to some extent through the theoretically predicted correlation with a style variable 'reflectivity–impulsivity.' Advance preparation was significantly, positively related to reflectivity ($r=.50$; $p<.001$); we would expect that this strategy 'would logically be associated with the slow, careful aspect of the reflective learner' (Jamieson & Chapelle, 1987: 538).

Despite this justification, however, there remain alternative explanations for learners waiting before responding (e.g., looking up a word in a dictionary). In retrospect, several other lines of construct validity evidence could have been gathered. First, ideally, evidence consisting of learners' verbal reports might indicate that they were thinking about and planning what they would type between the time they heard the input and the time they began to respond. Second, the authors might also have provided correlations not only with a measure of a related construct but also with another measure of the same construct. The other measure would have assessed advance preparation through a different method of measurement to ensure that performance was the same regardless of the context in which it was measured. Third, some form of experimental data could also contribute to the validity argument. For example, an experiment might compare response latency data of participants who had been trained to stop and plan with those who were told not to think before responding. If performance reflected the expected patterns for the two groups, results could be used as justification for making inferences about advance preparation from performance.

In addition to the additional construct validity argument, the usefulness analysis requires empirical data pertaining to authenticity, interactiveness, impact, and practicality. These were not examined systematically in the original research, but methods of investigation are described in Chapter 4.

Usefulness issues in CASLR assessments

The usefulness analysis obviously expands the scope of evaluative criteria that have been considered for assessment in CASLR. By so doing, it raises issues that have to be sorted out if CASLR assessments are to contribute to research and practice. The most critical of these, of course, is related to construct validity.

Construct validity

Assessments made through CASLR seem to invite a larger degree of scepticism than those using other means. This scepticism provides an opportunity to clarify issues that are important for all assessments in

SLA research, particularly the inter-related issues of construct definition and construct validity evidence.

The types of constructs investigated in SLA research can be thought to encompass a relatively broad or narrow scope, depending how they are defined (Chapelle, 1998c). A *trait-oriented* definition covers a large domain because it conceptualizes an attribute of an individual as independent of the context in which it is observed. A trait-oriented approach to defining the strategy 'monitoring' would define it as something that is done all of the time regardless of whether a person is listening to an academic lecture, writing an e-mail message to a colleague, or speaking to a close friend. A trait-oriented construct definition assumes that a researcher will be able to generalize the inferences made about a construct on the basis of performance on a test (i.e., performance in one context) to inferences about the construct in other contexts. In other words, if an individual is found to be a strong monitor user on the basis of a test of monitoring, the trait definition would assume that the individual would be a strong monitor user in the other contexts mentioned above.

Theoretical constructs defined more narrowly take an *interactionalist* perspective. An interactionalist definition views an attribute of an individual as dependent in part on the characteristics of the context in which it is observed. From an interactionalist approach, 'monitoring' would not be defined in a global sense. Instead, the definition would refer to 'monitoring while listening to academic lectures' for example. The definition of the strategy would have to include the contexts in which the strategy is used. To interpret results of a test of 'monitoring while listening to academic lectures,' the researcher would generalize results only to monitoring in this context. In short, the distinction between the two approaches rests on how far the strategy definition assumes the researchers can generalize the results of strategy assessment.

Both approaches to strategy definition have been used in computer-assisted strategy research. The assessment of 'advance preparation' described above illustrates a trait-oriented definition in computer-assisted strategy research (Jamieson & Chapelle, 1987). The strategy is defined in a general way; even though the definition mentions the word 'task,' it does not refer to any particular task, implying that the strategy is conceived as one that could apply equally to a linguistic task in any context. Advance preparation was measured as described above through response latency in an instructional setting in which learners were expected to be working at their own pace. The inferences made on the basis of summed response latencies were the degree to which the language learner was an advance preparer in general, rather than the degree to which he or she used advance preparation while working on the CALL materials. Accordingly, the scores for advance preparation were used in this research context to investigate the relationship between this strategy and other variables, which were also defined in a context-independent manner.

The assessment of 'resourcing' provides an example of an inter-actionalist approach to strategy definition (Chapelle & Mizuno, 1989). It is defined in this research as a learner's use of target language reference materials in learner-controlled CALL materials. The definition is interactionalist because it includes the 'learner-controlled CALL materials' as the context to which inferences about the strategy use generalize. Measurement of the strategy was calculated by tabulating the number of times the learners requested help per unit of activity (defined by construction of one sentence). The inferences were intended to be limited to contexts of learner-controlled CALL, and the scores were used to evaluate the value of offering learners optional help in learner-controlled CALL. Table 5.4 outlines the key characteristics of these examples of trait and interactionalist construct definitions.

These differences in approaches do not delineate right from wrong ways of approaching construct definition. Instead, they are different ways of conceptualizing the measurement problem. The point is that the construct needs to be defined in a way that the scope of the generalizability is made clear. The nature of the definition also influences the way in which empirical construct validity studies are conceptualized and interpreted.

The need for construct validation in CASLR is evident, particularly in cases where inferences about the same construct have been drawn on the basis of performance on different tasks, and where similar behaviors have been used as evidence for different constructs. For example, the assessment of automaticity has been accomplished in different ways. Hagen (1994) used response times on a grammaticality judgement task. Doughty and Fought (1984) operationalized controlled and automatic processing by documenting students' requests or non-requests for help from a computer program while they were working on grammar items. In other cases, the same performance across studies is used as evidence for different constructs. For example, Hagen's interpretation of response times as automaticity is different than Jamieson and Chapelle's interpretation of response times as advance preparation.

The need for construct validation is equally evident in studies in

Table 5.4. *Examples of trait and interactionalist approaches to defining L2 strategies*

	Trait-oriented definition	Interactionalist definition
Example	advance preparation (Jamieson & Chapelle, 1987)	resourcing (Chapelle & Mizuno, 1989)
Definition	'planning for and rehearsing linguistic components necessary to carry out an upcoming linguistic task' (O'Malley *et al.*, 1985)	'use of target language reference materials' (Chapelle & Mizuno, 1989: 28–29) in the context of controlled CALL materials (1989: 26)
Measurement	the amount of time (to .5 second accuracy) between the time that a prompt was given (in a CALL activity) and the time that the student began to respond (averaged over the number of items that student responded to over the course of the semester)	the frequency of the number of requests for help a student made divided by the number of sentences the student produced in a sentence constructing and editing CALL activity (help = dictionary, semantic/ pragmatic facts, and grammar)
Inference	performance was assumed to indicate the degree to which the learner was an 'advance preparer'	performance was assumed to indicate the degree to which learners used resourcing within the learner-controlled CALL activity
Use	to investigate the relationship between advance preparation and cognitive style as well as the relationship between advance preparation and subsequent language proficiency	to investigate the extent to which learners use resourcing in a set of learner-controlled CALL activities for practicing grammar and editing (as a means of evaluating the pedagogical potential of optional help)

which justification for construct validity rests on the authors' judgemental analysis of the construct meaning of observed performance. For example, in the study of the learners' use of resourcing strategies in a sentence-constructing task, the authors used the following justification: 'The computer provides help only upon request so students must ask for the help they need when they need it. Students' requests for help are [therefore] evidence of their use of resourcing'

(Chapelle & Mizuno, 1989: 28). This is an important logical justification, but the need remains to provide some empirical evidence for validity as well.

The methods outlined for empirical construct validation offer some possible directions. First, the researchers might have consulted learners' verbal reports indicating that learners had chosen help in order to assist with the sentence construction task, rather than for other purposes (e.g., to see what the help looked like). Second, they could have demonstrated consistency in the use of help over the several weeks the activity was used. Third, they might have supplied correlations between help use on their learner-controlled CALL activity and help use on another learner-controlled CALL activity. To act as correlational validity evidence for the interactionalist definition of the strategy, the covariate must be similar to the original assessment in terms of assessing resourcing *in learner-controlled CALL* as well. Fourth, they could have used an experimental study comparing subjects who had been trained to use help with those who were not told to use help.

In short, construct validity refers to the justifications provided for interpretations and therefore can be evaluated as a strong or weak argument for particular inferences. The type of justifications are chosen from several possibilities. Decisions about what kind of evidence to consider in a construct validity argument for a CASLR assessment depend on the way that the construct is defined in the research. The appropriate scope for generalization is critical for all assessments, but those based on CASLR raise particularly salient questions because of the need to interpret any influences of computer delivery on performance.

Reliability

The reliability of assessments in SLA research needs to be considered in view of construct theory. In the example of advance preparation, the expected strong reliability of the assessment across time was hypothesized because of the trait-type definition of advance preparation. Reliability was important in this case because scores from the assessment were to be used to calculate correlations with other tests. In other cases, reliability may be less important; moreover, it may be impossible to hypothesize strong reliability across different tasks and across time because some strategies may be expected to vary across tasks and time. In other words, the assessment of reliability of performance on CASLR assessments needs to be considered in a way that is motivated by the construct theory of what is being assessed.

Authenticity and interactiveness

CASLR assessments hold strong potential for authenticity because they can be built into instructional materials that are seen by learners to be a normal and useful part of their learning. As researchers gain a deeper understanding of how the learner's perception of the situation affects performance (e.g., Bruner, 1990; Coughlan & Duff, 1994), they become more interested in investigating the learner's behavior as it is situated within the context of interest – the language or content area classrooms where learning occurs, rather than in laboratories where an experimental rubric may be the learner's primary focus or out-of-class situations where communicative pressures may override learning. The majority of the assessments exemplified in this chapter were built into instructional materials, and therefore provide a model for future assessments that are strong in authenticity. Their degree of interactiveness can be strengthened by looking toward instructional materials with a clear meaning focus.

Impact and practicality

Researchers using CASLR in the past have suggested that impact of the assessment on the students was minimal because learners' attention was dedicated to the instructional task while data were collected unobtrusively. However, this observation barely scratches the surface of the impact-related issues for CASLR. One has to consider the possibility that learners' knowledge of data collection may disturb some students, particularly those who are less accustomed to using the computer. Learners obviously have the right to refuse to have data gathered during instruction in order to preclude negative impact. The more interesting and demanding issue, however, is the need to use assessments made during instruction to improve instruction. An assessment of learners' level of vocabulary knowledge during the writing process might best be used as input for subsequent vocabulary instruction. An assessment of monitoring or resourcing strategies might be used for strategy instruction. These possibilities have been hinted at throughout the history of CASLA, but CASLR assessments might also move the profession forward by experimenting with some of these potentials. The final chapter suggests that CASLR projects become practical as ongoing concerns in an environment in which teaching, testing, and research practices are integrated into a single program.

These usefulness issues are relevant to all measurements in SLA research, but CASLR assessments bring them into sharper focus. In general, researchers seem to be quicker to be critical of the meaning of performance within a computer-assisted task than they are with other SLA research tasks. Moreover, the precision of the data that can be gathered by a computer program and the well-defined algorithms that can be written to analyze some data direct researchers' attention to new questions about the meaning of inferences. The data the computer gathers can be used as evidence of processes (either processing during the task or longitudinal processes), and therefore offer a stimulating challenge to the problems of data interpretation.

Progress in data interpretation clearly rests on a synthesis of approaches from language testing and SLA research, but in order to see how the two areas can synthesize, it is also necessary to acknowledge the complementarity between language testing and SLA research. First, SLA researchers tend to focus on assessment of specific aspects of language abilities whereas educational uses of assessments often measure more broadly defined constructs. For example, an SLA researcher might measure 'knowledge of relative clauses' whereas an educational assessment might measure 'grammatical ability.' A second and related difference is the greater interest of SLA researchers in assessment of processing aspects of language ability relative to educational language testers, who have tended to define constructs in terms of static abilities. For example, in SLA research, assessment may need to measure *automaticity of access to linguistic knowledge* and would do so on the basis of response time to a prompt. Educational tests would be more likely to assess *linguistic knowledge* and would do so on the basis of number of correct responses to questions. Third, in practice SLA researchers are often interested in assessment for the purpose of detecting change in specific aspects of ability over time. This need motivates interest in assessments that are sensitive to change. The value of these complementary perspectives is taken up in the final chapter.

Conclusion

Early attempts at constructing CASLR for assessment have demonstrated their potential for investigating some questions of interest in SLA such as assessment of learners' language knowledge and strategies. The perspective taken in this chapter was that CASLR used for assessment is governed by the same principles as those of language testing and is therefore subject to the same evaluation principles as those outlined for CALT in Chapter 4. Engaging these fundamental measurement issues is essential if the next generations of CASLR assessment are to move beyond what has been done in the past.

6 Directions for CASLA

The start of the new millennium prompts visions of high-tech solutions to problems in applied linguistics. The past 20 years of research and development in CASLA provide a foundation – if only a fragile one – upon which such solutions might be built. However, past work also clearly demonstrates the need to develop and investigate computer applications from the relevant perspectives in applied linguistics rather than relying solely on work in related fields. To do so it is useful to recognize the overlapping themes running through the three areas discussed in previous chapters. The benefits to be gained through drawing connections among L2 teaching, assessment, and research have begun to be explored in recent volumes in applied linguistics (Bachman & Cohen, 1998; Doughty & Williams, 1998b; Skehan, 1998). The insights offered by these approaches are essential for progress in CASLA because of the need to marshall coherent and detailed professional knowledge to develop, use, and evaluate CASLA tasks. This chapter reviews the shared themes, suggesting how contributions from each area should help to advance knowledge to the benefit of all. Some potential benefits are illustrated through discussion of how software tools might be improved for CASLA.

Overlapping themes

The focus on evaluation issues in the previous chapters pointed to a number of shared perspectives for CALL, CALT, and CASLR. Evaluation of all materials – whether they be for instruction, assessment, or research – is seen as an argument about appropriateness for a particular purpose rather than as a categorical quality judgement. This view, drawn from work in language testing and applied to the other areas, suggested that an argument about the quality of materials for their purpose should be made on the basis of both judgemental and empirical analyses and that evaluative criteria should be based on up-to-date, field-specific criteria and research methods. Criteria outlined in the chapters of this book were developed on the basis of interpretation of current work in L2 instruction, assessment, and research but will need to evolve as this knowledge develops. Whatever the specific criteria, however, they will always need to be applied in view of the purpose of CASLA materials. The centrality of construct validity in CALT and of language learning potential in CALL underscores the point that concerns about language need to be given highest priority despite the many factors to be considered in choosing and developing materials. The criteria for each area also express consistent themes, as summarized in Table 6.1. These point toward ways in which substantive discipline-specific theory and research is needed to guide progress in CASLA.

Reliability and learner fit

Reliability, one criterion for test usefulness, requires test tasks that fall at an appropriate level of difficulty, making it possible to detect the level of ability of the examinee on the construct tested. In most cases, test tasks that all examinees answer correctly and those that are too difficult for all examinees do not contribute to the reliability of the test scores. In part because of the relationship between difficulty and reliability, empirical methods for predicting and estimating item difficulty are a mainstay in testing. In CALL, the difficulty of the materials relative to learners' needs is also important, and is therefore one aspect of learner fit, but in CALL, difficulty has typically been evaluated through judgemental analysis of the teacher. In SLA research, one of the recent themes has been to estimate and control task difficulty through systematic manipulation of task characteristics (e.g., planning time), as well as to explore methods for estimating task difficulty through examination of aspects of performance such as fluency, accuracy and complexity (Skehan, 1998); however, these methods remain to be developed in CASLR. Such measures of difficulty might fruitfully be applied in all areas of CASLA to improve understanding of task difficulty.

In CALL, learner fit refers not only to appropriate difficulty but also to appropriate instructional strategy relative to individual differences. Individual differences other than differences in language ability are considered in language testing from the perspective of how they may influence test performance, thereby contributing to test bias. In all areas, better, more context-specific measures of individual differences are needed. The suggestion from research in SLA and CALL that learner difference variables might be assessed through data gathered while learners work through CASLA tasks may hold promise.

Table 6.1. *Overlapping themes among teaching, testing, and research tasks with their implications*

Theme	Implication for research and development
Reliability and learner fit	Statistical methods from language testing and theoretical principles from SLA research might be applied to estimating task difficulty. Data on learners' working styles may contribute to measurement of individual differences.
Authenticity and generalizability	Use of CALL methods may improve authenticity of language tests and generalizability of SLA research.
Construct validity and operationalization of learning conditions	Definition of language abilities and validation methods from language testing might strengthen the quality of materials for teaching and research. Detailed construct definition from SLA may help to improve scoring routines as well as processing perspectives for construct validation.
Language learning potential and operationalization of learning conditions	Hypotheses about ideal learning conditions are useful for CALL and unobtrusive data collection in instructional settings might be applied for SLA research.
Interactiveness and meaning focus	Tasks with meaning focus from CALL might be applied to CALT and CASLR.
Positive impact	Positive impacts of CALL might also be considered in the investigation of impacts of CALT and CASLR.
Practicality	Software tools serving all areas of CASLA are needed.

Authenticity and generalizability

Authenticity, one concern for language testing and for CALL, is related to generalizability of CASLR. In all three, the issue is the relationship of the task for assessment, learning, or research to tasks of interest beyond the institutional setting. CALL provides software tools and concepts for constructing a variety of authentic tasks, including video input and interactive communication. As computer use continues to increase, more of these activities are authentic relative to tasks outside the classroom (Warschauer, 1999; Hawisher

& Self, 2000). Such tasks may hold potential for expanding the scope of CALT and CASLR. With a few exceptions, CALT and CASLR tasks have tended to adopt a narrow set of practices, modeling themselves on computer-adaptive testing or experimental psychology in part to take advantage of software tools developed for these more general purposes. Authenticity of a test might be improved by creating input which more closely resembles the input test takers encounter in the non-test environment, for example, spoken language accompanied by visual cues. The computer-delivered version of the TOEFL listening test described in Chapter 4 illustrates one project in which the authenticity of a listening test has been improved through the use of images.

Task authenticity in terms of learners' perceptions may be improved for both testing and research tasks if CALL can be used, when appropriate, for assessment and for testing hypotheses about learning conditions. Use of instructional CALL tasks, rather than laboratory tasks, for assessment and for testing hypotheses about instructed SLA opens the possibility of collecting longitudinal data of interest to SLA researchers while learners work on tasks that they perceive as relevant for their learning.

Construct validity and operationalization of learning conditions

Construct validity in language testing and operationalization of learning conditions in research tasks are both critical issues because they refer to the degree to which the theory-based intentions are actually carried out in tasks. Although these issues are in clearest focus within their respective areas, each has important implications for other areas.

Construct validity for CALL and CASLR

Perspectives from language testing may be useful for CALL and CASLR in several ways. Most important, language testing offers the conceptual foundations for defining language constructs, which are often the object of measurement in both CALL research and CASLR. To study learning outcomes successfully in CALL, researchers need to define what learners are to achieve so they can assess the extent to which CALL was successful. This process requires a clear definition of the targeted abilities, and therefore frameworks for ability outlined in language testing research are critical for assessing outcomes. A second construct-related contribution from testing to some types of CALL is conceptual guidance in the design of intelligent tutoring systems which rely on interpretation of learners' performance as evidence of their abilities in order to maintain a student model. Research in artificial intelligence has demonstrated a variety of approaches for modeling learners' knowledge and misconceptions across a number of disciplines, but discipline-specific articulation of the contents of language learner models is needed.

Principles of test design and validation might be considered a third contribution because they specify procedures for defining what is to be measured and how tests can be justified for purposes such as assessment of outcomes. Such procedures would help the CALL researcher refine learning goals to be precise about what is to be acquired. As Skehan put it, 'it is often said in applied linguistics that testing is where the buck stops' (Skehan, 1998: 180). In CALL research, this hasn't been said enough.

SLA research and CALT

Adding to the perspective on construct definition from language testing is the detailed view SLA research offers about L2 processes and knowledge which is necessary to gain more information about learners from computer-assisted tests than what has been gained through proficiency testing. One way of pursuing this objective is through scoring rubrics developed for constructed responses on language tests. Tests requiring learners to produce linguistic output are not used in many settings because they are seen as prohibitively impractical unless computer-assisted response analysis can be implemented. Moreover, if a computer-assisted scoring rubric for test takers' linguistic output can produce a more consistent measure of learners' abilities than human raters and a more precise measure than a dichotomous scoring rubric, then computer-assisted scoring will improve reliability.

A variety of methods exists for evaluating responses (Pusack, 1983), but the most difficult issues in using computer-assisted evaluation of linguistic output go beyond these technical problems to the conceptual ones requiring research directed at defining the inferences about language ability that can be made on the basis of information provided by computer-assisted analysis of linguistic output. This important construct defining research can go unnoticed when test items are scored dichotomously. For example, exploratory work investigating a partial-credit scoring algorithm for responses on a C-test yielded the following observation:

One can evaluate a C-test item as correct or incorrect without hypothesizing the ability responsible for the correct response . . . Decisions about partial correctness, in contrast, cannot be made without knowing the ability the item is intended to measure. For example, in evaluating the C-test items as indicators of productive vocabulary ability, we marked [an incorrect spelling] as partially correct but if we wanted to use that item as an indicator of reading comprehension, we would mark it correct to reflect the test takers' understanding of the previous text. (Chapelle, 1993: 30)

Logical consideration of construct validity includes the following questions. First, 'Is the construct clearly and unambiguously defined?' Second, 'To what extent do the scoring procedures reflect the construct definition?' (Bachman & Palmer, 1996: 150–151)

Both the assignment of multiple scores and partial credit scoring need to be based on a clear specification of the components of language ability required for correct responses, and the criteria for correctness [and levels of partial correctness], which must themselves derive from the definition of the construct to be measured. (Bachman & Palmer, 1996: 201)

Because a construct-motivated scoring program requires an unambiguous construct definition, its development can provide a more detailed perspective on construct validation.

A second way of increasing the amount of information obtained from test scores is to explore the processing perspective taken by some SLA researchers. Process-oriented data – the test taker's timing during task completion, their language, and their observations about their test-taking processes – continue to hold potential for language testing research. Language testing research has tended to focus on the products of performance rather than the processes – and with good reason. Most testing researchers would agree that the complexity inherent in a processing perspective toward language far exceeds what is needed for interpretation of test scores. Despite the propensity of testing researchers to stick to simply stated product-oriented construct definitions, investigation of test-taking processes is one of the ways of investigating construct validity. As a consequence, there is a need to understand the construct meaning of process data. In L2 testing, the relevant processing perspective needs to be derived from SLA research (Skehan, 1998); however, attempts to synthesize research in SLA and language testing are in their infancy (e.g., Bachman, 1989; Bachman & Cohen, 1998; Chapelle, 1994), and a striking discontinuity can exist between the ways in which researchers in the two areas perceive the basic constructs they work with. Synthesis of work in these two areas will require that both expand and revise the ways in which they go about their business;

research and development of computer-assisted language tests creates a strong motivation to do so.

Construct theory based on SLA research needs to work with new psychometric models (Mislevy, 1994; 1995) if substantive theory is ultimately to improve language testing. Typically, testing practices have obscured the details of learners' L2 knowledge and process by recording them as holistically scored performances or dichotomously scored items, which are assumed to fit within a unidimensional psychometric model. Snow and Lohman (1989) point out the distinction between such 'educational-psychometric models' (EPM) and the cognitive information-processing models (CIM) which psychologists use to explain performance, suggesting that the latter are needed to help provide meaningful explanations for test performance.

Language learning potential and operationalization of learning conditions

The particular features defined as contributing to language learning potential in CALL tasks were identified on the basis of some of the learning conditions suggested from second language research. Research recording learners' working styles on CALL may provide fruitful directions for SLA research.

Learning conditions for CALL

Even though much remains to be learned about SLA, existing research results support some hypotheses that are relevant to the design of CALL and its evaluation. Even more promising, however, are the perspectives evident in current SLA research with clear implications for classroom instruction in general, and CALL in particular (e.g., Gass, 1997; R. Ellis, 1999). The discussion of CALL in Chapter 3 attempted to reflect some of these perspectives; however, much more can be accomplished if CALL designers regularly consider CALL task design in view of the conditions hypothesized for SLA. Findings and research methods provide a means to construct and evaluate CALL in a way that can inform SLA research through classroom studies, creating the links that are needed for progress in both areas.

CALL for operationalizing learning conditions

A promising direction for improving the generalizability of SLA research is reflected in studies investigating hypotheses about conditions for learning through CALL. One such study comparing the effects of explicit versus implicit instruction described the materials as follows:

> Throughout the course, the target structures were presented among other input material in communicative settings, in order to increase the authenticity of the course material and to avoid too obvious a focus on the target structures. The target structures were presented in small structured doses. In the selection of topics and activities, the experimental course material resembled genuine (self-study) materials as much as possible.
> (de Graaff, 1997a: 104)

Results of such research investigating acquisition of the L2 by motivated learners in classroom settings are more generalizable to classroom instruction than are results of laboratory experiments. CALL affords a unique opportunity to control the type of instruction received in some aspects of classroom settings. The unobtrusive data collection methods used in some CALL and CASLR research also offer a valuable means of classroom assessment.

Interactiveness and meaning focus

Interactiveness in language testing and meaning focus in CALL both refer to the learners' engagement of their communicative language ability to express and interpret meaning through language. Such engagement is different than that involved in completing multiple-choice grammar or vocabulary items on a test or a structural transformation exercise in a grammar class. Neither language testing nor task-based instruction theory view such engagement as possible only outside the classroom; instead, each challenges task developers to construct tasks in a way that fosters learners' meaningful use of language. The quality of tasks conducive to 'language engagement,' van Lier suggests, is determined 'by characteristics of the *language* (contextuality, accessibility), of the *interaction* (particularly various forms of assistance that may be available), and of the *sociocultural setting*. All in all, if we were to put the quality in one word, it would have to be something like "participatability"' (van Lier, 1996: 47–48; emphasis in original).

Work in CALL has prioritized construction of learning tasks with participatability, to the point that some argue that the inherent value of CALL is that many learners like it. CALL tasks can be designed to allow learners to work with materials of interest to them in project-based, collaborative tasks. Possibilities for applying engagement-provoking concepts from CALL to CALT or CASLR have barely been explored. One of many that might be experimented with would include assessment tasks that select, or ask test takers to choose, topics from a database of appropriate materials. Choice of appropriate topical input would be expected to increase the test takers' involvement of topic knowledge and interest, thereby increasing the interactiveness of the task.

Positive impact

In teaching, testing, and research, professionals strive to conduct practice in a manner that is responsible to learners and teachers. At the same time, theory and research on change and innovation in language education demonstrates the systemic influences of any single change (Markcc, 1997). In language testing, the impact of computer-delivered tests is often framed in negative terms: How might the use of computers in testing disadvantage learners who have not had a lot of experience using computers? The other side of the impact question, however, asks how the introduction of CALT might ultimately advantage learners by prompting them to seek opportunities to learn to use computers, by encouraging teachers to help learners become computer literate, and by motivating language programs to maintain up-to-date computers and computer literacy opportunities.

This other side is evident from work in CALL that argues for the value of CALL on the basis that it helps to increase computer literacy in addition to literacy in the target language at a time when both literacies may be critical for success. The following is a telling comment from a Brazilian teacher in a study of perceptions about English teaching in Brazil:

> There are three kinds of illiterate people: the one who does not know how to read or write [in Portuguese], the one who does not know how to use the computer, and the one who does not know English. (Cox & de Assis-Peterson, 1999: 442).

So pervasive is the use of technology by successful, educated people in Brazil that this teacher's comment about the instrumental role of English apparently had to be coupled with one about technological literacy, even though technology was not an issue brought up in the question. Those who focus their CALL research on the impacts of CALL emphasize the need to examine 'how computer-mediated language and literacy practices are shaped by broader institutional and social factors, as well as what these new practices mean from the perspective of the learner' (Warschauer, 1998: 760). Research on the impact of computer-assisted practices in testing and research might also consider such questions.

Practicality

Practicality, which is affected by similar issues across the three areas, is among the most persistent stumbling blocks for the future of CASLA. Examination of practicality issues reveals disheartening disjunctures among expectations and realities. Administrators at some institutions appear to beam with excitement over the money-making potential of computer-assisted distance education, whereas in reality a good distance education course for language is likely to be more time intensive to produce and deliver than is face-to-face instruction. Testing programs aim to launch computer-based tests with the intent of modernizing language testing practices only to find the expense prohibitive, field resources sparse, and psychometric theory fragile. Teachers embark on developing labs and materials for computer-assisted learning only to find that their program has devoted no resources to the necessary technical support. Researchers set out to build sophisticated systems for the study and banking of interlanguage data only to find the computational linguistic issues are beyond their resources. Through a combination of blind enthusiasm and lack of experience with technology, practicality issues are regularly set aside until a project is underway.

One result has been the failure of research projects targeted at developing sophisticated applications for SLA to see their way into practice. Instead, the majority of CASLA in widespread use is developed using general-purpose software. What may help to con-tribute to the practicality of more sophisticated software in the future are efforts to develop software tools that can be used across areas. This suggestion goes beyond the general ideal that assessment be integrated with instruction, that L2 testing and SLA research seek common ground, or that instruction benefit from theory and research in SLA. It suggests that the design of software tools be informed by all three areas and that they be designed to serve in all three areas. The next section outlines some of the overlapping needs and suggested directions.

CASLA software development

Progress in CASLA over the next years will depend on the sophistica-tion of software available and the ability of applied linguists to use it. Therefore it is necessary to at least touch on the software issues implied by discussion in the previous chapters even though they have not been the focus of this book. An appreciation of software implications of the above themes for CASLA requires basic knowledge about how software for CASLA is developed through the use of *high-level programming languages, specific-purpose programming languages, tools, and templates.* What is needed for progress in CASLA is development of the latter three – specific-purpose software – targeted directly to the needs of second language teaching, testing, and research. Without such tools, software is prohibitively difficult and time-consuming to author, as seen in many projects dedicated to developing intelligent tutoring systems over the past decades (e.g., Holland, Kaplan, & Sams, 1995). Some such authoring systems have been developed for CALL (e.g., Brücher, 1993); in fact, the pages of CALL journals are filled with descriptions of CALL authoring systems. However, work remains in putting these to use in other CASLA applications in addition to strengthening the theoretical and empirical bases for decisions about the capabilities built into authoring tools.

Many of the software concepts used in CASLA are the familiar ones from wordprocessing, e-mail, and the World Wide Web. Word-processing relies on software editors that allow for entry and manipulation (e.g., cut and paste) of text into a computer file. Similar editors are used to enter and edit computer programs into files. Files are the units used to hold not only wordprocessor documents but also computer programs and Web pages. E-mail has made the concept of network-based computer-mediated communication an everyday practice. The World Wide Web provides examples of media, including text, graphics, audio, and video as well as links, which allow the user to navigate through information on the Web by interaction with a browser (e.g., Netscape). Users of the Web and other electronically stored linguistic data such as documents in wordprocessing software are familiar with conducting searches for particular words or phrases. These familiar technologies provide a good foundation for discussion of the software concepts underlying CASLA, but they need to be augmented by a brief discussion of the software that makes word processors, e-mail, Web documents, and CASLA applications work: programming languages.

A programming language consists of a set of commands which provide a means for a programmer to communicate with a computer to make it perform the desired functions. Programming languages, like natural languages, consist of a lexicon governed by syntactic and discourse rules. Programming languages such as BASIC, C, Java or LISP, are not interpreted directly by any computer. Each of these is a high-level language which adheres to rules that a person can learn to use, but which must be translated into machine language in order for the computer to interpret it. When a new language such as Java is

Human: software author → High-level programming language → Translation software → Machine language → Computer

Figure 6.1 Facets of the communication process from the author to the computer

designed, the developers must construct the software required to translate from the high-level language to machine language. Figure 6.1 illustrates the sequential process beginning with communication of the author's intentions into a high-level programming language, which is translated into the machine language that the computer can recognize and act on.

From this perspective, the high-level language meets the user half way by allowing the author to use a system whose linguistic rules are learnable rather than a set of machine language instructions that require coding actions at an extreme level of detail. A high-level language consists of statements such as the few lines of Java code illustrated in Figure 6.2, which says that if the value for the variable 'grade' is greater than or equal to 60, then print 'Passed' on the computer screen; otherwise, print 'Failed' on the computer screen. This short segment does not include any information about how the value of 'grade' is to be assigned; it is not a complete program, but just a few lines from a program that illustrate the type of language a programmer uses to specify the decisions that the computer is to make on the basis of a value.

If a general-purpose programming language meets the author half way, it is evident that some *specific-purpose programming languages* and *software tools* can be thought of as meeting the author more than half way, as illustrated in Figure 6.3. One approach appears in tools that allow the author to write descriptive statements of how objects are to be displayed or interpreted rather than spelling out the step-by-step instructions that the computer is to follow in accom-

```
if ( grade >= 60 )
          System.out.println( 'Passed' );
else
          System.out.println( 'Failed' );
```

Figure 6.2 Lines from a Java program (Deitel & Deitel, 1997: 68)

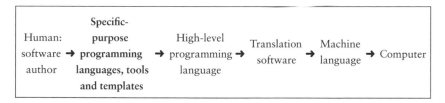

Figure 6.3 Software tools within the communication process from the author to the computer

plishing the display or interpretation. Writing about this approach for specific-purpose software for linguists, Shieber (1985) explained the need:

> Programming languages fail miserably as linguistic tools because they encode analyses at the wrong level linguistically . . . Linguists typically state grammars *declaratively*, as rules, filters and constraints – that is they describe *what* the strings of the language are like; with few exceptions, programming languages are too procedural to be used in this manner – they describe *how* to compute [or recognize] certain properties of a string.
> (1985: 194)

The best known of the linguistic software tools is Prolog, which allows the author to describe sentences with a notation similar to a phrase structure grammar specifying the form against which input sentences are to be evaluated to test their grammaticality next to the linguist's grammar (Pereira & Shieber, 1987). Prolog and other linguists' tools have been used for CASLA; however, more common are the general-purpose tools such as HTML, which provide a mechanism for authors to specify how text and graphics, for example, should be displayed on the screen. These mark-up or declarative tools are also incorporated into some of the specific-purpose programming languages designed for educational applications and used for CALL. However, development of specific-purpose tools ideally suited to CASLA will require a precise description of the software needs in CASLA.

A second approach to meeting the author more than half way is the authoring *template*. The person who builds a template can use a high-level programming language to construct a system that prompts the author for the material to be included. For example, computer-adaptive tests are often developed using such templates, which prompt for the question, the alternatives, the correct response, and the essential statistical information about the item. Computer-assisted learning is often developed using template systems such as

Authorware or *WebCT*.[1] Such systems prompt the author, who inputs decisions about the types of questions to be asked and their content, for example. Research tasks are developed through templates designed for psychological experiments (Hulstijn, 2000). These types of templates developed for a range of testing, instruction and research purposes do not make it practical to pursue some of the needs identified above.

Needs for CASLA authoring tools

Based on the needs identified through the overlapping themes in CASLA, development would benefit from software tools that allow for functions beyond those typically included in software for education or psychology. Ideally, software for CASLA would provide the capabilities summarized in Table 6.2.

A means for estimating task difficulty

A focal issue in SLA and language testing research is the need to better understand task difficulty (Norris *et al.*, 1998). This issue has been explored using a variety of empirical methods. Language testing research points to the promise of considering the complexity of the linguistic input used in a task in addition to other factors. As theory of task difficulty develops, ideally some task conditions contributing to task difficulty can be estimated automatically. For example, a finding that texts with more abstract vocabulary are more difficult as reading tests would point to one variable in a text that might be identified through automatic analysis of such texts. At the item level, research investigating difficulty of cloze items might contribute to predicting difficulty of potential cloze items, from which the author might develop a test. These tools need to be available within an authoring environment for development of a variety of CASLA tasks.

Functions for analysis of learners' linguistic output

A number of needs could be met by software tools that analyze the language produced by the learner. First, empirical research investigating task authenticity relies in part on estimating the quality of the language the learner produces while engaging in the task. Second, if the quality of learners' constructed responses are to be quantified for

---

[1] The *CALICO Journal: Special Issue on Language Courseware Design*, 17 (1), 1999, provides a number of current examples of approaches to courseware development used by professionals.

Table 6.2. *Functions needed in CASLA software tools and their purposes*

Software function	Purpose
Estimate task difficulty	Select appropriate level of tasks for intended learners Provide feedback for task development
Analyze learners' linguistic output	Assess task authenticity Assign point values and collect diagnostic data for language assessment Gather learner data for research
Analyze the language of objects (written text, audio, video)	Assess task authenticity Assess linguistic complexity of input
Support objects ordered in a database	Store examples of a variety of content and genres to be used directly or as models for language tasks
Gather process-oriented data	Assess participation in learning condition Assess learner characteristics in specific tasks
Support a structure for a learner model	Store learner data for intelligent tutoring, assessment Explore the nature of learner models for research
Author learning conditions	Develop tasks for instruction and research that operationalize SLA theory

language assessment, the language must first be analyzed. Third, SLA research relying on careful analysis of learners' language would use the results of such analysis as a means of gaining evidence about a learners' grammatical competence. Fourth, CALL software that identifies errors in learners' comprehensible output would require such analyses.

Over the past 40 years, computational linguists have refined methods for computer recognition and analysis of proficient-speaker language (Winograd, 1983; Gazdar & Mellish, 1989). These methods of parsing, or recognizing the structural constituents in, natural language apply in principle to recognition of non-proficient-speaker language and therefore have been applied to some CASLA projects, including SLA research (e.g., Huiskens, Coppen, & Jagtman, 1991) and CALL activities (e.g., Hull *et al.*, 1987; Imlah & du Boulay, 1985). In short, analysis of learners' language is a difficult, but not impossible, problem that has been the topic of research in CALL for many years and more recently in SLA research, as well. As mentioned in the first chapter, many CALL projects have implemented error recognition, and this can be done in a number of ways (Pusack, 1983). The problem is that after years of such research and small-scale development efforts, software tools that work across applications have barely benefited from this experience. Tools available to CASLA developers need to include these capabilities.

Functions for analyzing the language of objects

'Objects' in computer programming can refer to segments of video, still images, text, and audio, each of which can be called upon by a computer program or by a user writing a program or a document. The fact that objects consisting of different types of items can all be treated in the same way by a computer program is useful for programming, but to use such objects efficiently in applied linguistics, objects need to be tagged with particular types of relevant contextual and linguistic information. The types of analyses conducted by corpus linguists (Biber, Conrad & Reppen, 1998) concerning the lexicogrammatical characteristics of texts, for example, would be useful in selecting texts for testing and instruction. As research such as Gruba's (1999) develops farther, it may also be possible to analyze video in a way that is useful for task construction. These analyses need to be accessible as functions within a set of authoring tools so that the author can select a video from existing electronic sources, and have the function return useful information about its contents.

A means of organizing and creating objects

An increasing number of linguistic 'objects' exists in cyberspace, but to use these for work in CASLA, they need to be not only analyzed, but also gathered and organized. A database structure is needed to organize texts, audio, and videos according to registers. Moreover, functions are needed to develop such objects into the genres used in applied linguistics. The most obvious example is the function that changes a text into a cloze test. Even the simplest authoring software of the early 1980s provided this option. Such a function takes as input an electronic text and responses to questions such as where the first blank should start, whether it is to be a rational or fixed-ratio cloze, and how many items should be created, for example. The output is a cloze exercise that is presented to the student on a screen with instructions and an example and a set of correct responses for the computer to use in judging learners' responses. These and functions for producing other types of language tasks need to be accessible within a single system.

A means for gathering process-oriented data

Across all three areas, the need exists to explore context-appropriate, process-oriented assessment of learner characteristics. To do so requires a means for gathering and storing data about learners' working processes in CASLA tasks. Such a store of information is essential for assessing the degree and manner of task participation to help in interpreting CALL and SLA research. Software exists in many authoring packages for tracking learners' performance, but ideally the future will see such capabilities built into a complete suite of tools for CASLA. Research using such tools will hopefully make it possible for them to be developed into more sophisticated aids that not only gather specific information, but also combine that information in ways that are meaningful in SLA.

A structure for learner models

The learner models described in research on intelligent tutoring systems are databases in which information (or a summary of information) gathered about learners' performance is stored. The research in this area has focused on models that can be called upon by the computer program to inform subsequent instruction. However, these models might be equally or more valuable for assessment of language ability, particularly for purposes requiring detailed, longitudinal assessment (e.g., diagnostic, progress, or research). At present, however, such models have been constructed for individual projects with little discussion of the form of the databases, and no attempt to construct tools that would allow for an author to plug a student model into another piece of software. Such a plug-in might allow the author to set certain parameters such as the particular aspects of language the database was to collect, and the form for the output, which would reveal the information in the database in such a way that it could be used by another program. This type of tool would build upon the existing knowledge about learner models of L2 knowledge, and provide a means for others to experiment with them.

A means for authoring learning conditions

Two hypotheses about SLA drawn from interactionist research serve as an example of how theoretical work might inform options provided in authoring software. One suggestion from SLA theory is that software should provide a means for the author to make salient key linguistic characteristics of the target language input that learners receive. Linguistic features can be made salient in CALL activities by highlighting them in a different color when they appear in writing on the screen. When they occur in aural input, phrases containing linguistic elements may be transcribed on the screen, again with highlighting of the significant parts. The authoring software needs to provide a mark-up language that will allow for particular items to be marked for possible highlighting. However, marking up input is time-consuming, and so what the tools should do is to provide some automatic tagging and mark-up.

A useful mark-up scheme might allow the learner to select a grammatical feature, such as adverbial phrases, for highlighting. One might also request that the language exhibiting interpersonal functions (e.g., evaluation) or textual functions (e.g., cohesion through similarity chains of related lexical items) be highlighted. If this or other relevant tagging were automatically provided by the authoring software, the CALL developer would be in the position to construct materials that would make salient upon demand the linguistic features of interest at any given time (Mills, 2000). This type of sophisticated tagging of texts is what corpus linguists do, but these practices would need to be built into authoring software specifically for developing CASLA.

The second suggestion would be for authoring software to provide a means for offering modifications of linguistic input to learners. Modifications of input can come in the form of repetition, simplification through restatements, non-verbal cues, decreased speed, reference materials, or change of input mode, for example. Authoring tools need to provide these types of modifications automatically. For example, the software author would enter or choose a text to be used for comprehension materials in a language learning task. The authoring software would contain the linguistic analysis procedures to construct the oral version of the text, simplifications, and definitions, for example. These modifications would stay in the background until the learner called them to help with comprehension.

A means for delivering CASLA via a familiar interface

All the capabilities described above have been implemented in one project or another on a variety of platforms over the past 30 years. Part of the explanation for the lack of accumulated results in this area is that the platforms for implementing CASLA have constantly changed. The fact that software capabilities change with the start of each new project has had the effect of encouraging researchers to start anew when beginning a project rather than seeking existing software modules (or conceptual models) that can be built upon. As has always been the case with CALL, the technical expertise of developers differs depending on the computer and software they have been using for development. If SLA software tools are to be created in a way that allows them to be plugged into various applications successfully, standardization issues will need to be solved through the construction of updatable tools implemented on the Web and accessible by all standard browsers. This standardization is also needed for the accumulation of knowledge and for the education of future CASLA developers and users.

Conclusion

The accomplishments and needs of CALL, CALT, and CASLR make apparent that the three areas hold complementary strengths and needs. Identifying areas of overlap is useful because progress in CASLA rests in part on progress with the software tools available for producing the desired applications. These software needs seem to be basic to the infrastructure of developing CASLA to a level that reaches the sophistication of other computer applications of the early 21st century. At the same time, the process of developing software reveals that the state of knowledge in the field will benefit from its application to these detailed issues within a domain which offers extensive opportunity for empirical investigation. The CASLA retrospective of the 20th century portrays it as a time of idiosyncratic learning, quirky software development, and naive experimentation. The results set the stage for the 21st century to host collaborative development of infrastructure for large-scale use by the profession, and research essential for development of theories of language assessment and acquisition.

References

Abraham, R. (1985). Field independence-dependence and the teaching of grammar. *TESOL Quarterly, 19*, 689–702.

Abraham, R., & Liou, H.-C. (1991). Interaction generated by three computer programs: analysis of functions of spoken language. In P. Dunkel (ed.), *Computer-Assisted Language Learning and Testing: Research Issues and Practice* (pp. 85–109). New York: Newbury House.

Ackerman, T. (1994). Creating a test information profile for a two-dimensional latent space. *Applied Psychological Measurement, 18* (3), 257–275.

Adair-Hauck, B., Willingham-McLain, L., & Yongs, B. E. (2000). Evaluating the integrations of technology and second language learning. *CALICO Journal, 17* (2), 269–306.

Ahmad, K., Corbett, G., Rogers, M., & Sussex, R. (1985). *Computers, Language Learning, and Language Teaching*. Cambridge: Cambridge University Press.

Aijmer, K., & Altenberg, B. (eds.) (1991). *English Corpus Linguistics: Studies in Honour of Jan Svartvik*. London: Longman.

Alderman, D. (1978). *Evaluation of the TICCIT Computer-Assisted Instructional System in the Community College*. ERIC ED 167 606.

Alderson, J. C. (1990). Learner-centred testing through computers: institutional issues in individual assessment. In J. H. A. L. de Jong & D. K. Stevenson (eds.), *Individualizing the Assessment of Language Abilities* (pp. 20–27). Clevedon, England: Multilingual Matters.

Alderson, J. C. (1991). Innovation in language testing: can the microcomputer help? *Language Testing Update: Special Report No. 1.*

Alderson, J. C. (1993). Judgements in language testing. In D. Douglas & C. Chapelle (eds.), *A New Decade of Language Testing Research* (pp. 46–57). Alexandria, VA: TESOL.

Alderson, J. C. (2000). *Assessing Reading*. Cambridge: Cambridge University Press.

Alderson, J. C., & Hamp-Lyons, L. (1996). TOEFL preparation courses: a study of washback. *Language Testing, 13* (3), 280–297.

Alderson, J. C., & Wall, D. (1993). Does washback exist? *Applied Linguistics, 14*, 115–129.

Allwright, D. (1988). *Observation in the Language Classroom.* London: Longman.

Allwright, D., & Bailey, K. M. (1991). *Focus on the Language Classroom: An Introduction to Classroom Research for Language Teachers.* Cambridge: Cambridge University Press.

Altenberg, B. (1991). A bibliography of publications relating to English computer corpora. In S. Johansson & A.-B. Stenstrom (eds.), *English Computer Corpora: Selected Papers and Research Guide* (pp. 355–396). Berlin: Mouton de Gruyter.

American Educational Research Association (AERA), American Psychological Association (APA), National Council on Measurement in Education (NCME) (1999). *Standards for Educational and Psychological Testing.* Washington, DC: AERA.

Ashworth, D. & Stelovsky, J. (1989). Kanji City: an exploration of hypermedia applications for CALL. *CALICO Journal,* 6 (4), 27–39.

Atkinson, R. C. (1972). Optimizing the learning of a second-language vocabulary. *Journal of Experimental Psychology,* 96, 124–129.

Atkinson, R. C., & Hansen, D. N. (1966). Computer-assisted instruction in initial reading: the Stanford project. *Reading Research Quarterly,* 2 (1), 5–25.

Ayoun, D. (2000). Web-based elicitation tasks in SLA research. *Language Learning & Technology,* 3 (2), 77–98.

Ayoun, D. (forthcoming). The role of negative feedback in French L2 acquisition. *Modern Language Journal.*

Bachman, L. F. (1989). Language testing–SLA research interfaces. *Annual Review of Applied Linguistics,* 9, 193–209.

Bachman, L. F. (1990). *Fundamental Considerations in Language Testing.* Oxford: Oxford University Press.

Bachman, L. F. (1997). Generalizability theory. In C. Clapham and D. Corson (eds.), *Encyclopedia of Language and Education. Volume 7: Language Testing and Assessment* (pp. 255–262). Dordrecht, The Netherlands: Kluwer Academic Publishers.

Bachman, L. F., & Cohen, A. D. (eds.) (1998). *Interfaces between Second Language Acquisition and Language Testing Research.* Cambridge: Cambridge University Press.

Bachman, L. F., Kunnan, A., Vanniarajan, S., & Lynch, B. (1988). Task and ability analysis as a basis for examining content and construct comparability in two EFL proficiency tests. *Language Testing,* 5, 128–159.

Bachman, L. F., Lynch, B., & Mason, M. (1995). Investigating variability in tasks and rater judgements in a performance test of foreign language speaking. *Language Testing,* 12 (2), 238–258.

Bachman, L. F., & Palmer, A. S. (1982). The construct validation of some components of communicative competence. *TESOL Quarterly,* 16 (4), 449–465.

Bachman, L. F., & Palmer, A. S. (1996). *Language Testing in Practice.* Oxford: Oxford University Press.

Baecker, R. M., & Buxton, W. A. S. (1987). *Readings in Human–Computer Interaction: A Multidisciplinary Approach*. San Mateo, CA: Morgan Kaufmann Publishers.

Bailey, K. (1996). Working for washback: a review of the washback concept in language testing. *Language Testing*, 13 (3), 257–279.

Bailin, A. (ed.) (1991). *CALICO Journal: Special Issue on ICALI Research*, 9 (1).

Baker, F. B. (1989). Computer technology in test construction and processing. In R. L. Linn (ed.), *Educational Measurement* (3rd edn) (pp. 409–428). New York: Macmillan Publishing.

Beauvois, M. H. (1992). Computer-assisted classroom discussion in the foreign language classroom: conversation in slow motion. *Foreign Language Annals*, 25 (5), 455–464.

Beauvois, M. H. (1997). High-tech, high-touch: from discussion to composition in the networked classroom. *Computer Assisted Language Learning*, 10 (1), 57–69.

Beauvois, M. H. (1998). E-talk: Computer-assisted classroom discussion – attitudes and motivation. In J. Swaffar, S. Romano, P. Markley, & K. Arens (eds.), *Language Learning Online: Theory and Practice in the ESL and the L2 Computer Classroom* (pp. 99–120). Austin, TX: Labyrinth Publications.

Bejar, I. I. (1985). Speculations on the future of test design. In S. Embretson (ed.), *Test Design – Developments in Psychology and Psychometrics* (pp. 279–294). Orlando, FA: Academic Press.

Bejar, I., & Braun, H. (1994). On the synergy between assessment and instruction: early lessons from computer-based simulations. *Machine-Mediated Learning*, 4 (1), 5–25.

Bennett, R. E. (1993). On the meanings of constructed responses. In R. E. Bennett & W. C. Ward (eds.), *Construction Versus Choice in Cognitive Measurement: Issues in Constructed Response, Performance Testing, and Portfolio Assessment* (pp. 1–27). Hillsdale, NJ: Lawrence Erlbaum Associates.

Bennett, R. E., Rock, D. A., Braun, H. I., Frye, D., Spohrer, J. C., & Soloway, E. (1990). The relationship of expert-system scored constrained free-response items to multiple-choice and open-ended items. *Applied Psychological Measurement*, 14 (2), 151–162.

Bennett, R. E., Ward, W. C., Rock, D. A., & LaHart, C. (1990). *Toward a Framework for Constructed-Response Item*. Report No. ETS RR-90–7. Princeton, NJ: Educational Testing Service.

Bialystok, E. (1981). The role of linguistic knowledge in second language use. *Studies in Second Language Acquisition*, 4, 31–45.

Biber, D. (1988). *Variation Across Speech and Writing*. Cambridge: Cambridge University Press.

Biber, D., Conrad, S., & Reppen, R. (1994). Corpus-based approaches to issues in applied linguistics. *Applied Linguistics*, 15 (2), 169–189.

Biber, D., Conrad, S., & Reppen, R. (1998). *Corpus Linguistics*. Cambridge: Cambridge University Press.

Biber, D., Johansson, S., Leech, G., Conrad, S., & Finegan, E. (1999). *The Longman Grammar of Spoken and Written English.* Harlow: Pearson Education.

Birenbaum, M., & Tatsuoka, K. K. (1987). Open-ended versus multiple-choice response formats – It does make a difference for diagnostic purposes. *Applied Psychological Measurement,* 11 (4), 385–395.

Blais, J.-G., & Laurier, M. D. (1993). The dimensionality of a placement test from several analytical perspectives. *Language Testing,* 10 (2), 72–98.

Bland, S. K., Noblitt, J. S., Armington, S., & Gay, G. (1990). The naive lexical hypothesis: evidence from computer-assisted language learning. *Modern Language Journal,* 74, 440– 450.

Bley-Vroman, R., & Chaudron, C. (1994). Elicited imitation as a measure of second language competence. In E. E. Tarone, S. M. Gass, & A. D. Cohen (eds.), *Research Methodology in Second-Language Acquisition* (pp. 245–261). Hillsdale, NJ: Lawrence Erlbaum Associates.

Borrás I., & Lafayette, R. C. (1994). Effects of multimedia courseware subtitling on the speaking performance of college students of French. *The Modern Language Journal,* 78, 61–75.

Bowers, C. A. (1988). *The Cultural Dimensions of Educational Computing.* New York: Teachers College Press.

Bowers, C. A. (1993). Critical essays on education, modernity, and the recovery of the ecological imperative. New York: Teachers College Press.

Boyle, T. A., Smith, W. F., Eckert, R. G. (1976). Computer-mediated testing: a branched program achievement test. *Modern Language Journal,* 60, 428–440.

Bradin, C. (1999). CALL issues: instructional aspects of software evaluation. In J. Egbert & E. Hanson-Smith (eds.), *Computer-Enhanced Language Learning* (pp. 159–175). Alexandria, VA: TESOL Publications.

Brock, M. N. (1993). Three disk based text analysers and the ESL writer. *Journal of Second Language Writing,* 2 (1), 19–40.

Brock, M. N. (1995). Computerised text analysis: roots and research. *Computer Assisted Language Learning,* 8 (2–3), 227–258.

Brown, J. D., & Hudson, T. (1998). The alternatives in language assessment. *TESOL Quarterly,* 32 (4), 653–675.

Brown, A., & Iwashita, N. (1996). The role of language background in the validation of a computer-adaptive test. *System,* 24 (2), 199–206.

Brown, G., & Yule, G. (1983). *Discourse Analysis.* Cambridge: Cambridge University Press.

Brown, H. D. (1980). *Principles of Language Learning and Teaching.* Englewood Cliffs, NJ: Prentice-Hall.

Brown, J. D. (1997). Computers in language testing: present research and some future directions. *Language Learning & Technology,* 1 (1), 44–59.

Brown, J. S., & Duguid, P. (2000). *The Social Life of Information.* Boston: Harvard Business School Press.

Brown, J. S., Burton, R. B., & de Kleer, J. (1982). Pedagogical, natural language and knowledge engineering techniques in SOPHIE I, II and III. In D. Sleeman & J. S. Brown (eds.), *Intelligent Tutoring Systems* (pp. 227–282). New York: Academic Press.

Bruce, B., Peyton, J. K., & Batson, T. (eds.) (1993). *Network-Based Classrooms: Promises and Realities*. Cambridge: Cambridge University Press.

Brücher, K. H. (1993). On the performance and efficiency of authoring programs in CALL. *CALICO Journal*, 11 (2), 5–20.

Brumfit, C., Phillips, M., & Skehan, P. (eds.) (1986). *Computers in English Language Teaching: A View from the Classroom*. Oxford: Pergamon Press.

Bruner, C. (1990). *Acts of Meaning*. Cambridge, MA: Harvard University Press.

Buck, G. (1991). The testing of listening comprehension: an introspective study. *Language Testing*, 8 (1), 67–91.

Burstein, J., Frase, L., Ginther, A., & Grant, L. (1996). Technologies for language assessment. *Annual Review of Applied Linguistics*, 16, 240–260.

Burston, J. (1998). From CD-ROM to the WWW: coming full circle. *CALICO Journal*, 15 (1–3), 67–74.

Burston, J., & Monville-Burston, M. (1995). Practical design and implementation considerations of a computer-adaptive foreign language test: the Monash/Melbourne French CAT. *CALICO Journal*, 13 (1), 26–46.

Burton, R. R., & Brown, J. S. (1982). An investigation of computer coaching for informal learning activities. In D. Sleeman & J. S. Brown (eds.), *Intelligent Tutoring Systems* (pp. 79–98). New York: Academic Press.

CALICO Journal: Special Issue on Language Courseware Design, 17 (1), 1999.

Cameron, K. C., Dodd, W. S., & Rahtz, S. P. Q. (eds.) (1986). *Computers and Modern Language Studies*. West Sussex, England: Ellis Horwood.

Canale, M. (1986). The promise and threat of computerized adaptive assessment of reading comprehension. In C. Stansfield (ed.), *Technology and Language Testing* (pp. 30–45). Washington DC: TESOL Publications.

Canale, M. (1987). Language assessment: the method is the message. In D. Tannen & J. E. Alatis (eds.), *The Interdependence of Theory, Data, and Application* (pp. 249–262). Washington, DC: Georgetown University Press.

Carroll, J. B. (1989). Intellectual abilities and aptitudes. In A. Lesgold & R. Glaser (eds.), *Foundations for a Psychology of Education* (pp. 137–197). Hillsdale, NJ: Lawrence Erlbaum.

Chalhoub-Deville, M. (1997). Theoretical models, assessment frameworks, and test construction. *Language Testing*, 14 (1), 3–22.

Chalhoub-Deville, M. (ed.), (1999). *Development and Research in Computer Adaptive Language Testing* (pp. 122–135). Cambridge: University of Cambridge Examinations Syndicate / Cambridge University Press.

Chalhoub-Deville, M., Alcaya, C., & Lozier, V. M. (1996). *An Operational Framework for Constructing a Computer-Adaptive Test of L2 Reading Ability: Theoretical and Practical Issues.* CARLA Working Paper Series #1. Minneapolis, MN: Center for the Advanced Research on Language Acquisition, University of Minnesota.

Chang, K.-Y. R., & Smith, W. F. (1991). Cooperative learning and CALL/ IVD in beginning Spanish: an experiment. *The Modern Language Journal, 75,* 205–211.

Chanier, T., Pengelly, M., Twidale, M., & Self, J. (1992). Conceptual modelling in error analysis in computer-assisted language learning systems. In M. L. Swartz & M. Yazdani (eds.), *Intelligent Tutoring Systems for Foreign Language Learning* (pp. 125–150). Berlin: Springer Verlag.

Chapelle, C. A. (1993). Issues in computer-assisted analysis for one-word test responses, *Assessment – Transactions of the 1993 CALICO Symposium* (pp. 28–32). Durham, NC: CALICO.

Chapelle, C. A. (1994). Are C-tests valid measures for L2 vocabulary research? *Second Language Research,* 10 (2), 157–187.

Chapelle, C. A. (1997). CALL in the year 2000: still in search of research paradigms? *Language Learning and Technology,* 2 (1), 22–34.

Chapelle, C. A. (1998a). Multimedia CALL: lessons to be learned from research on instructed SLA. *Language Learning & Technology,* 2 (1), 22–34.

Chapelle, C. A. (1998b). Research issues: analysis of interaction sequences in computer-assisted language learning. *TESOL Quarterly,* 32 (4), 753–757.

Chapelle, C. (1998c). Construct definition and validity inquiry in SLA research. In L. F. Bachman & A. D. Cohen (eds.), *Second Language Acquisition and Language Testing Interfaces* (pp. 32–70). Cambridge: Cambridge University Press.

Chapelle, C. A. (1999a). Investigation of 'authentic L2 tasks.' In J. Egbert & E. Hanson-Smith (eds.), *Computer-Enhanced Language Learning* (pp. 101–115). Alexandria, VA: TESOL Publications.

Chapelle, C. A. (1999b). Validity in language assessment. *Annual Review of Applied Linguistics,* 19, 254–272.

Chapelle, C., & Abraham, R. (1990). Cloze method: what difference does it make? *Language Testing,* 7 (2), 121–145.

Chapelle, C. A., & Green, P. (1992). Field independence/dependence in second language acquisition research. *Language Learning,* 42, 47–83.

Chapelle, C., & Jamieson, J. (1983). Language lessons on the PLATO IV system. *System,* 11 (1), 13–20.

Chapelle, C., & Jamieson, J. (1986). Computer-assisted language learning as a predictor of success in acquiring English as a second language. *TESOL Quarterly,* 20, 27–46.

Chapelle, C., & Jamieson, J. (1989). Research trends in computer-assisted language learning. In M. Pennington (ed.), *Teaching Language with Computers: The State of the Art* (pp. 47–59). San Francisco: Athelstan Publishing.

Chapelle, C., & Jamieson, J. (1991). Internal and external validity issues in research on CALL effectiveness. In P. Dunkel (ed.), *Computer Assisted Language Learning and Testing – Research Issues and Practice* (pp. 37–57). New York: Harper & Row-Newbury House.

Chapelle, C., Jamieson, J., & Park, Y. (1996). Second language classroom research traditions: how does CALL fit? In M. Pennington (ed.), *The Power of CALL*. Houston, TX: Athelstan Publishing.

Chapelle, C., & Mizuno, S. (1989). Students' strategies with learner-controlled CALL. *CALICO Journal*, 7 (2), 25–47.

Chapelle, C., & Read, J. (1996). Toward a framework for vocabulary assessment. Work-in-progress presentation at the Language Testing Research Colloquium, Tampere, Finland, July 31–August 3, 1996.

Charniak, E., & McDermott, D. (1985). *Introduction to Artificial Intelligence*. Reading, MA: Addison-Wesley Publishing.

Chaudron, C. (1988). *Second Language Classrooms: Research on Teaching and Learning*. Cambridge: Cambridge University Press.

Choi, I.-C., & Bachman, L. F. (1992). An investigation into the adequacy of three IRT models for data from two EFL reading rests. *Language Testing*, 9 (1), 51–78.

Chun, D. M. (1994). Using computer networking to facilitate the acquisition of interactive competence. *System*, 22, 1, 17–31.

Chun, D. M., & Brandl, K. K. (1992). Beyond form-based drill and practice: meaning-enhancing CALL on the Macintosh. *Foreign Language Annals*, 25 (3), 255–267.

Chun, D. M., & Plass, J. L. (1996). Effects of multimedia annotations on vocabulary acquisition. *The Modern Language Journal*, 80, 183–198.

Clark, J. L. D. (1989). Multipurpose language tests: is a conceptual and operational synthesis possible? In J. E. Alatis (ed.), *Georgetown University Round Table on Language and Linguistics, 1989. Language Teaching, Testing, and Technology: Lessons from the Past with a View toward the Future* (pp. 206–215). Washington, DC: Georgetown University Press.

Clark, R. E. (1985). Confounding in educational computing research. *Journal of Educational Computing Research*, 1 (2), 137–148.

Clark, R. E. (1994). Media will never influence learning. *Educational Technology Research & Development*, 42 (2), 21–29.

Cohen, A. (1984). On taking language tests: what the students report. *Language Testing*, 1 (1), 70–81.

Cohen, A. (1998). Strategies and processes in test-taking and SLA. In L. F. Bachman & A. D. Cohen (eds.), *Interfaces between Second Language Acquisition and Language Testing Research*. Cambridge: Cambridge University Press.

Cohen, A., & Hosenfeld, C. (1981). Some uses of mentalistic data in second language research. *Language Learning*, 31, 285–313.

Cole, N. (1993). Comments on Chapters 1–3. In N. Frederiksen, R. J. Mislevy, & I. I. Bejar (eds.), *Test Theory for a New Generation of Tests* (pp. 72–77). Hillsdale, NJ: Lawrence Erlbaum Associates.

Coleman, D. W. (1985). TERRI: A CALL lesson simulating conversational interaction. *System*, 13 (3), 247–252.

Collett, M. J. (1980). Examples of applications of computers to modern language study 1: the step-wise development of programs in reading, grammar, and vocabulary. *System*, 8, 195–204.

Collentine, J. (2000). Insights into the construction of grammatical knowledge provided by user-behavior tracking technologies. *Language Learning & Technology*, 3 (2), 44–57.

Collombet-Sankey, N. (1997). Surfing the net to acquire communicative competence and cultural knowledge. In R. Debski, J. Gassin, & M. Smith (eds.), *Language Learning Through Social Computing. Applied Linguistics of Australia Occasional Papers Number 16* (pp. 141–158). Melbourne: University of Melbourne Printing Services.

Computers and the Humanities: Special Issue on Intelligent Computer-Assisted Language Instruction, 23 (1), 1989.

Coniam, D. (1996). Computerized dictation for assessing listening proficiency. *CALICO Journal*, 13 (2–3), 73–85.

Coniam, D. (1998). Interactive evaluation of listening comprehension: how the context may help. *Computer-Assisted Language Learning*, 11 (1), 35–53.

Conrad, S. (2000). Will corpus linguistics revolutionize grammar teaching in the 21st century? *TESOL Quarterly*, 34 (3), 548–560.

Cook, V. (1985). Bridging the gap between computers and language teaching. In C. Brumfit, M. Phillips, & P. Skehan (eds.), *Computers in English Language Teaching: A View from the Classroom* (pp. 13–24). Oxford: Pergamon Press.

Cook, V. (1988). Designing a BASIC parser for CALL. *CALICO Journal*, 6 (1), 50–67.

Corbel, C. (1993). *Computer-Enhanced Language Assessment*. In G. Brindley (Series Editor), Research Report Series 2. Sydney, Australia: National Centre for English Language Teaching and Research, Maquarie University.

Coughlan, P., & Duff, P. A. (1994). Same task, different activities: Analysis of SLA task from an activity theory perspective. In J. P. Lantolf & G. A. Appel (eds.), *Vygotskian Approaches to Second Language Research* (pp. 173–191). Norwood, NJ: Ablex Publishing.

Cox, M. I. P., & de Assis-Peterson, A. A. (1999). Critical pedagogy in ELT: images of Brazilian teachers of English. *TESOL Quarterly*, 33 (3), 433–452.

Craven, M.-L., Sinyor, R., & Paramskas, D. (eds.) (1990). *CALL: Papers and Reports*. La Jolla, CA: Athelstan Publishing.

Crook, C. (1994). *Computers and the Collaborative Experience of Learning*. London: Routledge.

Crookes, G. (1989). Planning and interlanguage variation. *Studies in Second Language Acquisition*, 11, 367–383.

Crookes, G., & Gass, S. (eds.) (1993a). *Tasks in a Pedagogical Context: Integrating Theory and Practice*. Clevedon, England: Multilingual Matters.

Crookes, G., & Gass, S. (eds.) (1993b). *Tasks and language learning: Integrating Theory and Practice*. Clevedon, England: Multilingual Matters.

Culley, G., Mulford, G., & Milbury-Steen, J. (1986). A foreign language adventure game: progress report on an application of AI to language instruction. *CALICO Journal*, 4, 69–94.

Cummins, J., & Sayers, D. (1995). *Brave New Schools: Challenging Cultural Illiteracy through Global Learning Networks*. New York: St. Martin's Press.

Curtin, C., Avner, A., & Provenzano, N. (1981). Computer-based analysis of individual learning characteristics. *Studies in Language Learning*, 3, 201–213.

Davidson, F. (1996). *Principles of Statistical Data Handling*. Thousand Oaks, CA: Sage Publications.

Davies, G. (1985). *Using Computers in Language Learning: A Teacher's Guide* (2nd edn). London: Centre for Information on Language Teaching and Research.

Davies, G. (1989). CALL and NCCALL in the UK: past, present, and future. In W. F. Smith (ed.), *Modern Technology in Foreign Language Education*. Skokie, IL: National Textbook Company.

Davies, G. (1993). CALL in the New Europe: the spirit of cooperation. In P. Liddell (ed.), *CALL: Theory and Application: Proceedings of CCALL2/CCELAO2*. Victoria, Canada: University of Victoria.

Davis, K. (1995). Qualitative theory and methods in applied linguistics research. *TESOL Quarterly*, 29, 127–453.

Day, R. (ed.) (1986). *Talking to Learn: Conversation in Second Language Acquisition*. Rowley, MA: Newbury House.

Debski, R. (1997). Support of creativity and collaboration in the language classroom: a new role for technology. In R. Debski, J. Gaskin, & M. Smith (eds.), *Language Learning Through Social Computing. Applied Linguistics of Australia Occasional Papers Number 16* (pp. 39–65). Melbourne: University of Melbourne Printing Services.

Debski, R., Gassin, J., & Smith, M. (eds.) (1997). *Language Learning through Social Computing: Occasional Papers of the Applied Linguistics Association of Australia, 16*. The University of Melbourne: ALAA & The Horwood Language Centre.

Decker (1976). Computer-aided instruction in French syntax. *Modern Language Journal*, 60 (5&6), 263–267.

de Graaff, R. (1997a). Differential effects of explicit instruction on second language acquisition. Vrije Universiteit, The Netherlands.

de Graaff, R. (1997b). The eXperanto Experiment: effects of explicit instruction on second language acquisition. *Studies in Second Language Acquisition*, 19 (2), 249–276.

Deitel, H. M., & Deitel, P. J. (1997). *Java: How to Program*. Upper Saddle River, NJ: Prentice Hall.

DeKeyser, R. M. (1995). Learning second language grammar rules: an experiment with a miniature linguistic system. *Studies in Second Language Acquisition*, 17 (3), 379–410.

DeKeyser, R. M. (1997). Beyond explicit rule learning: automatizing second language morphosyntax. *Studies in Second Language Acquisition*, 19 (2), 195–221.

Desmarais, L., Duquette, L., Renié, D., & Laurier, M. (1998). Evaluating learning interactions in a multimedia environment. *Computers and the Humanities*, 22, 1–23.

DeSmedt, W. (1995). Herr Kommissar: an ICALL conversation simulator for intermediate German. In Holland, V. M., Kaplan, J., & Sams, M. (eds.), *Intelligent Language Tutors: Theory Shaping Technology* (pp. 153–174). Hillsdale, NJ: Lawrence Erlbaum.

Dick, W., & Carey, L. (1985). *The Systematic Design of Instruction* (2nd edn). Glenview, IL: Scott, Foresman.

Dick, W., & Carey, L. (1996). *The Systematic Design of Instruction* (4th edn). New York: Harper Collins College Publishers.

Doughty, C. (1987). Relating second-language acquisition theory to CALL research and application. In W. F. Smith (ed.), *Modern Media in Foreign Language Education: Theory and Implementation* (pp. 133–167). Lincolnwood, IL: National Textbook Company.

Doughty, C. (1991). Second language instruction does make a difference: evidence from an empirical study of SL relativization. *Studies in Second Language Acquisition*, 13, 431–469.

Doughty, C. (1992). Computer applications in second language acquisition research: design, description, and discovery. In M. Pennington & V. Stevens (eds.), *Computers in Applied Linguistics: An International Perspective* (pp. 127–154). Clevedon, England: Multilingual Matters.

Doughty, C., & Fought, C. (1984). On investigating variable learner response: toward achieving better CALL courseware design. Report from the language analysis project. Philadelphia: University of Pennsylvania. (Cited in Doughty, 1987.)

Doughty, C., & Pica, T. (1986). Information gap tasks: do they facilitate second language acquisition? *TESOL Quarterly*, 20 (2), 305–325.

Doughty, C., & Williams, J. (1998a). Pedagogical choices in focus on form. C. Doughty & J. Williams (eds.), *Focus on Form in Classroom Second Language Acquisition* (pp. 197–261). Cambridge: Cambridge University Press.

Doughty, C., & Williams, J. (eds.) (1998b). *Focus on Form in Classroom Second Language Acquisition*. Cambridge: Cambridge University Press.

Douglas, D. (1995). Developments in language testing. *Annual Review of Applied Linguistics*, 15, 167–187.

Douglas, D. (1998). Testing methods in context-based second language research. In L. F. Bachman & A. D. Cohen (eds.), *Interfaces between Second Language Acquisition and Language Testing Research* (pp. 141–155). Cambridge: Cambridge University Press.

Douglas, D. (2000). *Assessing Languages for Specific Purposes*. Cambridge: Cambridge University Press.

Douglas, D., & Myers, R. K. (2000). Assessing the communication skills of veterinary students: whose criteria? In A. Kunnan (ed.), *Fairness in*

Language Testing. Selected Papers from the 1997 Language Testing Research Colloquium. Cambridge: Cambridge University Press.

Douglas, D., & Selinker, L. (1993). Performance on general vs. field-specific tests of speaking proficiency. In D. Douglas & C. A. Chapelle (eds.), *A New Decade of Language Testing Research* (pp. 235–256). Alexandria, VA: TESOL Publications.

Douglas, S. A. (1995). LingWorlds: an intelligent object-oriented environment for second language tutoring. In V. M. Holland, J. S. Kaplan, & M. R. Sams (eds.), *Intelligent Language Tutors: Theory Shaping Technology* (pp. 201–220). Mahwah, NJ: Lawrence Erlbaum Associates.

Duffy, T. M., & Jonassen, D. H. (1992). Constructivism: new implications for instructional technology. In T. M. Duffy & D. H. Jonassen (eds.), *Constructivism and the Technology of Instruction: A Conversation* (pp. 1–16). Hillsdale, NJ: Lawrence Erlbaum Associates.

Dunkel, P. (1999). Research and development of a computer-adaptive test of listening comprehension in the less commonly-taught language Hausa. In M. Chalhoub-Deville (ed.), *Development and Research in Computer Adaptive Language Testing* (pp. 91–121). Cambridge: University of Cambridge Examinations Syndicate / Cambridge University Press.

Dunkel, P. (1991). The effectiveness of research on computer-assisted instruction and computer-assisted language learning. In P. Dunkel (ed.), *Computer-Assisted Language Learning and Testing: Research Issues and Practice* (pp. 5–36). New York: Newbury House.

Dunkel, P., Henning, G., & Chaudron, C. (1993). The assessment of an L2 listening comprehension construct: a tentative model for test specification and development. *Modern Language Journal*, 77, 180–191.

Duquette, L., Renié, D., & Laurier, M. (1998). The evaluation of vocabulary acquisition when learning French as a second language in a multimedia environment. *Computer Assisted Language Learning*, 11 (1), 3–34.

Durrani, O. (1989). Designer labyrinths: text mazes for language learners. In K. Cameron (ed.), *Computer Assisted Language Learning: Program Structure and Principles* (pp. 38–48). Norwood, NJ: Ablex Publishing.

Egbert, J., Chao, C.-C., & Hanson-Smith, E. (1999). Computer-enhanced language learning environment: An overview. In J. Egbert & E. Hanson-Smith (eds.), *Computer-Enhanced Language Learning* (pp. 1–13). Alexandria, VA: TESOL Publications.

Egbert, J., & Hanson-Smith, E. (eds.) (1999). *Computer-Enhanced Language Learning.* Alexandria, VA: TESOL Publications.

Elling, B. (1995). The Stony Brook 'Experiment' and how it grew: an interview with John R. Russell. *CALICO Journal*, 12 (4), 128–136.

Ellis, N. C. (1995a). The psychology of foreign language vocabulary acquisition: implications for CALL. *Computer Assisted Language Learning*, 8 (2–3), 103–128.

Ellis, N. C. (1995b). Consciousness in second language acquisition: a review of field studies and laboratory experiments. *Language Awareness*, 4 (3), 123–146.

Ellis, R. (1999). *Learning a Second Language through Interaction*. Amsterdam: John Benjamins.

Embretson, S. (1983). Construct validity: construct representation versus nomothetic span. *Psychological Bulletin*, 93 (1), 179–197.

Embretson, S. (ed.) (1985). *Test Design: Developments in Psychology and Psychometrics*. Orlando, FA: Academic Press.

Emihovich, C. (1990). Ask no questions: sociolinguistic issues in experimental and testing contexts. *Linguistics and Education*, 2, 165–183.

Ericsson, K., & Simon, H. (1984). *Protocol Analysis–Verbal Reports as Data*. Cambridge, MA: The MIT Press.

Esling, J. (1991). Researching the effects of networking: evaluating the spoken and written discourse generated by working with CALL. In P. Dunkel (ed.), *Computer-Assisted Language Learning and Testing: Research Issues and Practice* (pp. 111–131). New York: Newbury House.

Færch, C., & Kasper, G. (eds.) (1987). *Introspection in Second Language Research*. Clevedon, England: Multilingual Matters.

Falbel, A. (1991). The computer as a convivial tool. In I. Harel & S. Papert (eds.), *Constructionism* (pp. 29–37). Norwood, NJ: Ablex Publishing.

Farrington, B. (1989). AI: 'Grandeur' or 'Servitude'? In K. Cameron (ed.), *Computer Assisted Language Learning: Program Structure and Principles* (pp. 67–80). Norwood, NJ: Ablex Publishing.

Feldmann, U., & Stemmer, B. (1987). Thin___ aloud a___ retrospective da___ in C-te___ taking: diffe___ languages – diff___ learners – sa___ approaches? In C. Færch & G. Kasper (eds.), *Introspection in Second Language Research* (pp. 251–267). Clevedon, England: Multilingual Matters.

Felshin, S. (1995). The Athena language learning project NLP system: a multilingual system for conversation-based language learning. In V. M. Holland, J. Kaplan, & M. Sams (eds.), *Intelligent Language Tutors: Theory Shaping Technology* (pp. 257–272). Hillsdale, NJ: Lawrence Erlbaum.

Ferrara, K., Brunner, H., & Whittemore, G. (1991). Interactive written discourse as an emergent register. *Written Communication*, 8 (1), 8–34.

Frase, L., Faletti, J., Ginther, A., & Grant, L. (1999). Computer analysis of the TOEFL Test of Written English. TOEFL Research Report RR-64. Princeton, NJ: Educational Testing Service.

Fredricksen, N. (1984). The real test bias: influences of testing on teaching and learning. *American Psychologist*, 39, 193–202.

Fulcher, G. (1996). Testing tasks: issues in task design and the group oral. *Language Testing*, 13 (1), 23–52.

Gagne, R. M., & Glasser, R. (1987). Foundations in learning research. In R. M. Gagne (ed.), *Instructional Technology: Foundations* (pp. 49–83). Hillsdale, NJ: Lawrence Erlbaum Associates.

Garrett, N. (1982). In search of interlanguage: a study of second language acquisition of German syntax. Unpublished doctoral dissertation, University of Illinois.

Garrett, N. (1987). A psycholinguistic perspective on grammar and CALL. In W. F. Smith (ed.), *Modern Media in Foreign Language Education: Theory and Implementation* (pp. 169–196). Lincolnwood, IL: National Textbook Company.

Garside, R., Leech, G., & Sampson, G. (eds.) (1987). *The Computational Analysis of English: A Corpus-Based Approach*. London: Longman.

Gass, S. (1997). *Input, Interaction, and the Second Language Learner*. Mahwah, NJ: Lawrence Erlbaum Associates.

Gass, S. M., & Madden, C. G. (eds.) (1985). *Input in Second Language Acquisition* (pp. 377–393). Rowley, MA: Newbury House.

Gazdar, G., & Mellish, C. (1989). *Natural Language Processing in PROLOG: An Introduction to Computational Linguistics*. Reading, MA: Addison-Wesley.

Gitomer, D. H., Steinberg, L. S., & Mislevy, R. J. (1995). Diagnostic assessment of troubleshooting skill in an Intelligent Tutoring System. In P. D. Nichols, S. F. Chipham, & R. L. Brennan (eds.), *Cognitively Diagnostic Assessment* (pp. 73–101). Hillsdale, NJ: Lawrence Erlbaum Associates.

Glasser, R., Lesgold, A., & Lajoie, S. (1987). Toward a cognitive theory for the measurement of achievement. In R. R. Ronning, J. A. Glover, J. C. Conoley, & J. C. Witt (eds.), *The Influence of Cognitive Psychology on Testing* (pp. 41–85). Hillsdale, NJ: Lawrence Erlbaum Associates.

Goodfellow, R., & Laurillard, D. (1994). Modeling lexical processes in lexical CALL. *CALICO Journal*, 11 (3), 19–46.

Grabinger, S., & Dunlap, J. C. (1996). Links. In P. A. M. Kommers, S. Grabinger, & J. C. Dunlap (eds.), *Hypermedia Learning Environments: Instructional Design and Integration* (pp. 89–114). Mahwah, NJ: Lawrence Erlbaum Associates.

Granger, S. (ed.) (1998). *Learner English on Computer*. London: Longman.

Green, B. F., Bock, R. D., Humphreys, L. B., Linn, R. L., & Reckase, M. D. (1984). Technical guidelines for assessing computer adaptive tests. *Journal of Educational Measurement*, 21, 347–360.

Grotjahn, R. (1986). Test validation and cognitive psychology: some methodological considerations. *Language Testing*, 3, 159–185.

Grotjahn, R. (1987). On the methodological basis of introspective methods. In C. Færch & G. Kasper (eds.), *Introspection in Second Language Research* (pp. 54–81). Clevedon, England: Multilingual Matters.

Gruba, P. (1999). The role of digital video media in second language listening comprehension. Unpublished Ph.D. dissertation, Department of Linguistics and Applied Linguistics, University of Melbourne.

Guillory, H. G. (1998). The effects of keyword captions to authentic French video on learner comprehension. *CALICO*, 15 (1–3), 89–108.

Hagen, L. K. (1994). Constructs and measurement in parameter models of second language acquisition. In E. E. Tarone, S. M. Gass, & A. D. Cohen (eds.), *Research Methodology in Second-Language Acquisition* (pp. 61–87). Hillsdale, NJ: Lawrence Erlbaum Associates.

Hainline, D. (ed.) (1987). *New Developments in Computer-Assisted Language Learning*. New York: Nichols Publishing Company.

Hardisty, D., & Windeatt, S. (1989). *CALL*. Oxford: Oxford University Press.

Hart, B. & Daisley, M. (1994). Computers and composition in Japan: notes on real and virtual literacies. Computers and *Composition*, 11, 37–47.

Hart, R. S. (ed.) (1981a). *Studies in Language Learning: Special Issue on the PLATO System and Language Study, 3*. Urbana, IL: Language Learning Laboratory, University of Illinois at Urbana-Champaign.

Hart, R. S. (1981b). Language study and the PLATO system. *Studies in Language Learning*, 3, 1–24.

Hartman, K., Neuwirth, C. M., Kiesler, S., Sproull, L., Cochran, C., Palmquist, M., & Zubrow, D. (1991). Patterns of social interaction and learning to write: some effects of network technologies. *Written Communication*, 8 (1), 79–113.

Hawisher, G. E., & Self, C. L. (eds.) (2000). *Global Literacies and the World-Wide Web*. London: Routledge.

Hegelheimer, V. (1998). Effects of textual glosses and sentence-level audio glosses on online reading comprehension and vocabulary recall. Unpublished doctoral dissertation, Department of Educational Psychology, College of Education, University of Illinois, Urbana, IL.

Hegelheimer, V., & Chapelle, C. A. (2000). Methodological issues in research on computer–learner interactions in CALL. *Language Learning & Technology*, 4 (1), 41–59.

Hendricks, H., Bennion, J. L., & Larson, J. (1983). Technology and language learning at BYU. *CALICO Journal*, 1 (3), 22–30 & 46.

Henning, G. (1992). Dimensionality and construct validity of language tests. *Language Testing*, 9 (1), 1–11.

Henning, G., Anbar, M., Helm, C., & D'Arcy, S. (1993). Computer-assisted testing of reading comprehension: comparisons among multiple-choice and open-ended scoring methods. In D. Douglas & C. Chapelle (eds.), *A New Decade of Language Testing Research* (pp. 123–131). Alexandria, VA: TESOL.

Henning, G., Hudson, T., & Turner, J. (1985). Item response theory and the assumption of unidimensionality. *Language Testing*, 2 (2), 141–154.

Henri, F. (1992). Computer conferencing and content analysis. In A. R. Kaye (ed.), *Collaborative Learning through Computer Conferencing* (pp. 117–136). Berlin: Springer Verlag.

Higgins, J. (1988). *Language, Learners, and Computers*. London: Longman.

Higgins, J. & Johns, T. (1984). *Computers in Language Learning*. Reading, MA: Addison-Wesley.

Hirst, G. (1991). Does conversation analysis have a role in computational linguistics? *Computational Linguistics*, 17 (2), 212–227.

Holland, M. (1994). Intelligent tutors for foreign languages: how parsers and lexical semantics can help learners and assess learning. In R. M. Kaplan & J. C. Burstein (eds.), *Proceedings of the Educational Testing Service Conference on Natural Language Processing Techniques and Technology in Assessment and Education* (pp. 95–107). Princeton, NJ: Educational Testing Service.

Holland, V. M. (1995). Introduction: the case for intelligent CALL. In V. M. Holland, J. D. Kaplan, & M. R. Sams (eds.), *Intelligent Language Tutors: Theory Shaping Technology* (pp. vii–xvi). Mahwah, NJ: Lawrence Erlbaum Associates.

Holland, V. M., Kaplan, J., & Sams, M. (eds.) (1995). *Intelligent Language Tutors: Theory Shaping Technology*. Hillsdale, NJ: Lawrence Erlbaum Associates.

Holmes, G., & Kidd, M. E. (1982). Second language learning and computers. *The Canadian Modern Language Review*, 38 (3), 503–516.

Hope, G., Taylor, H., & Pusack, J. (1984). *Using Computers in Teaching Foreign Languages*. Orlando, FA: Harcourt Brace Jovanovich.

Hosenfeld, C. (1976). Learning about learning: discovering our students' strategies. *Foreign Language Annals*, 9, 117–129.

Hsu, J. (1994). Computer assisted language learning (CALL): the effect of ESL students' use of interactional modifications on listening comprehension. Unpublished doctoral dissertation, Department of Curriculum and Instruction, College of Education, Iowa State University, Ames, IA.

Hsu, J., Chapelle, C., & Thompson, A. (1993). Exploratory environments: what are they and do students explore? *Journal of Educational Computing Research*, 9 (1), 1–15.

Huiskens, L., Coppen, P. A., & Jagtman, M. (1991). Developing a tool for the description of language acquisition. *Linguistics*, 29, 451–479.

Hull, G., Ball, C., Fox, J., Levin, L., & McCutchen, D. (1987). Computer detection of errors in natural language texts: some research on pattern-matching. *Computers and the Humanities*, 21, 103–118.

Hulstijn, J. (1993). When do foreign language learners look up the meaning of unfamiliar words? The influence of task and learner variables. *Modern Language Journal*, 77 (2), 139–147.

Hulstijn, J. H. (1997). Second language acquisition research in the laboratory: possibilities and limitations. *Studies in Second Language Acquisition*, 19, 131–143.

Hulstijn, J. H. (2000). The use of computer technology in experimental studies of some techniques and some ongoing studies. *Language Learning & Technology*, 3 (2), 32–43.

Hunt, E. (1987). Science, technology and intelligence. In R. R. Ronning, J. A. Glover, J. C. Conoley, & J. C. Witt (eds.), *The Influence of Cognitive Psychology on Testing* (pp. 11–39). Hillsdale, NJ: Lawrence Erlbaum Associates.

Imlah, W. G., & du Boulay, J. B. H. (1985). Robust natural language parsing in computer-assisted language instruction. *System*, 13 (2), 137–147.

Jagtman, M. (1994). *Computer-Aided Syntactic Analysis of Interlanguage Data*. Netherlands: Proefschrift Nijmegen.

Jagtman, M., Coppen, P.-A., & Bongaerts, T. (1991). Computational linguistics and language development data: some methodological considerations. *Gramma, tijdschrift voor taalkunde*, 15 (2), 127–146.

Jamieson, J., & Chapelle, C. (1987). Working styles on computers as evidence of second language learning strategies. *Language Learning*, 37, 523–544.

Jamieson, J., & Chapelle, C. (1988). Using CALL effectively: what do we need to know about students? *System*, 16, 151–162.

Jamieson, J., Campbell, J., Norfleet, L., & Berbisada, N. (1993). Reliability of a computerized scoring routine for an open-ended task. *System*, 21 (3), 305–322.

Johansson, S. (1991). Times change and so do corpora. In K. Aijmer & B. Altenberg (eds.), *English Corpus Linguistics: Studies in Honour of Jan Svartvik* (pp. 305–314). London: Longman.

Johns, T. (1994). From printout to handout: grammar and vocabulary teaching in the context of data-driven learning. In T. Odlin (ed.), *Perspectives on Pedagogical Grammar* (pp. 293–313). Cambridge: Cambridge University Press.

Johns, T. (1986). Micro-Concord, a language learner's research tool. *System*, 14 (2), 151–162.

Johnson, D. (1991). Second language and content learning with computers: Research in the role of social factors. In P. Dunkel (ed.), *Computer-Assisted Language Learning and Testing: Research Issues and Practice* (pp. 61–83). New York: Newbury House.

Johnson, K. E. (1995). *Understanding Communication in Second Language Classrooms*. Cambridge: Cambridge University Press.

Jonassen, D. H. (1985). Learning strategies: a new educational technology. *Programmed Learning and Educational Technology*, 22 (1), 26–34.

Jones, C. (1986). It's not so much the program, more what you do with it: the importance of methodology in CALL. *System*, 14 (2), 171–178.

Jones, C., & Fortescue, S. (1987). *Using Computers in the Language Classroom*. London: Longman.

Kasper, G. (1997). Can pragmatic competence be taught? (NFLRC NetWork #6) Honolulu, HI: Second Language Teaching & Curriculum Center, University of Hawai'i at Manoa. [Available at *http://www.lll.hawaii.edu/nflrc/NetWorks/NW6/* retrieved May 22, 2000]

Kaya-Carton, E., Carton, A. S., & Dandonoli, P. (1991). Developing a computer-adaptive test of French reading proficiency. Computer-adaptive testing of listening and reading comprehension: the Brigham Young approach. In P. Dunkel (ed.), *Computer-Assisted Language Learning and Testing: Research Issues and Practice* (pp. 259–284) New York: Newbury House.

Kelm, O. R. (1992). The use of synchronous computer networks in second language instruction: a preliminary report. *Foreign Language Annals*, 25 (5), 441–454.

Kemp, F. (1993). The origins of ENFI, network theory, and computer-based collaborative writing instruction at the University of Texas. In B. Bruce, J. K. Peyton, & T. Batson (eds.), *Network-Based Classrooms: Promises and Realities* (pp. 161–180). Cambridge: Cambridge University Press.

Kenning, M. J., & Kenning, M.-M. (1983). *Introduction to Computer-Assisted Language Teaching*. Oxford: Oxford University Press.

Kenning M.-M., & Kenning, M. J. (1990). *Computers and Language*

Learning: Current Theory and Practice. West Sussex, England: Ellis Horwood.

Kern, R. G. (1995). Restructuring classroom interaction with networked computers: effects on quantity and characteristics of language production. *Modern Language Journal,* 79, 457–476.

Kerr, S. T. (1996). Toward a sociology of educational technology. In D. H. Jonassen, *Handbook of Research for Educational Communications and Technology* (pp. 143–169). New York: Simon & Schuster Macmillan; London: Prentice-Hall.

Kirsch, I. S., & Mosenthal, P. B. (1988). *Understanding Document Literacy: Variables Underlying the Performance of Young Adults.* Report no. ETS RR-88-62. Princeton, NJ: Educational Testing Service.

Kirsch, I. S., & Mosenthal, P. B. (1990). Exploring document literacy: variables underlying performance of young adults. *Reading Research Quarterly,* 25 (1), 5–30.

Klingner, J. K., & Vaughn, S. (2000). The helping behaviors of fifth graders while using collaborative strategic reading during ESL content classes. *TESOL Quarterly,* 34 (1), 69–98.

Koschmann, T. (1996). Paradigm shifts and instructional technology: an introduction. In T. Koschmann (ed.), *CSCL: Theory and Practice of an Emerging Paradigm* (pp. 1–23). Mahwah, NJ: Lawrence Erlbaum Associates.

Kramsch, C., Morgenstern, D., & Murray, J. H. (1985). An overview of the MIT Athena language learning project. *CALICO Journal,* 2 (4), 31–34.

Krashen, S. (1982). *Principles and Practice in Second Language Acquisition.* Oxford: Pergamon.

Kud, J. M., Krupka, G. R., & Rau, L. F. (1994). Methods for categorizing short answer responses. In R. M. Kaplan & J. C. Burstein (eds.), *Proceedings of the Educational Testing Service Conference on Natural Language Processing Techniques and Technology in Assessment and Education* (pp. 31–40). Princeton, NJ: Educational Testing Service.

Kulik, C. C., Kulik, J. A., & Schwalb, B. J. (1986). The effectiveness of computer-based adult education: a meta-analysis. *Journal of Educational Computing Research,* 2, 235–252.

Kyto, M., Ihalainen, O., & Rissanen, M. (eds.) (1988). *Corpus Linguistics, Hard and Soft.* Amsterdam: Rodopi.

Lado, R. (1961). *Language Testing: The Construction and Use of Foreign Language Tests.* New York: McGraw-Hill.

Lam, W. S. E. (2000). Literacy and the design of the self: a case study of a teenager writing on the Internet. *TESOL Quarterly,* 34 (3), 457–482.

Lamy, M.-N., & Goodfellow, R. (1999a). Supporting language students' interactions in web-based conferencing. *Computer Assisted Language Learning,* 12 (5), 457–477.

Lamy, M.-N., & Goodfellow, R. (1999b). 'Reflective conversation' in the virtual language classroom. *Language Learning & Technology,* 2 (2), 43–61.

Lantolf, J. P., & Appel, G. (1994). Theoretical framework: an introduction to Vygotskian approaches to second language research. In J. P. Lantolf & G. Appel (eds.), *Vygotskian Approaches to Second Language Research*. Norwood, NJ: Ablex Publishing.

Larsen-Freeman, D., & Long, M. (1991). *An Introduction to Second Language Acquisition Research*. London: Longman.

Last, R. W. (1979). The role of computer-assisted learning in modern language teaching. *Association for Literary and Linguistic Computing Bulletin*, 7, 165–171.

Last, R. W. (1984). *Language Teaching and the Microcomputer*. Oxford: Basil Blackwell.

Last, R. W. (1989). *Artificial Intelligence Techniques in Language Learning*. New York: John Wiley & Sons.

Laufer, B., & Hill, M. (2000). What lexical information do L2 learners select in a CALL dictionary and how does it affect word retention? *Language Learning & Technology*, 3 (2), 58–76.

Laurier, M. (1999). The development of an adaptive test for placement in French. In M. Chalhoub-Deville (ed.), *Development and Research in Computer Adaptive Language Testing* (pp. 122–135). Cambridge: University of Cambridge Examinations Syndicate / Cambridge University Press.

Lawler, R. W., & Yazdani, M. (eds.) (1987). *Artificial Intelligence and Education. Volume 1: Learning Environments and Tutoring Systems*. Norwood, NJ: Ablex Publishing.

Lazerton, A. (1996). Interlocutor support in oral proficiency interviews: the case of CASE. *Language Testing*, 13 (2), 151–172.

Leech, G. (1991). The state of the art in corpus linguistics. In K. Aijmer & B. Altenberg, (eds.), *English Corpus Linguistics: Studies in Honour of Jan Svartvik* (pp. 8–29). London: Longman.

Leech, G. (1997). Teaching and language corpora: a convergence. In Wichmann, A., Fligelstone, S., McEnery, T., & Knowles, G. (eds.), *Teaching and Language Corpora* (pp. 1–24). New York: Addison Wesley Longman.

Leech, G., & Candlin, C. (eds.) (1986). *Computers in English Language Teaching and Research*. London: Longman.

Legenhausen, L., & Wolff, D. (1990). CALL in use – use of CALL: evaluating CALL software. *System*, 18 (1), 1–13.

Legenhausen, L., & Wolff, D. (1992). STORYBOARD and communicative language learning: results of the Dusseldorf CALL project. In M. L. Swartz & M. Yazdani (eds.), *Intelligent Tutoring Systems for Foreign Language Learning* (pp. 9–23). Berlin: Springer Verlag.

Lemay, L. (1995). *Teach Yourself Publishing with HTML in a Week*. Indianapolis, IN: Sams Publishing.

Levin, L. S., Evans, D. A., & Gates, D. M. (1991). The Alice system: a workbench for learning and using language. *CALICO Journal*, 9 (1), 27–56.

Levy, M. (1997). *Computer-Assisted Language Learning: Context and Conceptualization*. Oxford: Oxford University Press.

Lian, A.-P. (1984). Aspects of answer-evaluation in traditional foreign language CAL. In R. M. Russell (ed.), *Proceedings of the Conference on Computer-Aided Learning in Tertiary Education* (pp. 150–160). Brisbane, Australia: University of Queensland.

Lightbown, P., & Spada, N. (1990). Focus-on-form and corrective feedback in communicative language teaching. *Studies in Second Language Acquisition*, 25, 1–14.

Linacre, J. M. (1999). The development of an adaptive test for placement in French. In M. Chalhoub-Deville (ed.), *Development and Research in Computer Adaptive Language Testing* (pp. 182–195). Cambridge: University of Cambridge Examinations Syndicate / Cambridge University Press.

Linn, R., Baker, E., & Dunbar, S. (1991). Complex, performance-based assessment: expectations and validation criteria. *Educational Researcher*, November, 15–21.

Liou, H.-C. (1991). Development of an English grammar checker: a progress report. *CALICO Journal*, 9 (1), 57–70.

Liou, H.-C. (1993). Investigation of using text-critiquing programs in a process-oriented writing class. *CALICO Journal*, 10 (4), 17–38.

Lomicka, L. L. (1998). 'To gloss or not to gloss': an investigation of reading comprehension online. *Language Learning & Technology*, 1 (2), 41–50.

Long, M. H. (1980). Inside the 'black box': methodological issues in classroom research on language learning. *Language Learning*, 30, 1–42.

Long, M. H. (1985). Input and second language acquisition theory. In S. M. Gass & C. G. Madden (eds.), *Input in Second Language Acquisition* (pp. 377–393). Rowley, MA: Newbury House.

Long, M. H. (1988). Instructed interlanguage development. In L. Beebe (ed.), *Issues in Second Language Acquisition: Multiple Perspectives* (pp. 115–141). New York: Newbury House.

Long, M. H. (1996). The role of linguistic environment in second language acquisition. In W. C. Ritchie & T. K. Bhatia (eds.), *Handbook of Second Language Acquisition* (pp. 413–468). San Diego: Academic Press.

Long, M. H., & Robinson, P. (1998). Focus on form: theory, research and practice. In C. Doughty & J. Williams (eds.), *Focus on Form in Classroom Second Language Acquisition* (pp. 15–41). Cambridge: Cambridge University Press.

Loritz, D. (1986). An introductory LISP parser. *CALICO Journal*, 4 (4), 51–70.

Loritz, D. (1995). The adolescence of CALL. *CALICO Journal*, 12 (4), 7–14.

Loschky, L., & Bley-Vroman, R. (1993). Grammar and task-based methodology. In G. Crookes & S. Gass (eds.), *Tasks and Language Learning: Integrating Theory & Practice*, (pp. 123–167). Clevedon, England: Multilingual Matters, Ltd.

Luff, P., Gilbert, N., & Frohlich, D. (eds.) (1990). *Computers and Conversation*. London, Academic Press.

Lyman-Hager, M., Davis, J., Burnett, J., & Chennault, R. (1993). Une vie de boy: interactive reading in French. In F. L. Borchardt & E. M. T. Johnson (eds.), *Proceedings of the CALICO 1993 Annual Symposium on Assessment* (pp. 93–97). Durham, NC: Duke University.

MacIntyre, P. D., Clément, R., Dörnyei, Z., & Noels, K. A. (1998). Conceptualizing willingness to communicate in a L2: a situational model of L2 confidence and affiliation. *The Modern Language Journal*, 82, 545–562.

MacWhinney, B. (1995). *The Childes Project: Tools for Analyzing Talk* (2nd edn). Hillsdale, NJ: Lawrence Erlbaum Associates.

Madsen, H. S. (1991). Computer-adaptive testing of listening and reading comprehension: the Brigham Young approach. In P. Dunkel (ed.), *Computer-Assisted Language Learning and Testing: Research Issues and Practice* (pp. 237–257). New York: Newbury House.

Mandinach, E. B., & Linn, M. C. (1986). The cognitive effects of computer learning environments. *Journal of Educational Computing Research*, 2 (4), 411–427.

Markee, N. (1997). *Managing Curricular Innovation*. Cambridge: Cambridge University Press.

Markley, P. (1998). Empowering students: the diverse roles of Asians and women in the ESL computer classroom. In J. Swaffar, S. Romano, P. Markley, & K. Arens (eds.), *Language Learning Online: Theory and Practice in the ESL and the L2 Computer Classroom* (pp. 81–96). Austin, TX: Labyrinth Publications.

Markosian, L. Z., & Ager, T. A. (1983). Applications of parsing theory to computer-assisted instruction. *System*, 11 (1), 65–77.

Marty, F. (1981). Reflections on the use of computers in second language acquisition. *Studies in Language Learning*, 3 (1), 25–53.

Mason, R. (1992). Evaluation methodologies for computer conferencing applications. In A. R. Kaye (ed.), *Collaborative Learning through Computer Conferencing* (pp. 105–116). Berlin: Springer Verlag.

McEnery, T., Baker, J. P., & Wilson, A. (1995). A statistical analysis of corpus based computer vs. traditional human teaching methods of part of speech analysis. *Computer Assisted Language Learning*, 8 (2–3), 259–274.

McLaughlin, B. (1987). *Theories of Second Language Learning*. London: Edward Arnold.

McLaughlin, B. (1990). Restructuring. *Applied Linguistics*, 11 (2), 113–128.

McNamara, T. (1996). *Measuring Second Language Performance*. London: Longman.

Messick, S. (1989). Validity. In R. L. Linn (ed.), *Educational Measurement* (3rd edn) (pp. 13–103). New York: Macmillan Publishing.

Messick, S. (1995). Standards of validity and the validity of standards in performance assessment. *Educational Measurement: Issues and Practice*, 14 (4), 5–8.

Meunier, L. E. (1994). Computer adaptive language tests (CALT) offer a great potential for functional testing. Yet, why don't they? *CALICO Journal*, 11 (4), 23–39.

Meunier, L. E. (1996). Human factors in a computer-assisted foreign language environment: The effects of gender, personality, and keyboard control. *CALICO Journal*, 13 (2&3), 47–72.

Mills, D. (2000). Web-based technology as a resource for form-focused language learning. *TESOL Quarterly*, 603–615.

Mislevy, R. J. (1993a). Foundations of a new test theory. In N. Frederiksen, R. J. Mislevy, & I. I. Bejar (eds.), *Test Theory for a New Generation of Tests* (pp. 19–39). Hillsdale, NJ: Lawrence Erlbaum Associates.

Mislevy, R. J. (1993b). A framework for studying differences between multiple-choice and free-response test items. In R. E. Bennett & W. C. Ward (eds.), *Construction versus Choice in Cognitive Measurement: Issues in Constructed Response, Performance Testing, and Portfolio Assessment* (pp. 75–106). Hillsdale, NJ: Lawrence Erlbaum Associates.

Mislevy, R. J. (1994). Evidence and inference in educational assessment. *Psychometrika*, 59 (4), 439–483.

Mislevy, R. J. (1995). Test theory and language learning assessment. *Language Testing*, 12 (3), 341–369.

Mislevy, R. J. (1996). Test theory reconceived. *Journal of Educational Measurement*, 33 (4), 379–416.

Mohan, B. (1992). Models of the role of the computer in second language development. In Pennington, M., & Stevens, V. (eds.), *Computers in Applied Linguistics: An International Perspective* (pp. 110–126). Clevedon, England: Multilingual Matters.

Molholt, G., & Presler, A. M. (1986). Correlation between human and machine ratings of Test of Spoken English passages. In C. W. Stansfield (ed.), *Technology and Language Testing* (pp. 111–128). Washington DC: Teachers of English to Speakers of Other Languages.

Moss, P. (1992). Shifting conceptions of validity in educational measurement: implications for performance assessment. *Review of Educational Research*, 62 (3), 229–258.

Munnich, E., Flynn, S., & Martohardjono, G. (1994). Elicited imitation and grammaticality judgements: what they measure and how they relate to one another. In E. E. Tarone, S. M. Gass, & A. D. Cohen (eds.), *Research Methodology in Second-Language Acquisition* (pp. 227–243). Hillsdale, NJ: Lawrence Erlbaum Associates.

Murray, D. E. (1991). *Conversation for Action: The Computer Terminal as a Medium of Communication*. Amsterdam: John Benjamins.

Murray, D. E. (1995). *Knowledge Machines: Language and Information in a Technological Society*. London: Longman.

Murray, D. E. (2000). Protean communication: the language of computer-mediated communication. *TESOL Quarterly*, 34 (3), 397–421.

Murray, J. H. (1995). Lessons learned from the Athena language learning project: using natural language processing, graphics, speech processing, and interactive video for communication-based language learning. In V. M. Holland, J. Kaplan, & M. Sams (eds.), *Intelligent Language Tutors:*

Theory Shaping Technology (pp. 243–256). Hillsdale, NJ: Lawrence Erlbaum.

Nagata, N. (1993). Intelligent computer feedback for second language instruction. *The Modern Language Journal*, 77 (3), 330–339.

Nation, P. (1993). Using dictionaries to estimate vocabulary size: essential but rarely followed procedures. *Language Testing*, 9, 27–40.

Nelson, G. E., Ward, J. R., Desch, S. H., & Kaplow, R. (1976). Two new strategies for computer-assisted language instruction (CALI). *Foreign Language Annals*, 9 (1), 28–37.

Newman, F., & Holzman, L. (1993). *Lev Vygotsky: Revolutionary Scientist*. New York: Routledge.

Nichols, P. D. (1994). A framework for developing cognitively diagnostic assessments. *Review of Educational Research*, 64 (4), 575–603.

Nissan, S., DeVincenzi, F., & Tang, K. L. (1996). An analysis of the factors affecting difficulty of the dialogue items in the TOEFL listening comprehension. TOEFL Research Report 51. Princeton, NJ: Educational Testing Service.

Nitko, A. J. (1989). Designing tests that are integrated with instruction. In R. L. Linn (ed.), *Educational Measurement* (3rd edn) (pp. 447–474). New York: Macmillan Publishing.

Norris, J. M., Brown, J. D., Hudson, T., Yoshioka, J. (1998). *Designing Second Language Performance Assessments: Technical Report #18*. Honolulu, HI: Second Language Teaching & Curriculum Center, University of Hawai'i at Manoa.

Nutta, J. (1998). Is computer-based grammar instruction as effective as teacher-directed grammar instruction for teaching L2 structures? *CALICO Journal*, 16 (1), 49–62.

Olson, C. P. (1987). Who computes? In L. W. Livingstone (ed.), *Critical Pedagogy and Cultural Power*. South Hadley, MA: Bergin & Garvey Publishers.

O'Malley, J., Chamot, A., Stewner-Manzanares, G., Kupper, L., & Russo, R. (1985). Learning strategies used by beginning and intermediate ESL students. *Language Learning*, 35, 21–46.

Ortega, L. (1997). Processes and outcomes in networked classroom interaction: defining the research agenda for L2 computer-assisted classroom discussion. *Language Learning & Technology*, 1 (1), 82–93.

Otto, S. (1989). Assessment, articulation, accountability: new roles for the language lab. In J. E. Alatis (ed.), *Georgetown University Round Table on Languages and Linguistics, 1989. Language Teaching, Testing, and Technology: Lessons from the Past with a View toward the Future* (pp. 276–287). Washington, DC: Georgetown University Press.

Oxford, R. L. (1990). *Language Learning Strategies: What Every Teacher Should Know*. New York: Newbury House.

Paiva, V. (1999). CALL and on-line journals. In R. Debski & M. Levy (eds.), *WORLDCALL: Global Perspectives on Computer-Assisted Language Learning* (pp. 249–265). Lisse, The Netherlands: Swets & Zeitlinger Publishers.

Papert, S. (1987). Computer criticism vs. technocentric thinking. *Educational Researcher*, Jan.–Feb., 22–23.

Papert, S. (1980). *Mindstorms*. New York: Basic Books.

Paramskas, D. M. (1983). Courseware-software interfaces: some designs and some problems. *CALICO Journal*, 1 (3), 4–6.

Paramskas, D. M. (1993). Computer-assisted language learning (CALL): increasingly integrated into an ever more electronic world. *The Canadian Modern Language Review*, 50 (1), 124–143.

Paramskas, D. M. (1995). Meanwhile, up north: the beginnings of CALL in Canada. *CALICO Journal*, 12 (4), 97–105.

Park, Y. (1994). Incorporating interactive multimedia in an ESL classroom environment: learners' interactions and learning strategies. Unpublished doctoral dissertation, Department of Curriculum and Instruction, College of Education, Iowa State University, Ames, IA.

Pederson, K. M. (1987). Research on CALL. In W. F. Smith (ed.), *Modern Media in Foreign Language Education: Theory and Implementation* (pp. 99–132). Lincolnwood, IL: National Textbook Company.

Pellettieri, J. (2000). Negotiation in cyberspace: the role of chatting in the development of grammatical competence in the virtual foreign language classroom. In M. Warschauer & R. Kern (eds.), *Network-Based Language Teaching: Concepts and Practice* (pp. 59–86). Cambridge: Cambridge University Press.

Pennington, M. (ed.) (1989). *Teaching Languages with Computers: The State of the Art*. La Jolla, CA: Athelstan.

Pennington, M. (1996). *The Computer and the Non-Native Writer: A Natural Partnership*. Cresskill, NJ: Hampton Press.

Pennington, M., & Brock, M. N. (1992). Process and product approaches to computer-assisted composition. In M. Pennington & V. Stevens (eds.), *Computers in Applied Linguistics: An International Perspective* (79–109). Clevedon, England: Multilingual Matters.

Pennington, M., & Stevens, V. (eds.) (1992). *Computers in Applied Linguistics: An International Perspective*. Clevedon, England: Multilingual Matters.

Pereira, F. & Shieber, S. (1987). *Prolog and Natural-Language Analysis: CSLI Lecture Notes Number 10*. Palo Alto, CA: Center for the Study of Language and Information.

Perkins, K., & Linnville, S. (1987). A construct definition study of a standardized ESL vocabulary test. *Language Testing*, 4 (2), 125–141.

Phillips, M. (1985). Educational technology in the next decade: an ELT perspective. In C. Brumfit, M. Phillips, & P. Skehan (eds.), *Computers in English Language Teaching: A View from the Classroom* (pp. 99–119). Oxford: Pergamon Press.

Pica, T. (1994). Research on negotiation: what does it reveal about second-language learning conditions, processes, and outcomes? *Language Learning*, 44 (3), 493–527.

Pica, T., Kanagy, R., & Falodun, J. (1993). Choosing and using communication tasks for second language instruction. In G. Crookes & S. Gass (eds.), *Tasks and Language Learning: Integrating Theory & Practice* (pp. 9–34). Clevedon, England: Multilingual Matters.

Pica, T., Lincoln-Porter, F., Paninos, D., & Linnell, J. (1996). Language learners' interaction: how does it address the input, output, and feedback needs of L2 learners? *TESOL Quarterly*, 30 (1), 59–84.

Pienemann, M. (1992). COALA – a computational system for interlanguage analysis. *Second Language Research*, 8 (1), 59–92.

Pierce, B. (1995). Social identity, investment, and language learning. *TESOL Quarterly*, 29, 9–31.

Piper, A. (1986). Conversation and the computer: a study of the conversational spin-off generated among learners of English as a second language working in groups. *System*, 14, 187–198.

Powers, D. E., Fowles, M. E., Farnum, M., & Ramsey, P. (1994). Will they think less of a handwritten essay if others wordprocess theirs? Effects on essay scores of intermingling handwritten and word-processed essays. *Journal of Educational Measurement*, 31 (5), 220–233.

Purpura, J. (1996). *Modeling the relationship between test takers' reported cognitive and metacognitive strategy use and performance on language tests*. Unpublished doctoral dissertation, Department of Applied Linguistics, University of California at Los Angeles.

Pusack, J. (1983). Answer-processing and error correction in foreign language CAI. *System*, 11 (1), 53–67.

Rassool, N. (1999). *Literacy for Sustainable Development in the Age of Information*. Clevedon, England: Multilingual Matters.

Reid, J. (1986). Using the Writer's Workbench in composition teaching and testing. In C. Stansfield (ed.), *Technology and Language Testing* (pp. 167–188). Washington DC: TESOL Publications.

Reiser, R. A. (1987). Instructional technology: a history. In R. M. Gagne (ed.), *Instructional Technology: Foundations* (pp. 11–48). Hillsdale, NJ: Lawrence Erlbaum Associates.

Renié, D., & Chanier, T. (1995). Collaboration and computer-assisted acquisition of a second language. *Computer Assisted Language Learning*, 8 (1), 3–29.

Riel, M., & Harasim, L. (1994). Research perspectives on network learning. *Machine-Mediated Learning*, 4 (2&3), 91–113.

Robinson, G., Underwood, J., Rivers, W., Hernandez, J., Rudisill, C., & Enseñat, C. (1985). *Computer-Assisted Instruction in Foreign Language Education: A Comparison of the Effectiveness of Different Methodologies and Different Forms of Error Correction*. San Francisco: Center for Language and Crosscultural Skills. ERIC ED 262 626.

Robinson, P. (1995). Attention, memory and the 'noticing' hypothesis. *Language Learning*, 45, 285–331.

Robinson, P. (1996). Learning simple and complex second language rules under implicit, incidental, rule-search, and instructed conditions. *Studies in Second Language Acquisition*, 18, 27–67.

Saettler, L. P. (1990). *The Evolution of American Educational Technology*. Englewood, CO: Libraries Unlimited.

Salaberry, R. (1999). CALL in the year 2000: still developing the research agenda. A commentary on Carol Chapelle's 'CALL in the Year 2000: still in search of research paradigms.' *Language Learning & Technology*, 3 (1), 104–107.

Sampson, G. (1987). Probabilistic models of analysis. In R. Garside, G. Leech, & G. Sampson (eds.), *The Computational Analysis of English: A Corpus-Based Approach* (pp. 16–29). London: Longman.

Sanaoui, R., & Lapkin, S. (1992). A case study of an FSL senior secondary course integrating computer networking. *The Canadian Modern Language Review*, 48 (3), 525–552.

Sanders, A., & Sanders, R. (1987). Designing and implementing a syntactic parser. *CALICO Journal*, 5 (1), 77–86.

Sanders, A., & Sanders, R. (1989). Syntactic parsing: a survey. *Computers and the Humanities*, 23, 13–30.

Sanders, D., & Kenner, R. (1983). Whither CAI? The need for communicative courseware. *System*, 11 (1), 33–39.

Sanders, R. (1991). Error analysis in purely syntactic parsing of free input: the example of German. *CALICO Journal*, 9 (1), 72–89.

Sanders, R., & Sanders, A. (1995). History of an AI spy game: Spion. *CALICO Journal*, 12 (4), 114–127.

Schaeffer, R. H. (1981). Meaningful practice on the computer: is it possible? *Foreign Language Annals*, 14, 133–137.

Schmidt, R. W. (1990). The role of consciousness in second language learning. *Applied Linguistics*, 11 (2), 129–158.

Schmidt, R., & Frota, S. (1986). Developing basic conversational ability in a second language: a case study of an adult learner of Portuguese. In R. Day (ed.), *Talking to Learn: Conversation in Second Language Acquisition* (pp. 237–326). Rowley, MA: Newbury House.

Schneider, E. W., & Bennion, J. L. (1983). Veni, vidi, vici via videodisc: a simulator for instructional conversations. *System*, 11 (1), 41–46.

Schrupp, D. M., Busch, M. D., & Mueller, G. A. (1983). Klavier im haus – an interactive experiment in foreign language instruction. *CALICO Journal*, 1 (2), 17–21.

Scott, T., Cole, M., & Engel, M. (1992). Computers in education: a cultural constructivist perspective. *Review of Research in Education*, 18, 191–251.

Scott, V. M., & New, E. (1994). Computer aided analysis of foreign language writing process. *CALICO Journal*, 11 (3), 5–18.

Self, C. L., & Meyer, P. R. (1991). Testing claims for on-line conferences. *Written Communication*, 8 (2), 163–192.

Sharwood-Smith, M. (1993). Input enhancement in instructed SLA: theoretical bases. *Studies in Second Language Acquisition*, 15, 165–179.

Shepard, L. (1993). Evaluating test validity. *Review of Research in Education*, 19, 405–450.

Shieber, S. M. (1985). Criteria for designing computer facilities for linguistic analysis. *Linguistics*, 23, 189–211.

Shin, D. (1995). A comparison of audiotaped and videotaped listening comprehension placement tests for ESL learners. Unpublished Masters thesis, Department of English, Iowa State University, Ames, IA.

Skehan, P. (1989). *Individual Differences in Second Language Acquisition*. London: Edward Arnold.

Skehan, P. (1998). *A Cognitive Approach to Language Learning*. Oxford: Oxford University Press.

Skinner, B. F. (1954). The science of learning and the art of teaching. *Harvard Educational Review*, 24 (3), 86–97.

Skinner, B. F. (1961). Teaching machines. *Scientific American*, November, 2–13.

Sleeman, D., & Brown, J. S. (eds.) (1982a). *Intelligent Tutoring Systems*. New York: Academic Press.

Sleeman, D., & Brown, J. S. (1982b). Introduction: intelligent tutoring systems. In D. Sleeman & J. S. Brown (eds.), *Intelligent tutoring systems* (pp. 1–11). New York: Academic Press.

Smith, W. F. (ed.) (1987). *Modern Media in Foreign Language Education: Theory and Implementation*. Lincolnwood, IL: National Textbook Company.

Snow, R. E., & Lohman, D. F. (1989). Implications of cognitive psychology for educational measurement. In R. L. Linn (ed.), *Educational Measurement*, (3rd edn) (pp. 263–331). New York: Macmillan Publishing.

Spolsky, B. (1989). *Conditions for Second Language Learning: Introduction to a General Theory*. Oxford: Oxford University Press.

Stevenson, D. K. (1981). Beyond faith and face validity: the multitrait-multimethod matrix and the convergent and discriminant validity of oral proficiency tests. In A. S. Palmer, P. J. M. Groot, & G. A. Trosper (eds.), *The Construct Validation of Tests of Communicative Competence* (pp. 37–61). Washington, DC: TESOL Publications.

Swaffar, J., Romano, S., Markley, P., & Arens, K. (eds.) (1998). *Language Learning Online: Theory and Practice in the ESL and the L2 Computer Classroom*. Austin, TX: Labyrinth Publications.

Swain, M. (1985). Communicative competence: some roles of comprehensible input and comprehensible output in its development. In S. M. Gass & C. G. Madden (eds.), *Input in Second Language Acquisition* (pp. 235–253). Rowley, MA: Newbury House.

Swain, M. (1993). Second language testing and second language acquisition: is there a conflict with traditional psychometrics? *Language Testing*, 10 (2), 193–207.

Swain, M. (1998). Focus on form through conscious reflection. In C. Doughty & J. Williams (eds.), *Focus on Form in Classroom Second Language Acquisition* (pp. 64–81). Cambridge: Cambridge University Press.

Swain, M., & Lapkin, S. (1995). Problems in output and the cognitive processes they generate: a step towards second language learning. *Applied Linguistics*, 16, 371–391.

Swartz, M. L. (1992). Issues for tutoring knowledge in foreign language intelligent tutoring systems. In M. L. Swartz & M. Yazdani (eds.),

Intelligent Tutoring Systems for Foreign Language Learning (pp. 219–233). Berlin: Springer Verlag.

Swartz, M. L., & Yazdani, M. (eds.) (1992). *Intelligent Tutoring Systems for Foreign Language Learning: The Bridge to International Communication*. New York: Springer Verlag.

Tarone, E. E., Gass, S. M., & Cohen A. D. (eds.) (1994). *Research Methodology in Second-Language Acquisition*. Hillsdale, NJ: Lawrence Erlbaum Associates.

Taylor, C., Jamieson, J., & Eignor, D. (2000). Trends in computer use among international students. *TESOL Quarterly*, 34 (3), 575–585.

Taylor, C., Kirsch, I., Eignor, D., & Jamieson, J. (1999). Examining the relationship between computer familiarity and performance on computer-based language tasks. *Language Learning*, 49 (2), 219–274.

Traub, R. E. (1993). On the equivalence of the traits assessed by multiple-choice and constructed-response tests. In R. E. Bennett & W. C. Ward (eds.), *Construction versus Choice in Cognitive Measurement: Issues in Constructed Response, Performance Testing, and Portfolio Assessment* (pp. 29–44). Hillsdale, NJ: Lawrence Erlbaum Associates.

Tribble, C. (1991). Some uses of electronic text in English for Academic purposes: working papers from a seminar. In J. C. Milton & K. S. T. Tong (eds.), *Text Analysis in Computer Assisted Language Learning* (pp. 4–14). The Hong Kong University of Science & Technology and City Polytechnic of Hong Kong.

Tribble, C., & Jones, G. (1990). *Concordances in the Classroom: A Resource Book for Teachers*. Harlow: Longman.

Tucker, G. R. (2000). The applied linguist, school reform and technology: challenges and opportunities for the coming decade. *CALICO Journal*, 17 (2), 197–221.

Tung, P. (1986) Computer adaptive testing: implications for language test developers. In C. Stansfield (ed.), *Technology and Language Testing* (pp. 13–28). Washington DC: TESOL Publications.

Turbee, L. (1995). What can we do in a MOO? Suggestions for language teachers. In M. Warschauer (ed.), *Virtual Connections: On-Line Activities & Projects for Networking Language Learners* (pp. 235–238). Honolulu, HI: Second Language Teaching & Curriculum Center, University of Hawai'i at Manoa.

Underwood, J. (1984). *Linguistics, Computers, and the Language Teacher*. Rowley, MA: Newbury House.

Underwood, J. (1989). On the edge: intelligent CALL in the 1990s. *Computers and the Humanities*, 23, 71–84.

Van Campen, J. (1981). A computer-assisted course in Russian. In P. Suppes (ed.), *University-Level Computer-Assisted Instruction at Stanford: 1968–80* (pp. 603–646). Stanford, CA: Institute for Mathematics Studies in the Social Sciences.

van Lier, L. (1996). *Interaction in the Language Curriculum: Awareness, Autonomy & Authenticity*. London: Longman.

van Lier, L. (1988). *The Classroom and the Learner*. London: Longman.

VanPatten, B., & Cadierno, T. (1993). Explicit instruction and input processing. *Studies in Second Language Acquisition*, 15, 225–243.

Wainer, H., & Braun, H. I. (eds.) (1988). *Test Validity*. Hillsdale, NJ: Lawrence Erlbaum Associates.

Wainer, H., Dorans, N. J., Flaugher, R., Green, B. F., Mislevy, R. J., Steinberg, L., & Thissen, D. (1990). *Computer Adaptive Testing: A Primer*. Hillsdale, NJ: Lawrence Erlbaum Associates.

Wainer, H., & Kiely, G. L. (1987). Item clusters and computer adaptive testing: a case for testlets. *Journal of Educational Measurement*, 24, 185–201.

Wall, D. (1997). Impact and washback in language testing. In C. Clapham & D. Corson (eds.), *Encyclopedia of Language and Education. Volume 7: Language Testing and Assessment* (pp. 291–302). Dordrecht, The Netherlands: Kluwer Academic Publishers.

Warschauer, M. (ed.) (1995a). *Virtual Connections: On-Line Activities & Projects for Networking Language Learners*. Honolulu, HI: Second Language Teaching & Curriculum Center, University of Hawai'i at Manoa.

Warschauer, M. (1995b). *E-mail for English Teaching*. Alexandria, VA: TESOL Publications.

Warschauer, M. (1997a). Comparing face-to-face and electronic discussion in the second language classroom. *CALICO Journal*, 13 (2&3), 7–25.

Warschauer, M. (1997b). Computer-mediated collaborative learning: theory and practice. *The Modern Language Journal*, 81, 470–481.

Warschauer, M. (1998). Researching technology in TESOL: determinist, instrumental, and critical approaches. *TESOL Quarterly*, 32 (4), 757–761.

Warschauer, M. (1999). *Electronic Literacies: Language, Culture, and Power in Online Education*. Mahwah, NJ: Lawrence Erlbaum Associates.

Warschauer, M. (2000). The changing global economy and the future of English teaching. *TESOL Quarterly*, 34 (3), 511–535.

Warschauer, M., & Kern, R. (2000). *Network-Based Language Teaching: Concepts and Practice*. Cambridge: Cambridge University Press.

Warschauer, M., & Lepeintre, S. (1997). Freire's dream or Foucault's nightmare? Teacher–student relations on an international computer network. In R. Debski, J. Gassin, & M. Smith (eds.), *Language Learning through Social Computing. Applied Linguistics of Australia Occasional Papers Number 16* (pp. 67–89). Melbourne: University of Melbourne Printing Services.

Watson-Gegeo, K. A. (1988). Ethnography in ESL: defining the essentials. *TESOL Quarterly*, 22, 575–592.

Wertsch, J. V. (1985). *Vygotsky and the Social Formation of the Mind*. Cambridge, MA: Harvard University Press.

Wichmann, A., Fligelstone, S., McEnery, T., & Knowles, G. (eds.) (1997). *Teaching and Language Corpora*. New York: Addison Wesley Longman.

Wiggins, G. P. (1993). *Assessing Student Performance: Exploring the Purpose and Limits of Testing*. San Francisco: Jossey-Bass Publishers.

Wigglesworth, G. (1997). An investigation of planning time and proficiency level on oral test discourse. *Language Testing*, 14 (1), 85–106.

Winograd, T. (1972). *Understanding Natural Language*. New York: Academic Press.

Winograd, T. (1983). *Language as a Cognitive Process. Volume I: Syntax*. Reading MA: Addison-Wesley Publishing.

Wolfe-Quintero, K., Inagaki, S., & Kim, H-Y. (1998). *Second Language Development in Writing: Measures of Fluency, Accuracy, & Complexity. Technical Report #17*. Honolulu, HI: Second Language Teaching & Curriculum Center, University of Hawai'i at Manoa.

Wresch, W. (1993). The imminence of grading essays by computer – 25 years later. *Computers and Composition*, 10 (2), 45–58.

Wyatt, D. (1984). *Computers and ESL*. Orlando, FL: Harcourt Brace Jovanovich.

Yang, L., & Givón, T. (1997). Benefits and drawbacks of controlled laboratory studies of second language acquisition: the Keck second language learning project. *Studies in Second Language Acquisition*, 19, 173–193.

Yang, L., & Givón, T. (1993). *Tracking the Acquisition of L2 Vocabulary: The Keki Language Experiment*. Institute of Cognitive & Decision Sciences, Technical Report No. 93–11. Eugene, OR: University of Oregon.

Yates, S. J. (1996). Oral and written linguistic aspects of computer conferencing. In S. C. Herring (ed.), *Computer-Mediated Communication: Linguistic, Social, and Cross-Cultural Perspectives* (29–46). Amsterdam: John Benjamins.

Yazdani, M. (1989). Language tutoring with Prolog. In K. Cameron (ed.), *Computer Assisted Language Learning: Program Structure and Principles* (pp. 101–111). Norwood, NJ: Ablex Publishing.

Yi'an, W. (1998). What do tests of listening comprehension test? A retrospection study of EFL test-takers performing a multiple-choice task. *Language Testing*, 15 (1), 21–44.

Young, R., Shermis, M. D., Brutten, S., & Perkins, K. (1996). From conventional to computer adaptive testing of ESL reading comprehension. *System*, 24 (1), 32–40.

Author index

Subject index

211